A HISTORY OF THE MEDIEVAL
CHURCH, 590–1500

BY THE SAME AUTHOR

THE LOLLARD BIBLE. Cambridge.

THE INCENDIUM AMORIS OF RICHARD
ROLLE. Manchester.

HOW CHRISTIANS WORSHIP: the Parish
Church in the Middle Ages. S. C. M.
Press.

Uniform with this volume

By J. W. C. WAND

A HISTORY OF THE EARLY CHURCH.
TO A.D. 500.

A HISTORY OF THE MODERN CHURCH.
From 1500 to the present day.

A HISTORY OF THE MEDIEVAL CHURCH
590—1500

BY

M. DEANESLY, M.A.

FORMERLY PROFESSOR OF HISTORY IN THE UNIVERSITY OF LONDON

WITH TWO MAPS

SEVENTH EDITION

METHUEN & CO. LTD.
36 ESSEX STREET W.C.
LONDON

This book was originally published November 26th 1925
It has been reprinted six times
(Fifth edition, 1947, revised)
Seventh edition, 1951

CATALOGUE NO. 3407/U

PRINTED IN GREAT BRITAIN

PREFACE

THIS short study of medieval church history was planned partly for the use of the general reader, and partly for that of theological students, in particular for those taking the General Ordination Examination, or those following some such course as that of the B.D. in the University of Manchester. As far as possible, in a small space set apart for the treatment of a large subject, the social and personal aspects of church history have been dwelt on, as against the political. It seemed above all desirable to give some idea of the medieval attitude towards life, religion and the church, of the faith and ideals of medieval churchmen, and of the actual working of the medieval church system.

As to the period covered by this book, it seemed clear that a study of the middle ages should end before the Reformation: and on the whole, it seemed desirable to start with the pontificate of Gregory the Great, as best marking the watershed between early and medieval church history. An introductory chapter has been added, however, for the sake of students who may have been reading for a course on early church history which ended with the council of Chalcedon.

M. DEANESLY

June, 1925

PREFACE
TO THE SEVENTH EDITION

EXPERIENCE shows that to suggest too many books for further reading to those with only a limited time to read them defeats its own object. Nevertheless, a few additions have been made at times to the select book list since this book was first published, and a word may perhaps be said here about one or two books published of recent years of outstanding interest to such students of Church history as are likely to read this book. There have been two dealing with the history of religious orders. The first is Pierre Mandonnet's *Saint Dominique*, 2 vols., 1937, which sheds a flood of light, incidentally, on the early and persisting conception in the Church of the apostolic life as communal, on the springs of the Hildebrandine Reform and on the history of the Austin canons in the twelfth century. The second is Dom David Knowles' *The Monastic Order in England*, 1940, and *Religious Orders in England*, 1948; this is a history of the Benedictine and other orders both in Europe and England, in which the studies of Bernard of Clairvaux, Aelred of Rievaulx and others will not easily be forgotten. Mr. Dickinson's *Origins of the Austin Canons*, 1950, helps to complete the picture. Fliche et Martin's general *Historie de l'Église*, in many volumes, some still to come, is a most useful reference book for all sides of Church history. Professor Stenton's *Anglo-Saxon England*, 1943, is authoritative for many obscure points of English church history up to and round about the Norman Conquest. And finally, for those interested in the plans and forms of early churches, there are Mr. A. W. Clapham's *English Romanesque Architecture before the Conquest*, with its beautiful plans and illustrations, and his *English Romanesque Architecture after the Conquest*, which takes the history of the round-arched church, its figure sculpture and its carved ornament down to the twelfth century.

M. D.

19 *March*, 1951.

CONTENTS

MAPS

INTRODUCTION

FROM THE COUNCIL OF CHALCEDON TO GREGORY THE GREAT, 451–590

The Roman empire at Constantinople—The Christian church in east and west—Nestorians and Monophysites after Chalcedon—Justinian and the church: legislation: S. Sophia: the Monophysites and Rome—Britain and Gaul

IN the greater part of the period between the holding of the council of Chalcedon in 451 and the accession of pope Gregory the Great in 590 the Roman empire was ruled from Constantinople. In earlier days the Roman emperors had ruled Europe as far north as the Rhine and the Danube, north Africa, and Asia to the Caspian and Mesopotamia ; and though Rome was not always the seat of imperial government, that government had been broadly western. But the defence of the eastern frontiers from the barbarian had always been a pressing imperial duty, and as early as the fourth century the empire had been given a second capital in Constantinople, New Rome. This city, joining as it did two seas and two continents, and situated much farther east than Rome, was a better strategic position for the holding of the Danube frontier against the barbarian. In 395 the empire was divided between the two sons of the emperor Theodosius, and two emperors ruled for a time, in Old and New Rome. But while the barbarians from beyond the Danube pressed into the Balkans in spite of the military defence of the emperors at Constantinople, they proved more dangerous to the west, whither they passed on and settled. Real power in Italy was in the fifth century exercised rather by the greatest general for the time being than the emperor

2 HISTORY OF THE MEDIEVAL CHURCH

himself, and in 476 the last Roman emperor in the west was deposed by the barbarians. Theodoric the Ostrogoth at the end of the century settled with his followers in north Italy, and the east Roman emperor, powerless to stop him, formalised his rule over the Italian provincials by allowing him the title of Patrician. Meanwhile the east Roman emperors retained from their court at Constantinople the nominal rule of the whole empire, though Europe west of the Balkans, and north Africa, had for the most part passed to the various barbarian tribes who settled in them. This lapse of the imperial government at Rome had two important results for church history. It left the bishop of Rome, sole patriarch of the west, unchecked by a superior local secular power. Though some of the old municipal officials were still maintained in Rome by Theodoric, none of them enjoyed a greater prestige or power than the bishop, or pope. At Constantinople, on the other hand, the presence of the semi-sacred emperor was, after a struggle, to eclipse the spiritual dignity and actual power of the patriarch. Secondly, the government of the empire from Constantinople kept the centre of gravity in church matters swung to the east ; the main stream of Christian history continued eastern rather than western.

Between 451 and 590 Christianity was the official religion of the emperors, though in some of the outlying portions of the empire its hold was slight. The eastern churches held the Balkans, Asia Minor, Egypt, Palestine, Syria and Mesopotamia ; western Christianity was mainly a Mediterranean religion, strong in Italy, in north Africa before the Vandal invasions, in the Rhone valley and in Spain. In north Gaul, Britain and Ireland a portion of the population were converted, but neither the empire nor Christianity had made any progress beyond the Rhine. In east and west Christianity had conquered the towns before the countryside : its organisation had developed while the Christian population consisted mainly of city groups, and from the cities it had spread slowly outwards over the countryside. By the middle of the fifth century the normal unit of church government was the city group of Christians, headed by the bishop and his " familia " of clergy. The see or sphere of the bishop's authority included a larger or smaller territory round his city, very small in the east and Italy where cities were plentiful and Christianity was old, very large in the west where conditions were the opposite. This sphere of authority was known usually as the " parochia " or parish of the bishop. Episcopal sees had already become grouped in provinces, under the authority of the metropolitan or bishop of the mother see. His authority was exercised in a supervision of episcopal elections, (which were made by the clergy, nobles and people of the parochia under the direction of neighbouring bishops summoned to perform the obsequies of the late bishop), and in the summons and presidency of the provincial synod. At these synods bishops and representatives of their clergy attended, and canons or rulings on points of discipline and doctrine were laid down by the metropolitan after discussion in the synod : these canons were the chief standard and rule for the governance and life of the church.

Beyond this, the provinces of the church had become grouped into eparchates or patriarchates, round some parochia or see situated in a city of world wide importance, and usually where the first preaching of the faith had been the work of an apostle. There were four eastern and one western patriarchates. In the east, Antioch had been the chief city of Asia Minor and Syria : its first conversion was connected with the residence of the apostle Peter, and it had been the chief eastern centre of Christianity after the destruction of Jerusalem. Jerusalem, the birthplace of Christianity, was now a patriarchate, and Alexandria was a third. Here Mark, the disciple of Peter, had taught, and here the schools of Greek philosophy were ready to argue out the theological implications of the narrative of the gospels. Constantinople, founded only in the years 336–339, could not of course claim apostolic origin, but it was an imperial city, and as New Rome was declared a patriarchate, (eparchate), equal in rights and privileges to Old Rome, by the council of Chalcedon. Territorially and politically this patriarchate was of greater importance than those of Antioch and Alexandria. Its boundaries included the greater part of the Balkans, south of the

Danube, the Aegean islands and Asia Minor. In the west, the patriarchate of Rome claimed foundation from the preaching of the apostles Peter and Paul, and covered, in its strict canonical sense, central and north Italy, and, in a newer and wider sense, the whole of western Europe and north Africa.

The visible organisation of the church was broadly the same in all the patriarchates, and rested upon the locally trained and ordained family of clergy and the locally elected but provincially sanctioned bishop. The common holding of the scriptures, and appeal to the Fathers or great doctors of east and west for their interpretation, was a further means of unity. Yet another link sprang from this common holding of the scriptures and the Fathers, the common doctrine and practice of the church with regard to the Christian life, to morals, and to the sacraments, as means of grace for that life. To preserve this unity of belief and practice, general, oecumenical or universal councils had been held in the past, particularly to decide between rival doctrines, each claiming to be the one apostolic Christian faith. Though the summons to the bishops and certain clergy to attend these councils had been general, in fact they had been attended mainly by eastern bishops and the language spoken at them had been Greek. The last of these oecumenical councils had been that of Chalcedon in 451, which had further defined the faith about the person of Christ, the relation, that is to say, of His godhead to His manhood.

Between 451 and 590 Christian history in the east differed from Christian history in the west. In the east, the patriarchs and the emperor were still occupied with the question as to whether the decisions of the council of Chalcedon were to stand, and to be enforced on all. This struggle over the final definition of the faith, together with that over the imperial right to define it, was the main drama played upon the Christian stage, involving as it did the relations of the emperor with the patriarchs both of Old and New Rome. In the west the main problem, apart from the Roman patriarch's or pope's share in the former struggle, was the maintenance of Christianity under a barbarian rule that was usually pagan or Arian, and the conversion of the barbarians to baptism or catholic orthodoxy.

To take the eastern side of church history first. The council of Chalcedon claimed to have added nothing to the authoritative declarations of earlier councils, but to have safeguarded them by certain canons. By so doing it succeeded in imposing a certain measure of uniformity of belief on the greater part of the Christian world. The doctrines it condemned were those held by the remnant of the Nestorians, (which had been refuted earlier), and by the Monophysites, (which had not). The Nestorians, following the tenets of Nestorius, patriarch of Constantinople, denied that certain acts and attributes of human life, especially birth and infancy, could be attributed to God, the second person of the blessed Trinity : they " could not speak of God as being two or three months old," or being born of a woman. Their opponents answered that this position implied the existence of two " persons " of Christ, a divine and a human : the Nestorians were " dividing the person " of Christ. The result of the Nestorian position was to emphasise Christ's humanity, at the expense of His godhead. The error of the Monophysites was exactly the opposite, and had arisen from the teaching of Eutyches, a strong opponent of Nestorius. They held that Christ had but one nature, and that divine. They asserted His godhead and denied His humanity, which became phantasmal, and not, in the contemporary philosophical sense of the term, " substantial." It was the errors of the Nestorians and Monophysites respectively which were condemned later in the clauses of the *Quicunque vult*, " Yet He is not two, but one Christ," and " One altogether : not by confusion of substance, but by unity of person." The importance of these heresies after the council of Chalcedon is that neither of their holders acquiesced and became part of catholic Christendom, but both were eventually pushed out and founded schismatic eastern churches.

The Nestorians had been strong in the " far east " of the Roman empire, especially at Edessa. The schools of Edessa were Nestorian in tendency, as was Barsumas, their most famous teacher at the time of the council of Chalcedon.

In the anti-Nestorian effort which followed that council
the schools were attacked, many teachers banished, and
Barsumas himself forced to withdraw to Persia. Here
he influenced the existent Christian church, and opposed
the opposite heresy of Monophysitism, which was strong
in Syria. In 489 the emperor Zeno closed the schools of
Edessa and more scholars crossed the frontier to Barsumas.
The great episcopal see of the Persian church had been
fixed at Seleucia-Ctesiphon, and here and at Nisibis the
Nestorians founded schools. The Persian Christians had
enjoyed for the most part peace and patronage under
the Sassanid dynasty, and it was Barsumas' policy to
persuade the king that his opponents were ready to side
with the Roman empire if war broke out, while Nestorianism
was consistent with loyalty to Persia. The Nestorian
church of Persia was in fact regarded in the Roman empire
as pro-Persian, and hated for that as well as doctrinal
reasons. Nevertheless, it grew and flourished, was a great
home of monasticism, and sent missions to India and China
which maintained themselves for hundreds of years.

The Monophysites after Chalcedon were strong in the
patriarchates of Jerusalem and Alexandria, and to some
extent in Syria and Mesopotamia. In Jerusalem they
ejected the orthodox patriarch and set up a Monophysite,
whose eventual imprisonment by the emperor did not
prevent the persistence of his views among the Christian
population. In Alexandria the patriarch was murdered,
and a Monophysite consecrated. From about this time
dates the rise of the Monophysite Coptic church, and the
sinking of the great Alexandrian patriarchate, now represented only by the orthodox remnant, to a position of
nullity. There had always been two elements in the
patriarchate, the Greek represented by the great theological
school of Alexandria, and the cosmopolitan population
of that great seaport, and the purely Egyptian people of
the Nile valley. The Monophysite schism in Egypt
represented a national Coptic reaction against Greek rule ;
and in the institutions of the Coptic church like those of
the Nestorian the influence of monasticism was strong.
In the patriarchate of Antioch too a violent Monophysite
was elected in 461. His election led to much rioting and

rival singing in church, and though he was twice ejected, his influence long continued.

An imperial effort to reconcile orthodox and Monophysites only succeeded in producing a schism between the patriarchates of Rome and Constantinople, which lasted for thirty-five years. The emperor Zeno was forced into exile for two years by a pretender, supported mainly by the Monophysites, who anathematised the council of Chalcedon and recalled Monophysite bishops. Zeno therefore desired to end the Monophysite schism as a political danger to himself, and sought to accomplish this by the issue of a *Henotikon*, or edict for reunion, in 482. The edict was addressed to the bishops, clergy and laity of the Alexandrian patriarchate, and set forth the sufficiency of the faith as declared at Nicaea and Constantinople. It further anathematised both Nestorius and Eutyches, and declared against the division of Christ's person, and the confusion of the substance of the manhood and the godhead. All this was quite orthodox : but the point of the edict was the further statement that if anyone had taught any contrary doctrine, whether at Chalcedon or elsewhere, he was to be anathematised. The suggestion was, that the fathers at Chalcedon had erred. Most Alexandrians and Egyptians were willing to adopt the *Henotikon*, though the extremists would have liked the condemnation of Chalcedon to have been explicit. The Monophysite patriarch of Alexandria and probably also the patriarch of Constantinople regarded the *Henotikon* as permission openly to repudiate Chalcedon, and the *Tome* of pope Leo I, which had been accepted there. Rome was naturally indignant. Pope Simplicius, after a bitter correspondence and the sending of two embassies, excommunicated both patriarchs and Zeno himself. Schism followed. Zeno died and his successor was a pious old Monophysite who degraded two patriarchs of Constantinople for wishing to make peace with Rome. But his successor Justin on his accession in 518 solemnly reaffirmed the decisions of Chalcedon, and thus ended the schism. The result for the Monophysites was their permanent severance from catholicism. During the schism, their communities both in Syria and Egypt had been largely organised by the bishop of Antioch and by the more famous Monophysite leader, Jacobus Baradaeus, (578), after whom the Syrian Monophysites were often called Jacobites. The existence of these schismatic and largely unsupported churches was to account in part for the rapidity of Mahometan conquest in Egypt and Syria in the seventh century.

The reign of Justinian (527–565) was the most splendid period in the history of the Byzantine emperors, and of great importance to the church. Justinian's reconquest of Africa from the Vandals and Italy from the Ostrogoths brought him great glory, but no security to the church in those lands. His campaign against the Vandals was partly occasioned by religious motives, and as an orthodox Crusade against persecuting Arianism was welcomed by the subject catholic bishops. But though after fifteen years of war Africa was restored to the empire and to orthodoxy, in less than a hundred years afterwards African Christianity was to be wiped out by the Arabs. Justinian's reconquest of Italy was to be even less permanent ; a fresh band of barbarians, the Lombards, were almost at once to undo his work, and plant themselves as firmly in north Italy as ever the Ostrogoths had done. But the achievements of Justinian's reign were peaceful as well as warlike, and in this respect greatly affected the church. His codification of Roman law, his passion for building, and his claim to supervise and protect the church in matters both of discipline and doctrine were of outstanding importance.

Roman law at Justinian's succession was a confused and unharmonised mass of earlier legal material, which he caused to be re-edited, and which in this form became the *Corpus Juris Romani*. The language of his *Code* was Latin, for the Byzantine court was still " Roman " and Latin-speaking. The issue of the *Corpus* was of double importance to the church. It greatly influenced the later canon or church law : principles and methods of procedure were borrowed by the church courts, and the varied elements of the " sacred canons " were harmonised in the twelfth century on the model of Justinian's *Code*. The elements of Roman law were taught to the barbarian nations of Europe largely by the church : the

transfer of landed property by will was unknown to
Germanic folk-law and first practised in northern and
western Europe for the endowment of churches. Secondly,
Justinian's *Code* abounded in laws dealing with the organisation of the clergy, their morals, the foundation and
government of monasteries, the administration of ecclesiastical property and the jurisdiction over clerics. Imperial law had long taken cognisance of heresy, but Justinian
in 527 and 528 issued especially severe laws for the punishment of heretics. They might not hold public office,
engage in the liberal professions, hold meetings or maintain
churches of their own, or even enjoy all the civil rights
of the Roman citizen : for them, said Justinian, " to
exist is sufficient."

Justinian's passion for building led him to plant fortresses along the boundaries of his empire, monasteries
and churches all over it, and above all to build the great
church of Christ the Holy Wisdom (S. Sophia) at Constantinople. Byzantine architecture, the development
of Latin architecture in an eastern city under the tradition
of dome building, had produced some wonderful churches
before Justinian, but nothing on the scale or with the
inspiration of S. Sophia. They had been built with
circular, square or rectangular naves, and roofed with a
single or composite dome ; they had been fine experiments
in form and in the equilibrium of domes, but relatively
small. S. Sophia was completely built in six years, and
dedicated on Christmas Day 537 ; it was a vast domed
hall, square in plan, opening on to semicircular domed
apses, the outline of these apses being broken again by
semicircular clustering chapels. Expanse rather than
height was aimed at. The structure and equipoise of the
small and large domes was a wonderful achievement,
and the materials used extraordinarily rich. The great
altar under its covering was of gold and precious stones,
its screen and the stalls of the priests of silver, the pulpitum,
or raised platform, where the gospel was read and the
emperor was crowned, was of precious marbles, silver
and ivory. While the columns, door and window frames,
and carved window lattices, were of porphyry or marbles,
some white and some coloured, the rest of the building

was of rough brickwork, entirely covered with fine marbles and patterned or figured mosaics, glowing with suffused splendour against a golden background. "Who shall describe," wrote a chronicler, " the fields of marble gathered on the pavement and lofty walls of the church ? Fresh green from Carystus, and many-coloured Phrygian stone of rose and white, deep-red and silver ; porphyry powdered with bright spots, green of emerald from Sparta, and Iassian marble with waving veins of blood-red on white : streaked red stone from Lydia, and crocus-coloured marble from the hills of the Moors : Celtic stone like milk poured out on glittering black, the precious onyx with gold shining through it, and fresh green from the land of Atrax." Byzantine reverence for and delight in S. Sophia were expressed by one writer who declared that " Words worthy of it are not to be found : after we have spoken of it we cannot speak of anything else ; " and by another who claimed that God must certainly have extended His mercy to Justinian, if only because he built S. Sophia.

During his whole reign Justinian claimed the complete mastery of the church. Through his generosity numbers of churches, hospitals and monasteries were founded, and the bishops were encouraged to call in the aid of the secular power to spread the faith and suppress heresy : but Justinian believed it his own paramount duty to guide as well as protect the church. He had missions sent against the Monophysites of Asia, he closed the yet remaining sanctuaries of Isis at Philae and Ammon at Augila, he strove to suppress alike Jews, Manichaeans, Montanists, Arians and Donatists, he conciliated at first the Roman church. But he soon found that nothing short of armed force would suppress the Monophysites, and his wife, the empress Theodora, was herself inclined to their side, and urged conciliation even at the price of alienating the pope. Justinian therefore adopted a course similar to, though less extreme than, that of Zeno. He invited to Constantinople the Monophysite ex-patriarch of Antioch, for whom Theodora had great admiration, arranged a conference with the Monophysites, and prepared a declaration of faith reminiscent of Zeno's *Henotikon*. He allowed the Monophysites to carry on propaganda in Constantinople,

and even under Theodora's protection in the palace : in
535 a bishop with Monophysite leanings was elected to
the throne of Constantinople. The year following pope
Agapetus came himself to Constantinople, declared the
patriarch deposed, and stirred up a fresh persecution of
Monophysites in the east, including even Egypt, their
stronghold : Justinian so far acquiescing. But when a
new pope was elected in 537, Justinian's general arrested,
deposed him and caused Theodora's favourite, Vigilius,
to be elected in his place. Though Vigilius proved less
tractable when pope than had been expected, Theodora
encouraged Jacob Baradaeus to ordain Monophysite
bishops in Asia and Syria and even in 550 a Monophysite
patriarch of Antioch : Theodora was in fact the patroness
of the new Jacobite church.

Justinian's second attempt to conciliate the Monophysites was by the condemnation of the works of three
eastern doctors, moderate and learned Nestorians, or
quasi-Nestorians, whose works had been summarised
as the " Three Chapters " and formally approved at
Chalcedon : he issued the edict condemning these " Three
Chapters " in 543. The Monophysites were delighted,
and Justinian meant to stand no intervention by the pope
this time. Vigilius was carried off by force to Constantinople, and talked over by the emperor, Theodora, and
the court theologians : on Easter Eve, 548, he formally
condemned the Three Chapters. Theodora died two
months later.

The matter was not, however, ended. The bishops of
Africa and Illyricum protested against Vigilius's action,
and in spite of their deposition by the emperor, the whole
west was troubled. Vigilius was alarmed at the result
of his action, and demanded an oecumenical council.
Fearing Justinian's anger he took refuge in a church, where
he was found by the soldiers sent to seize him : his clerks
were seized, and when he clung to the altar pillars, the
soldiers pulled him so violently that the altar collapsed
upon him, to the horror of the crowd. The council he
desired was summoned to Constantinople in 553 ; it
formally condemned the Three Chapters, and with them
Vigilius. The east had been conciliated at the expense of

the west : the bishops of Milan and Aquileia firmly refused
to remain in communion with Vigilius, who had "be-
trayed his trust" and "deserted the orthodox cause,"—
the sanctity of all the decrees of Chalcedon. The reign
of Justinian proved throughout a period of deep humilia-
tion for the papacy. Two popes had suffered indignity,
and Vigilius's next two successors were elected under
imperial pressure, and were forced to continue the humble
servants of the emperor. The church of Ravenna, the
capital of reconquered Italy, was deliberately exalted
at the expense of Rome. The subjection of the patriarch
of Old Rome to the emperor seemed likely to continue
as absolute as that of New Rome, and his prestige suffered
during the reign far more than his colleague's. The
Byzantine system of the imperial patronage and complete
dominance of the church had seen its most splendid phase.

Meanwhile in the west Christianity struggled with
barbarism. Ten years after the council of Chalcedon
S. Patrick died in Ireland : he was by birth a Briton, and
he worked not only to Christianize Ireland, but to prepare
there a fresh stock of missionaries for the reconversion of
Britain. Christianity in Britain had perished before the
invading Saxons in the eastern part of the island : the
invaders, as Bede said, "like men mowing down ripe
corn," drove the Britons back to the west. Five years
before Chalcedon the wretched remnant of the Britons
had sent their famous appeal to Aetius in Italy for help,
entitled : "The groans of the Britons : " but no help
could be spared. British Christianity persisted in the
monasteries of Wales and Strathclyde, and its miseries
found expression in the lament of Gildas († c. 570). In
his *Liber Querulus de Excidio Brittanniae*, probably written
at the monastery he founded in Brittany, Gildas lamented
the triumphs of the Saxons and the weakness of the petty
kings of Wales, among whom his youth had been spent.
But the Irish followers of S. Patrick were already working
to convert the Picts of northern Britain, and hoping from
that vantage ground to send missionaries south among the
Saxons,—with whom they had not, like Welsh Britons, a
personal quarrel. The Irish monk Columba crossed to
attempt missionary work in the Pictish kingdom of Dalriada.

He was given land by the king, founded his monastery on the island of Hii, or Iona, in 563, and lived and worked there for thirty years. Many daughter houses to Iona were founded, and the many early churches dedicated to him show his influence. But his work was not to spread southward till later : the Saxons continued heathen, worshipping Woden the All-Father, and the war-god Thor with his hammer.

In Gaul also the barbarians had settled, Visigoths and Burgundians and Franks, but the Christian population had remained instead of retreating gradually before them, as in Britain. Visigoths and Burgundians were Arian : the Franks in the north east were pagan like the Anglo-Saxons, and a fierce fighting race. In the south the orthodox bishops were hard pressed, the imperial schools gradually perished and learning died, save where it was cherished for ecclesiastical purposes in the bishops' households. While the greatest secular event in the history of fifth century Gaul was the extension of the rule of the Frankish king Clovis over his fellow Franks and his neighbours of other races, the greatest event for Christian history was his conversion to orthodox Christianity in 496. His wife Clotilda was a Christian, and for some time Clovis hesitated over the rival merits of Christ and Thor as war-gods, showing some favour to the Christian bishops and even giving presents to monasteries. But when he had chased the Alemanni from their homes in Alsace, and defeated them in battle, he decided to accept Christian baptism. We are told that his decision was due to the answer to his prayer for success, made to Christ " whom Clotilda declares to be the son of the living God." Three thousand Franks accompanied their king to baptism, which was performed by bishop Remigius of Reims, of whose address to Clovis a chronicler has preserved the beginning : " Bow thy neck in meekness, O Sicambrian : adore what thou hast burned and burn that which thou hast adored." While the conversion of the Franks made possible intermarriage with the provincials, and the peaceful establishment of Frankish power, Frankish Christianity was at first, like that of Clovis himself, a rough and barbarous affair. The best picture of its

struggles, its barbarisms and its efforts is given in the works
of Gregory of Tours, († 594), an excellent bishop and the
first historian of the Frankish nation.   The most learned
Gallic bishop of the sixth century, however, was Venantius
Fortunatus, who at the end of his life was one of Gregory's
successors at Tours.   He had been born about 530, educated
in imperial Ravenna, and during his lifetime wrote a
prodigious amount of Latin verse, secular and sacred,
some of it very fine.   He left Ravenna about 565, and
travelled up the Rhine through Mainz, Cologne, Treves
and Metz, repaying hospitality by poems celebrating some
local event or building.   At the court of the Franks he
was the nucleus of Roman culture, wrote wedding songs
for princesses and eulogies for warriors, and finally settled
down as the friend of the Frankish princess Rhadegund,
who had founded a great nunnery at Poitiers.   He wrote
her religious poems, and charming little verses to accompany
baskets of violets and chestnuts : his whole career as poet
and man of letters was much more important than that
as bishop.   His fine poem for Easter, as others, has ever
since been used by the church :—

Hail to thee, festival day ! blest day that art hallowed for
     ever ;
Day wherein God overcame hell and arose from the dead.

He who was nailed to the cross is God and the ruler of all
     things :
All things created on earth worship the maker of all.

Rise now, O Lord, from the grave and cast off the shroud
     that enwrapped Thee :
Thou art sufficient for us : nothing without Thee exists.

Jesus has harrowèd hell : He has led captivity captive :
Darkness and chaos and death flee from the face of the
     light.

A History of the Medieval Church, 590–1500

CHAPTER I

GREGORY THE GREAT, 590–604

Gregory's youth, monastic profession and election as pope—Gregory, the empire, and the Lombards—His administration of the papal patrimony—His correspondence with bishops and patriarchs—His writings

THERE is much to be said for beginning a study of medieval church history with the pontificate of pope Gregory the Great (590–604). The great oecumenical councils were past, and with them one mode of expressing the will of catholic Christendom, both eastern and western. Since 476 there had been no emperor residing in the west, and the way was open for the extension of papal power in Italy. There a new race of barbarians had appeared, and it fell to the papacy to struggle with these new invaders, " fierce with more than the usual fierceness of the Germans," and finally to arrange terms of peace for the partition of Italy between these Lombards and the Roman Empire. The peace once made, and it was arranged by Gregory the Great himself, the papacy was left in a position of political advantage, able to play off the Lombards against the emperor at Constantinople. Had the seat of empire remained at Rome, or had Constantinople become permanently the real capital of Europe, the fortunes of the papacy as a temporal power must have been different. Gregory the Great not only ruled in

Rome for fourteen years when these issues were being shaped : he took a large part in shaping them. By his influence on the Lombard settlement, and no less by his influence on the administration, missions and doctrines of the church, as by his protection of nascent Benedictine monachism, Gregory stands out as the greatest statesman of the early medieval church.

Gregory himself was born in Rome about the year 540. The Rome of his boyhood was a beggared Rome, wasted by the Gothic wars. Only a handful of officials inhabited the civil offices on the Palatine mount. Pagan shrines and temples were disused and ruinous, and not as yet, for the most part, taken over and reconsecrated as Christian churches. Five great basilicas (the contemporary word for church) shared the reverence of the Christian population, and the two last of the " seven churches of Rome " were already growing in veneration. The mother church of Rome, the site of the pope's chair or " cathedra," was the basilica of S. John on the Lateran ; close by was the papal residence, the Lateran palace. The basilicas of S. Peter and S. Paul respectively were built on the traditional sites of their martyrdom, S. Peter's on the Vatican, and S. Paul's on the road to Ostia. The basilica on the Esquiline, S. Maria Maggiore, surpassed in size the comparatively small church on the Lateran ; the fifth basilica was dedicated to S. Lawrence, the sixth to S. Sebastian, and the seventh to S. Cross in Jerusalem. Of these seven churches, one was thus dedicated to the Blessed Virgin, one to the cross whose " invention " by Helena in Jerusalem sent a wave of veneration to the remotest parts of Europe, and four were erected over the graves of the martyrs, and hallowed by their relics. This close association of the living Christian with the dead, the living worshipper with the prayers and protection of the martyr, before whose " sacred pledges " lamps burned continually, was common to Christendom, and determined the architectural form of Christian churches for centuries. To the Christian of the sixth century, as earlier, there was no spot more hallowed than these " martyria," and the churches erected over them : and the dust of the apostle who had seen with his own eyes and touched with his hands the very body of the Saviour was in itself a link with Christ, inexpressibly precious.

Gregory's father and mother were a devout and wealthy couple of senatorial rank. His youth was spent at his father's house on the Caelian, opposite the deserted palaces of the Palatine. Of the old classical education, which Martianus Capella had just summarised in his treatise on the seven liberal arts, Gregory received instruction in the first three subjects, with some knowledge of Latin literature, the slight contemporary infusion of Porphyry's logic, or dialectic, and a considerable knowledge of rhetoric. Of the four remaining liberal arts, arithmetic, music, geometry and astronomy, he seems like his contemporaries to have known little or nothing.

While Gregory passed into the lower grades of the imperial civil service, the Lombard conquerors were passing down into north Italy. By 571 they had conquered the valley of the Po ; the next year they seized Benevento and Spoleto ; in 573 Rome itself was in danger. In this year we find Gregory prefect of the city, the highest civil dignitary in Rome. His duties included the nominal presidency of the senate : supreme civil jurisdiction within 100 miles of the capital : the provision of grain supplies : the care of aqueducts, sewers, and the bed of the Tiber : the leadership of such officials as remained in Rome, and a large financial authority. Gregory's early connexion with and training in administrative work is of importance. Through his father he must have been in touch with the administrative side of church work, and he himself obtained the highest administrative office in the imperial government. Just as the spirit of classical literature was passed on chiefly through the mind and writings of Augustine to the medieval world : so the Roman genius for administration and " government " became the heritage of the medieval church chiefly through Gregory the Great. Gregory might well have looked upon the exarchate at Ravenna as the next stage in his career ; but he chose rather to exchange his worldly chances for the life of Christian perfection.

In 574 Gregory sold his patrimony in Sicily, and founded six monasteries there. He then bestowed the remainder

c

of his patrimony upon the poor, keeping the paternal house on the Caelian as a monastery for himself and the brothers he collected there, and dedicated it to S. Andrew. S. Benedict had founded his monastery at Monte Cassino, and died about forty years earlier, and Gregory can hardly have been ignorant of his reputation. But there is no evidence that his new monastery on the Caelian adopted the Benedictine rule, or that he was acquainted with the rule before he became a monk. S. Benedict legislated for a house, not an order, and there is, in fact, no evidence that any house explicitly adopted his rule for its sole guide for a hundred years or more after his death. Gregory was later to be a great patron of monks, and the chief champion of their rights as against unprincipled or greedy diocesans. The monastic life attracted him, as he wrote in one of his later letters, as an opportunity for a life of detachment, prayer, or contemplation. " I remember with sorrow what I once was in the monastery : how I rose in contemplation above all changeable and decaying things, and thought of nothing but the things of heaven : how my soul, though pent within the body, soared beyond its fleshly prison, and looked with longing upon death itself as the means of entering into life. . . . And when I recall the condition of my former life, I sigh as one who looks back and gazes on the shore he has left behind."

For four years Gregory was left to learn the life which was to affect medieval Europe so profoundly ; but in 578 the pope, wishing to raise him ultimately to high office in the church, took him from the monastery, and ordained him " seventh " deacon. In the spring of the year following, 579, pope Pelagius sent him as his secretary to Constantinople. The Lombards were ravaging Italy, the exarch at Ravenna did nothing in her defence : " the district of Rome," Pelagius wrote, " is more than ever unguarded." It was Gregory's paramount duty to prevail upon the emperor to send help, money, or above all troops to Italy, but he had little success. Though Gregory lived in a palace, he did not give up his monastic habit of life : " for many of his brothers from the monastery followed him, led by brotherly love," and the seclusion in which he lived with them probably accounts for the fact that during his stay in Constantinople he learned no Greek. The court of the emperor was still Latin speaking, and Latin was still in the east the language of public life.

On his return to Rome Gregory was made abbot of his old monastery, which he ruled from 586 till 590. Among his monks whom he mentions in his letters were four who, like himself, were to be taken from the monastery and made bishops : Maximianus, whom Gregory made arch-bishop of Syracuse ; Marinianus, who was elected bishop of Ravenna ; Sabinus, bishop of Gallipoli, and Augustine, the first metropolitan of Canterbury. During these years Gregory re-edited the lectures on the book of Job, which he had given to his monks in Constantinople, as the *Magna Moralia*, which later scholars were to find a mine of mis-cellaneous theology in the form of a commentary ; was in close touch with pope Pelagius ; and even desired to start on that mission to the heathen Angles which he had contemplated since the sight of the Anglian boys in the slave market had filled him with pity.

To the perennial fears of the Lombards from which Rome suffered were added in 590 the horrors of bubonic plague. Pope Pelagius himself died in February, and the clergy and people of Rome immediately elected Gregory pope. During the summer, while the imperial confirma-tion was awaited from Constantinople, the plague raged in Rome. In April Gregory organised a sevenfold peni-tential procession, to march to the basilica of S. Maria Maggiore, and implore deliverance from the plague. As the procession of penitents crossed the bridge of Hadrian, a later legend tells of their vision of the archangel Michael in the sky over the mausoleum of Hadrian : he was re-storing his sword, the sword of pestilence, to its scabbard. The plague was stayed, and the mausoleum became for medieval Rome the castle of Sant' Angelo. The confirma-tion of the papal election arrived in the autumn, and on 3 September Gregory was hurriedly consecrated in the basilica of S. Peter.

For fourteen years, from September 590 till March 604, Gregory ruled as apostolic bishop of Rome, and the effec-tive protector of the civil population of central Italy from the " unspeakable Lombards." If there is any leading motive in his reign, any phrase that sums up his character, it is his insistence that all should live in expectation of the " terrible judgment " which the New Testament, and the world catastrophes of the day, made him believe imminent. He passed all his pontificate " among the swords of the Lombards," never sure but that some combination of Lombard dukes and king might reduce the sacred city itself to a wilderness, sometimes with their forces actually at the gates ; he had seen from the wall Christians tied by the necks like dogs, and led away to be sold as slaves in Gaul ; his ears were filled with the oppressions of the wretched peasants of the Campagna, starving refugees in Rome clamoured for shelter and food. To a noble who asked his influence with the emperor he wrote : " Why, my noble son, do you not reflect that the world is near at end ? Day by day all things are driven onward, and we are brought nearer to the trial we shall have to endure before the eternal, the terrible Judge. What then ought we to think of but His coming ? Our life is like a voyage : the voyager may stand or sit or lie, but all the time he is going on as the ship may bear him. So also are we : sleeping or waking, silent or talking, still or in movement, willing or unwilling, every day, every moment, we draw near the end." Filled with conviction of the shortness of the time, the imminence of the Judge, Gregory wore himself out in labours.

His pontificate is notable above all for its enhancement of the prestige of the apostolic see in Christendom, to which his passion for righteousness and ordered peace tended even more strongly than his zeal for the honour of the chair of S. Peter. His influence on the prestige of the apostolic see was fivefold. The papacy took over, under him, certain functions of the civil government which had earlier been performed by the officials of the emperor ; the policy of balance was begun between the Lombards and Constantinople ; the administration of the papal patrimony, and the whole apostolic see, profited from his civil experience ; the churches of the west were brought more closely into touch with Rome than for a hundred years earlier or later ; and the traditional claims of Rome were upheld against Constantinople.

When Gregory became pope imperial Italy consisted of three regions, each grouped round an important city. The centre of the northern region was Ravenna, the residence of the exarch ; the centre of the middle region was Rome ; the centre of the southern the city of Naples. The "patrimony of S. Peter" was not, however, co-extensive with these regions. It included estates round Rome, especially to the south, in the Campagna ; large estates in the toe and heel of Italy—Lucania and Apulia ; important grain bearing lands in Sicily; and less important groups of estates in Gaul, Illyricum and the Mediterranean islands. In virtue of these estates the Roman church was the richest landowner in Italy, and the largest taxpayer to the imperial treasury : it was thus natural that when the Lombard invasions broke up the imperial administration, and in particular, interrupted communications between Ravenna and Rome, the officials of the patrimony should have been charged with, or spontaneously assumed, the duties of imperial officials. The feeding of the large majority of the citizens by the imperial corn distributions devolved upon the pope, and was only maintained by large contributions from the papal patrimony. The land-tax was henceforward collected by officials of the patrimony. Gregory, moreover, interfered with secular officials to prevent oppression of the peasantry : " if your piety were to remain unaware," he once wrote to the empress, " of what is being done in these provinces, I should be punished by the severe Judge for my sin of silence."

Gregory's treatment of the Lombard problem redounded to the prestige of the papacy later, though not to his good relations with the emperor Maurice at the time. The Arian Lombards were, fortunately for Rome, not united : they ruled from three main centres. The valley of the Po was ruled from Pavia, from 590 by king Agilulf and queen Theudelinda : this group was the most menacing to the exarch at Ravenna. But from 591 two Lombard leaders became dukes of Spoleto and Benevento respectively. The duchy of Spoleto threatened the communications between Rome and Ravenna, and was a most dangerous neighbour to Rome. The duchy of Benevento, to the south, was a more immediate threat to Naples. For the provincials themselves, and for the pope, the pressing need was for the ending of the horrors of war, by ceding to the Lombards some such position as had been held by the Ostrogoths. To the exarch, safe amid his marshes, and not particularly moved by the miseries of the provincials, it seemed good above all things to play for time, without recognising the Lombard status by an imperial peace. In time, lessened stress at Constantinople might allow troops to be sent to help him : or the divisions of the Lombards might prove their own undoing. In face of the supineness of the exarch Gregory undertook the defence of central Italy. In the stress of an invasion, he appointed a military governor to Nepi, thirty miles north of Rome, and in 592 he arranged a peace with the duke of Spoleto. This was disregarded by the exarch, and king Agilulf in consequence marched to take Rome, possibly to make it his capital. But Gregory, interrupting his sermons on the prophet Ezekiel, inspired the defence, and at the end of the summer the Lombards retired. In 595 Gregory arranged a peace with Agilulf which provoked the wrath of the emperor ; but the peace stood, and henceforth the pope was a greater personage in Lombard politics than the exarch.

The prestige of the apostolic see was increased, again, by Gregory's administration of the revenue of the church. The question of the organisation of the Roman see is of great interest, as, since it was immensely richer and more advanced than all other sees in the west, it served to some extent as a model. Papal letters of advice often mentioned the custom of the apostolic see ; Frankish councils are found adopting a practice spontaneously " because it was the usual custom throughout all Italy." The patrimony of S. Peter has at this time been computed at from 1300–1800 square miles. Each local patrimony was subdivided into large groups of estates which were further subdivided into separate farms. Each patrimony was under a papal agent, the rector. Under him came a set of officials called defensors : beneath the defensors came the " actionarii," beneath them the conductors or farmers, who leased the farms and collected the rents, in money or in kind, from the " coloni " or " rustici." The church possessed slaves, like lay landowners : some did farm work, some were craftsmen or personal servants. The rectors and defensors of the patrimonies had before Gregory's reign been ecclesiastics : the actionarii and the conductors had been laymen. Gregory required the actionarii also to be ecclesiastics in minor orders : and it was in the case of the Sicilian actionarii that he first allowed the tonsure to be given separately from a minor order— a practice of great importance to European civilisation later, (see Chapter II). Gregory was in constant touch with the officials of the patrimonies, forced upon them in several cases mitigation of custom in favour of the peasant, and impressed upon them diligence and righteous dealing.

Not only the collection of the revenue, but its distribution was the subject of his anxious thought. He was bound, first of all, to provide for the stipends of the apostolic see. He must provide for all the clergy, and officials of the patrimony whom the church supported : except for those priests (presbyters) attached to some of the basilicas within the city of Rome which had separate endowments. Beyond this he was particularly bound to afford alms to ecclesiastics in distress, and such diocesan churches as had been almost entirely denuded of their clergy and population by the Lombards. Beyond this again, he must arrange for the feeding of the poor, the destitute population dependent on corn and food doles. Of Gregory's payments to his clergy John the Deacon tells us : " He turned into money the revenues of all the patrimonies [an exaggeration, as appears from Gregory's letters] according to the ledger of [pope] Gelasius, of whom he seems to have been a most faithful follower ; and having collected all the orders of the church [i.e., the clerical militia, see Chapter II], either from the palace, or the monasteries, or the churches, or the cemeteries, or the deaconries, or the urban or suburban xenodochia, he distributed to all their pensions, in silver or in gold, four times a year, according as the ledger of Gelasius indicated." In addition to this, early on Easter morning, sitting in the basilica of pope Vigilius, Gregory distributed a golden pound to all bishops, presbyters, and deacons General

relief was variously administered. At each of the seven
deaconries (not merely offices, but buildings at this date),
food was given to the starving on application ; the xenodochia sheltered the infirm, the sick, and strangers ,
monthly distributions were made to the poor of that
part of the revenue of the patrimony still collected in
kind (wine, cheese, vegetables, bacon, fish and oil), " thus
the church came to be regarded as a source of supply for
the whole community : "   special alms were given to
monasteries ; and in the papal palace strangers were
entertained, and food cooked to be borne by special officials
to the sick. So keen was Gregory's sense of his responsibility for the poor, that he held himself guilty and refused
to say mass for some days when a certain pauper had been
found dead without help in the back room of a common
lodging-house ; and John the Deacon tells us that a large
volume existed in his day, containing the names of all the
recipients of Gregory's bounty, not only in Rome and
the suburbs, but even in distant coast towns.

Over the churches within the old canonical patriarchate
in Italy Gregory exercised constant supervision, writing
directly to bishops, receiving appeals at Rome, and using
the officials of the patrimony to a certain extent as his
agents for the supervision of the local clergy. Italy was
divided up into a vast number of little dioceses, many
of them only a few miles in extent : " every town of
any size, and many that were little better than villages
possessed a bishop." In Italy church organisation had
crystallised early, at a stage when each local group of
Christians had its own bishop, who alone baptised, celebrated the mysteries, and reconciled after penance. The
Sicilian dioceses were relatively much larger. Gregory
in his letters is seen providing for dioceses destitute of
clergy ; joining one see to another ; allowing the moving
of a see from the plain to a hill town, for purposes of
defence ; remonstrating with neglectful bishops for failing
to convert the pagan and with those who would not pay
to their clergy the full canonical fourth, (see page 34),
of their revenue ; and showing extraordinary pains and
patience to procure the more decent behaviour of illiterate
old ruffians like the archbishop of Sardinia, who, (Gregory

heard), ploughed up his neighbour's corn fields before mass, celebrated mass himself, and then proceeded to remove his neighbour's boundary stones.

Outside the old canonical patriarchate Gregory corresponded with the bishops of Spain, Africa, Milan, Ravenna, Istria, Dalmatia and Illyricum. He heard with joy of the conversion of king Reccared of Spain from Arianism in 589, and sent a pallium to Leander of Seville ; in Africa he wrote urging the bishops to suppress the Donatist heresy ; he prevented the election of a Lombard, and probably Arian, bishop to the great metropolitan see of Milan, and to his joy, the child of Theudelinda and Agilulf received orthodox baptism in 602. With the bishops of Ravenna he had a protracted dispute over the wearing of the pallium. This vestment of white wool, draped over the shoulders, was originally that of an imperial official, and it was worn in the east in the sixth century by all bishops indiscriminately. In the west it was worn of right only by the pope and two other bishops, one of whom was the bishop of Ravenna ; the pope in addition conferred it as a mark of honour on metropolitans, and even certain simple bishops. The bishop of Ravenna's right to wear the pall was not challenged by Gregory, but only his custom of wearing it, not only during mass, but before, when he gave audience to the laity, and when he went in solemn processions. Although Gregory was gratified by the election of his own monk Marinianus as bishop of Ravenna in the midst of the dispute, he found to his surprise that the latter continued to defend the rights of the church of Ravenna in the matter, with the support of the exarch. The matter was finally allowed to drop. With the churches of Istria, Dalmatia and Illyricum Gregory was also in correspondence, for the eradication of simony and heresy.

Gregory's own view that the holder of the apostolic see was something far more than patriarch of the west is illustrated by his relations with the churches of the east, and particularly with the patriarch of Constantinople. To Gregory the apostolic see was " the chief of all the churches, whose bishop was responsible for the government of the whole church," at least by the duty of correcting transgressors. The Roman bishop was vested with this preeminence as the successor and vicar of S. Peter. All bishops and patriarchs could be corrected by the pope, if guilty of heresy or offence against the canons. The decrees of councils had no force " without the authority and consent of the apostolic see." " As regards the church of Constantinople," he wrote, " who can doubt that it is subject to the apostolic see ? Why both our most religious lord the emperor, and our brother the bishop of Constantinople, continually acknowledge it." Constantinople, the seat of the emperor, was in fact the only patriarchate likely to prove a dangerous rival to Rome in Gregory's day. Gregory was willing to allow a share in the apostolic primacy to the older patriarchates of Antioch and Alexandria, which neither historical fact nor political expediency could conçede to Constantinople.

Over three matters Gregory had difficulties with the patriarchs of Constantinople. The most important was over the title of oecumenical, or universal, bishop, which one of these had assumed at a synod in 588. Gregory protested, and wrote also to the other patriarchs of the east, eliciting however small support from them. In his letter to Constantinople Gregory explained that " oecumenical " could only mean " sole " bishop, and implored the patriarch not to incur the wrath of Christ at the last judgment by the use of so proud and sinful a title. To the emperor Maurice even, who had small enough love for him, he wrote, upbraiding him for his failure to rebuke the patriarch. Yet Maurice gave no help, the next patriarch continued to use the same title, and within a hundred years the popes themselves began to use the title which Gregory found so obnoxious. It was probably in connexion with this difficulty that the empress Constantia was induced to write to the pope ordering him to send the head of S. Paul, or some other large portion of his relics, to deposit within a basilica she was building in honour of the apostle, near her own palace. The request threw Gregory into consternation, and he wrote in answer explaining the dangers that such sacrilegious transfer of relics would almost infallibly provoke. Gregory's motive in stressing the blood-curdling nature

of the punishment incurrent by sacrilege is sufficiently
clear. In one more matter, an appeal from two presbyters
who had been condemned for heresy by the church of
Constantinople, Gregory vindicated the appellate jurisdiction of the Holy See.

An account of Gregory's despatch of Augustine for the
conversion of the English may be transferred to the
chapter on the conversion of Europe by the missionaries :
but it should be noted here that this mission also redounded
to the prestige of the papacy. Later English missionaries
in Europe, Wilfrid, Willibrord, and above all Boniface
and his disciples, were the ardent children and champions
of the apostolic see.

As a theologian, Gregory wrote nothing especially
profound or original ; his theology was based on the
creeds, supplemented by Augustine, for whom he had a
great admiration. " Holy scripture," he wrote, " is
incomparably superior to every form of knowledge and
science ; " Christ, as Augustine taught, is the centre of
the Old Testament as well as the New. " The Old Testament is the prophecy of the New, the New is the explanation of the Old." Christ is foreshadowed in the Old Testament, " every just man was, in a sense, a figure of Christ,"
and this was the justification for the interpretation of
the scriptures allegorically or mystically, for which
Gregory had so insatiable a thirst, and so prolific a faculty
in exposition. Gregory's conception of the church was
essentially that of Augustine, the City of God. " No
one is ignorant," he says, " that holy church is the city
of the Lord," whose foundation is Christ. The kingdom
of heaven, in the gospels, is the church : the church is
the body of Christ, and the union between the head and
the body is so close that " Christ still suffers many things
in His body, in the person of His members, while the church
is already glorified with her head in heaven." To be
separated from the church, the body, is to be separated
from Christ, the head : " the holy universal church pro-
claims that God cannot truly be worshipped, save within
herself, and asserts that all they who are without her
shall never be saved." Gregory's theology was expounded,
not in any great treatise upon doctrinal controversies,

but in his *Morals*, his lectures on Ezekiel, in the *Dialogues*, in his letters, and in the *Cura Pastoralis*. This last treatise, explaining the supreme office of a bishop in preaching, became perhaps the most popular of all his works, and was translated sooner or later into all the vernacular languages ; but all Gregory's works were immensely studied by succeeding generations, found a place in every monastic and cathedral library, and justify his title as the " fourth doctor of the church."

The changes effected by Gregory in liturgy and church music have been overestimated in the past. The so-called " Gregorian Sacramentary " represents the state of the Roman liturgy not in the days of Gregory, but of pope Hadrian, (772–795). According to tradition, Gregory completely revised the system of church music, compiled an antiphonary, or liturgical music book, and founded a school of church music, the schola cantorum. But the antiphonary in question was much later than Gregory, and plain chant, the system of church music with which his name is generally connected, much older. The " planus cantus " was the ordinary development of the old Graeco-Roman music, when applied to church hymns and chants : it was " open " (planus) or unbarred, not divided as modern music by a recurrent, regular accent. The music sung in the basilica of S. Peter under Gregory was simply the Graeco-Roman music of the day. The tradition by which Gregory himself trained and chastised the boy singers of the schola cantorum represents no historical impossibility. It was the duty and custom of all pious bishops at the time to instruct their young lectors or cantors in the chant-ing of the office, expositions which probably combined moral explanations with liturgical and musical directions : and there is no reason why even so great a bishop as Gregory should have omitted these instructions. All bishops at the day nourished young lectors or cantors in their household, and the bishops of Rome had certainly done so earlier than Gregory. These young lectors may have been separately housed even before Gregory's time. Gregory's later biographer states that he built a fresh schola for these boys near the Lateran, and the evidence though late, may be trustworthy.

CHAPTER II

THE SECULAR AND MONASTIC CLERGY, 600–750

The clerical militia—The bishop's parochia and familia—Bishops' schools—Revenue and stipends—Spiritual work of clergy—Celtic monachism—Benedictine monachism

ALTHOUGH dividing lines were not yet as sharply drawn as later in the middle ages, the clergy in this period were already recognised as secular or monastic : those living in the world under the immediate rule of the bishop, engaged in ministerial and apostolic work among the laity, and those engaged in contemplation and the celebration of the divine praises in a monastery. Both were clerks, for they had received the tonsure and been set apart for the service of the Lord : but the secular clergy were clerks in a special sense and par excellence. The special points which call for notice in connexion with them are the contemporary conception of the clerical militia, the work of the bishop in his see or parochia, ecclesiastical revenues and stipends, and the training and spiritual work of the clergy.

In the time of Gregory I the conception of the clergy as the " clerical militia " was already long developed. The imperial civil service had provided a ladder of offices, by which a candidate, beginning at the bottom, might proceed through the " cursus honorum " to the highest civil or military rank. The parallel between this ladder and the various grades of the Christian ministry had not been unnoticed by Christian bishops, and by 600 the commonest collective description of the clergy was the " clerical militia," or the " celestial " in opposition to the " secular " militia. The celestial militia consisted of seven orders, its sevenfold nature denoting the perfection of the divine service : ostiarius, exorcist, lector, acolyte, subdeacon, deacon, presbyter or sacerdos.   Pope Zosimus († 418) had compared the grades of the " saecularia officia " with those of the celestial militia, and forbidden that laymen should present themselves to the church, and expect ordination forthwith (saltu) to the higher grades : " Let him learn in the camp of the Lord in the grade of lector the rudiments of the divine service : nor let him esteem it base to be ordained exorcist, acolyte, subdeacon, and deacon, and this not at a bound, but at the times appointed by the ordination of the fathers.   Let such a man then approach that summit, the presbyterate, when his age fulfils the conditions which that name implies."   About the year 600 the first three minor orders were usually conferred together ; boys were ordained lectors at about seven years of age, and received the other grades at intervals of several years, till they were ordained to the presbyterate at the age of forty-five.   Gregory of Tours relates how, at the death of a Gallic bishop, the bishops summoned for his funeral encountered a claim from one Cato, a presbyter of his clergy, to be ordained bishop almost as of right, from his due canonical reception of the various grades. " For," he said, " I have been allotted these grades of clerkship ever with canonical institution.   I was a lector ten years, I ministered in the office of subdeacon for five years, fifteen years was I bound to the diaconate, and now for twenty years I have enjoyed the honour of the presbyterate.   What now remains for me but to receive . . . the episcopate ? "   Nevertheless, the desire of the citizens who shared with the clergy in the election of a bishop often, especially in the unsettlement of the barbarian invasions, led to the hasty consecration of some powerful lay noble, who had not been trained in the minor orders ; often with disastrous results to the discipline of the local church later.

The giving of the tonsure, apparently an old Roman ceremony of adoption, in the eastern church accompanied reception into the family of an abbot, or a bishop.   In the latter case it always accompanied the giving of the first minor order—(in the eastern church the clerical tonsure is still not given separately from a minor order). In the western church it accompanied the giving of a minor order till the pontificate of Gregory I; afterwards it was given separately to those attached in some way to the service of the church, but not intending to proceed to orders. All who received the tonsure, whether monks, anchorites, the secular clergy or church officials, by this ceremony became clerks (from clericus, κλῆρος, lot); this appears from early forms for the shearing of a clerk. At this ceremony the bishop said alternately with the candidate certain verses, usually from the sixteenth psalm: " The Lord himself is the portion of mine inheritance. . . . Thou shalt maintain my lot." By the year 600 the hair was not only shorn round the nape of the neck, but in a large circular patch on the crown, so that the remaining hair resembled a " corona : " in the east the whole top of the head was shaved, leaving no fringe in front. There was, however, no special significance in this difference of cut, except as denoting the eastern or the western obedience. Nor was there in origin any difference of significance between the monastic and clerical tonsures in east or west : both signified adoption into the family of the Lord. The status of clerkship was of legal as well as religious significance. No clerk might carry arms, and on the other hand the clerk was under special legal protection, and could be tried only by the bishop's court, over which, at this period, the bishop himself or his archdeacon presided.

The see or province of an archbishop or bishop about 600 was still normally spoken of as a " parochia," though the term " diocese " was beginning also to be used of the see of a bishop. The word " parochiae " was still used for bishoprics as late as the tenth and eleventh centuries. But in our period, 600–750, " the sacerdos and his parochia " meant almost always, the bishop and his see. Rural parishes, headed not by a bishop but by a priest, (presbyter), had only come into existence in the sixth century : the council of Vaison in 529 was the first to legislate for them. The whole see or parochia had earlier been served by the clergy of the bishop's church, his familia. As the countryside became Christian, the foundation of smaller, local units of clergy became necessary.

An episcopal familia in 600 contained the larger proportion of the clergy of the see ; it continued by far the
most important unit of clergy till three or four hundred
years later. It was recruited mainly from boys, for the
reason that, unless the bishop educated his clergy himself,
they were likely to get no education elsewhere. This
had not been the case under imperial Rome : as long as
the state schools, the schools of rhetoric, had educated
boys—primarily for the civil service,—the bishops could
get adult educated ordinands, at least for the higher
clerical offices. But the barbarian invasions had swept
away the schools of rhetoric in Gaul by c. 450 ; the Vandal
invasion destroyed them in Africa ; in Italy after the
Ostrogoth and Lombard invasions the state ceased to
pay the salary of the rhetors. As a result, there were no
schools in Gaul and Africa ; and though private rhetors
practised for fees in Italy, education had been dealt a
severe blow. Even in Italy it became advisable for
bishops to train up their lectors themselves, and elsewhere
it was indispensable. The episcopal order was "ordo
doctorum," and to the seventh century mind, the instruction of the clergy by the bishop in person was as important
an element in his doctorate, as the instruction of the laity
by sermons. The bishop's "cathedra" was as yet the
only academic "chair." Boys were sent to the bishop
by noble parents for ordination as lector, and training
for the sacerdotium : boys of free birth were taken, and
children of the coloni, or even the serfs on the bishop's
estates, were also so taken. The ordination of the last
two had, however, to be preceded by manumission. Many
persons of servile birth seem actually to have been ordained. All the personal service in the bishop's household,
all the " sacristan " work in his cathedra, and in the chapels
and hospitals, was performed by clerks who never rose
above the minor orders ; there was relatively a very large
number of married clerks in minor orders, practically the
domestic servants of the church. It is doubtful if many
boys of servile birth rose above this status : but there was
a career open to talent for all, through the minor orders.
The canonical prohibition for a bishop to ordain the lector
of another was connected originally with this question of

education : the council of Toledo (531) had stated that it
was unfair to the bishop who had taken the child " from
rustic and mean surroundings " that the clerk should
later, " when imbued with such an education, transfer
himself to another church."

There are many early references to episcopal household
schools, and the education afforded in them to young
lectors. The education consisted normally of Latin,
singing and the computus, (for reckoning the date of
Easter). The higher branches of knowledge, the seven
liberal arts, were not usually taught before the Carolingian
renaissance. Though bishops continued, between 600
and 750, to teach their young clerks themselves, this
most important duty began to devolve on the senior
presbyter of their familia. In large and well organised
familiae before the barbarian invasions, the senior presbyter
had been termed the archipresbyter, as the senior deacon
had been termed the archidiaconus. In sixth and seventh
century Gaul another title appears for the presbyter, who
in practice ranked as senior in the familia : this is the
" scholasticus " or " capischola." He trained the young
lectors, under the bishop's supervision, and he also wrote
the bishop's charters and privileges : by the ninth century
he was usually called the " magister scholarum," and
by the twelfth century (to look ahead), the chancellor.
The council of Toledo, 531, had enacted : " Of those whom
the will of their parents sets free from the years of their
first infancy for the clerical office, we decree that immediately they have received the tonsure they shall be handed
over to the ministry of the lectors : they ought to be
taught in the house of the church, in the bishop's presence,
by his deputy. But when they shall have completed
their eighteenth year, their wishes concerning the taking
of a wife ought to be scrutinised by the bishops, in the
presence of clerks and laity." The " domus ecclesiae "
signified the house near his cathedral where the bishop
lived ; that the young lectors lived with him is shown
from many contemporary lives, and from Gregory of
Tours' story of bishop Aitherius of Lisieux, who at night
" rested upon his couch, having around his bed the many
little beds of his clerks." If the boy lector chose to marry,

D

when his intention was solemnly scrutinised by his bishop,
he was not to be denied power to do so. The churches of
the rural parishes were served by similar familiae, though
of course on a smaller scale. The parish clerk of the
middle ages is the seventh century familia of clergy reduced
to a minimum.

The episcopal familia was supported from the estates
of the see, and from the offerings of the faithful in the
cathedral; and such basilicas as were directly served by
the familia. All endowments were vested in the bishop
and the senior clergy, who formed his " council " and
attested charters and leases. By 600 it was already
long established in Italy that the revenue of the see should
be divided into four portions, for the bishop, the clergy,
church fabrics, and the poor. The fourth for the poor
went to the maintenance of at least one " xenodochium "
(something between an almshouse, guest-house, and hospital), the payment of regular alms to certain of the poor,
(who were enrolled on the matricula of the familia), the
maintenance of " widows," " deaconesses," and in some
cases, orphan children, and in indiscriminate alms on
certain festivals. The fourth for the clergy was divided
up into stipends, the Vulgate word for wages, paid three
or four times a year to the individual clerks. In general
the stipends varied with the grade the clerk had attained :
but Gregory I stated more than once that they should
be absolutely at the discretion of the bishop, who ought
to reward the zealous with a higher stipend than the
slothful. Stipends consisted of payments both in money
and kind. Those of the higher clergy generally after the
seventh century consisted of a grant for life of certain
lands or vineyards.

To turn from the clergy themselves to their churches
and their work. In the seventh century " ecclesia " was
used for a church building, but much more often for the
clergy and people of a parochia, episcopal or rural. The
commonest word for the church building was " basilica,"
which had been originally used for a building of a certain
architectural type, but was now used for a church of
any shape. None the less, most of the " basilicas " of
the seventh and eighth centuries in southern Europe were

of the old basilica shape, i.e., rectangular churches, with, characteristically, a semicircular or apsidal recess at one end for the altar. There was often also a narthex or portico at the end opposite from the apse, containing sometimes the font for baptism by immersion ; sometimes the baptistery was a separate building near the church. Behind the altar a stone seat ran round the apse for the clergy, and at the back of the altar, raised on steps, was the semicircular cathedra or bishop's throne. Sitting on this, he could be seen by all the worshippers, and he seems to have sat on his throne to preach. When he celebrated the mysteries, he stood at the back of a low altar, facing the people.

The clergy were bound to say the canonical hours daily in the basilica ; the heaviest obligation was the saying of the long office of mattins at a very early hour. On Sundays and feast days the bishop, or the presbyter of the rural parochia, celebrated the divine mysteries, normally at nine o'clock, and those not undergoing penitential discipline communicated. If the church were too small to accommodate, on great festivals, the country folk who were bound to come from a considerable distance, mass was said earlier, and repeated as many times as was needed. The laity went to no other service on Sunday : but they attended the singing of the canonical hours on the vigils of great festivals. Baptisms were performed on Easter Eve, and before Pentecost, except in case of danger of death ; a Lombard king going to seek the archbishop of Milan on Easter Saturday, found him baptizing in the baptistery, but so confusing was the multitude of lights, so thick the clouds of incense, that he failed to recognise him. Absolution could still, in 600, only be conferred by the bishop : confession was only made after grave sin, schism, or heresy, and at death ; it was inevitable, however, that the presbyters of rural parishes should soon be allowed to absolve. Confirmation was given to young children ; unction with the sacred chrism was administered to the sick. Deaconesses were still enrolled on the matricula of the basilica and prepared women for baptism. The exorcist's peculiar function was still to cast out evil spirits, and particularly the evil spirits of heathenism, by catechising before baptism. The words in the church of England catechism : " Dost thou renounce the devil and all his works, etc.? " are the remnant of an exorcism, which in the eighth century ran : " Forsakest thou the devil ? And all devil-worship ? " and then went on to demand a special renunciation of the various forms of devil-worship, worship of Diana and the classical deities, and Woden and the Germanic gods and goddesses.

The monastic clergy in the period included those of the Benedictine and Celtic type, and those clerks in orders who lived in a monastery with their bishop or provost. Many of the stricter spirits of the period held, like S. Augustine of Hippo before them, that the secular clergy ought to live a communal life, like the apostles and early Christians in the Acts of the Apostles. Accordingly many bishops lived with their familiae, and provided a communal life of this kind, in a dwelling near the church called indifferently the bishop's monastery or house. Clerks who thus lived in the monastery were as frequently called monks as those who lived under a definite religious rule. They were the predecessors of the " Austin canons " of the twelfth century (see p. 129). Of the monks who lived under a rule, there were two chief types, the Celtic and the Benedictine.

Ireland, Britain, central Europe, Spain and even Italy were, about 600, largely under the influence of Celtic monachism : this was of an older type than Benedictine monachism, more closely allied with the east. The guides which it followed were the lives and rules of the Egyptian monks, Antony and Pachomius, and the Greek and Frankish monks, Basil and Cassian. The Celtic monks aimed at fulfilling the counsel of Christ to perfection : " If any man would be perfect, let him sell all that he hath." By renouncing the society of the world, its pleasures, ambitions and distractions, by renouncing all the pleasures of sense, and by renouncing their own will to an abbot, they hoped to practise a life of prayer, or contemplation. They lived usually in communities, though the tendency towards solitary or eremitical life was strong among them, as in the eastern monachism from which they sprang : they were not necessarily ordained to the grades of clerkship. Compared with Benedictine monks, they laid more stress on austerity of life as an instrument of perfection, and less on the sanctifying influence of community life itself. They said the canonical hours, and from the time when the labours of Patrick made Ireland their headquarters, they reverenced learning, and produced from among their numbers some of the greatest scholars of the seventh century. The seven British bishops mentioned by Bede at the time of the coming of Augustine were connected with monasteries of the Celtic type in Wales : but the largest Celtic monastery, and the most esteemed for its learning in the seventh century, was the Bangor on Belfast Lough. From this house had come Columbanus and twelve companions, who, after passing through Britain and Gaul, had founded his great Celtic monastery, Luxeuil, in " the vast wilderness " of the Vosges. Later Columbanus founded other houses at Fontaines, and at Bobbio in the Apennines, where the last part of his life was spent. He was the friend of queen Theudelinda, and took no small share in converting the Lombards from their Arianism ; while he paid the greatest deference to the apostolic see, he had a long correspondence with Gregory the Great over the date for the keeping of Easter, and refused to withdraw from the conservative, Celtic position. When confronted with the decisions of earlier popes, he quoted the proverb that " a living dog is better than a dead lion," and urged that Gregory, " a living saint, might well correct the omissions of one who went before him."

The discipline of the Columban monasteries was exceedingly severe : the rule enjoined on the monks to fast every day, pray every day, work every day, and read every day. " A monk must live under the rule of one father, and in the society of many brethren, that he may learn humility from one, patience from another, silence from a third, gentleness from a fourth. He is not to do what he likes. He is to eat what he is told to eat, he is to have only what is given to him, he must do the work which is set him, he must be subject to those whom he dislikes. He must go to bed so tired that he will fall asleep on the way, and he must rise before he has had as much sleep as he wants.   When he is ill-treated, he must be silent.   He must fear the prior of his monastery as a master, and yet love him as a father : he must believe that whatever orders he gives are good."   The manual labour demanded of the monks was exacting, for the new houses were generally planted in the wilderness, and the monks were dependent for their food on their agriculture. The penances assigned in the rule were also severe ;   yet crowds of postulants joined the monasteries, not only from the labouring class, but from the Frankish and Burgundian nobles.

At the beginning of the seventh century Benedictine monachism was but just beginning to be known outside Italy.   It was to hold parallel sway in Europe between 600 and 700, and after that date was gradually to be accepted, even by the Celtic houses themselves.   It became so important a factor in European civilisation that the eighth to the eleventh centuries, the centuries of its flowering, have been termed the " Benedictine centuries."

S. Benedict himself († 543) had founded the great monastery of Monte Cassino.   From the accounts of the crowds of parents, noble and otherwise, who brought their young sons and confided them to him to be made monks, he must have gained a reputation for eminent sanctity and wisdom in his lifetime.   But the older, Eastern monachism had a hold on Italy before S. Benedict : on several occasions he was brought into contact with monasteries and monks, probably of the Basilian type ; and his famous rule shows that he was familiar with the writings of the eastern fathers of the monastic life.   When Benedict died, or when Gregory the Great died, it was hardly realised that Benedict had originated a new type of monks, much less a definite " order."   His famous " rule " was the rule of one house, Monte Cassino ;   even in daughter houses of that monastery it appears to have been at first only one among the guides to perfection, and there is no evidence that it was accepted as the sole or pre-eminent rule of any house in Italy, except Monte Cassino, before the seventh century.   But since S. Benedict's conception of the monastic life was eventually to triumph in western Europe, it is of importance to realise the nature of the Benedictine rule, life and vows.

S. Benedict speaks of his rule in the prologue as a " very little rule for beginners : " not for ascetics, that is, of the Egyptian type, but of those who desired to find in a monastery a " school for the service of God." The monks were to live as a family under the government of the abbot, their father. At their profession they were to promise obedience to him, conversion of manners, (which implied obedience to the rule, with its obligations of poverty and chastity), and " stability." No monk might, as was usually allowed at the time, pass from one monastery to another as through successive schools of holiness : he must live all his life in the family which had accepted him. He must obey the abbot as Christ himself, and patiently bear with his fellow monks' infirmities, whether of body or character. He must share in the agricultural and domestic work of the community, and to do this he could not have been strictly, in the modern sense, " enclosed ; " but he passed most of his life within his monastery, within whose gates strangers, except those seeking succour or hospitality, were forbidden to enter. The monastery must, in most cases, have been just the Italian dwelling house of the time, whose colonnaded open court, or peristyle, became the typical monastic cloister. Here, in the open air, the monk worked, read, or learned the psalms of the divine office by heart ; in one of the halls he dined with his fellows, in another he slept with them. There were no separate cells, and there was no privacy. There was usually only one meal a day, meat was never eaten, and in material conditions the life must have approximated, not to the rigours of the Egyptian hermits, but to the poverty of the Italian peasant of the day.

The monks' time table was to be regulated by the performance of the " opus Dei," the recital of the seven canonical hours. This took less time at first than it did in later centuries, but it was the monks' paramount duty, with which nothing was to be allowed to interfere. The time table varied in winter and summer : for the offices were said at a stated hour, and this hour varied according to the length of the day. In mid March the average day worked out thus : the monks rose at 2, and said Vigils or the night office. An hour's meditation or reading followed. Lauds were said at dawn, at 4.30, Prime at sunrise, at 6, and reading filled the time till Terce at 9. From 9.15 till 4 work in the fields followed, with Sext said inter-mediately at 12. None was said at 4, Vespers at 4.30, the single meal was taken at 5 o'clock. Collation (which was still a reading and not a meal) was at 5.45, and the day ended with Compline in the dusk at 6. In mid-winter the monks would have had as much as $9\frac{1}{2}$ hours' sleep, in midsummer a very short night indeed : but a 2 hours' siesta broke, as with the peasants, the hot Italian working day. It is noticeable that the Benedictine night office was not said between two periods of sleep, as became the custom in strict monastic houses much later : it was said while it was still night, but at the end of the night's rest. Mass was said only on Sundays and holy days ; open breaches of the rule were publicly confessed in chapter, and private sins to the abbot or some " spiritual father or senior ; " but regular private confession was not yet used. The monastery did not necessarily include a presbyter among its inhabitants. The monks were drawn in S. Benedict's day from both the noble and the peasant classes, but the illiterate at first predominated : the average monk in the time of Gregory I seems not to have had the education which was considered necessary for the presbyterate. His work was in no sense pastoral, but a vocation to prayer, humility and mortification : numbers might be accepted as postulants by an abbot who were too old to undergo the long training by which peasant boys were fitted for holy orders.

Nevertheless, the spread of the Benedictine order affected the relations of the monks to the secular clergy. Insistence on a close community life produced a more " civilised " type of monk, whom it was possible in some cases to take from his monastery and promote to the orders of clerk-ship after a shorter training than that accorded to the lay ordinand. S. Augustine in the early fifth century had written that it was scarcely possible, out of even a good monk, to make a good clerk. Gregory the Great

found some of his best material for the clerical order in
the monasteries. But even he still conceived of the
monastic and clerical vocations as entirely separate, and
even incompatible, as various passages in his letters show
clearly. " No one," he said, " can both perform ecclesiastical (clerical) duties, and remain by due order under
monastic rule." " The duties of each office separately
are so weighty that no one can rightly discharge them.
It is therefore very improper that one man should be
considered fit to discharge the duties of both." Nevertheless, if a bishop wished for the services of a certain
monk, he might with the abbot's permission withdraw
him from the monastery and ordain him to the clerical
servitude ; but the ex-monk was then under no monastic
obligations. Monks were clerks because they had received
the tonsure : they could not be tried by the lay courts :
but they had not received any of the seven orders, and it
is for this reason that occasional medieval chroniclers
speak of them as laymen.

Knowledge and observance of the Benedictine rule
spread gradually. In seventh century Gaul it was quite
usual to enjoin on new monasteries the observance both
of the Columban and Benedictine rule. Even in the chief
Celtic house of Luxeuil a joint copy of the two rules is found
by the year 630, and in 631 a monastery was founded at
Limoges where the two rules were prescribed, " according
to the practice of the men of Luxeuil." As a result of
this double observance, the milder and more humane rule
of S. Benedict gradually replaced the Columban. The
synod of Autun, 670, was the first to make the Benedictine
rule obligatory on monasteries for at least part of France.
In the synods of 742 and 743, presided over by the missionary Boniface, the rule is emphatically mentioned as
the norm for all men's and women's cloisters. But it
was not till after the work of Benedict of Aniane (see
p. 164) that the Benedictine rule actually became the
standard for all continental monasteries.

CHAPTER III

THE MISSIONARIES : AUGUSTINE, AIDAN, WILLIBRORD, BONIFACE

Augustine's mission to Ethelbert of Kent—Missionary work from Canterbury—Aidan's mission to Northumbria—Archbishop Theodore —Willibrord's mission to Friesland—Boniface commissioned by Gregory II—Boniface founds German episcopate—Boniface reforms Frankish church

THE transformation of Christianity from a Mediterranean to a European religion was slow and gradual ; the years of unsettlement during the barbarian invasions were not favourable to missionary progress. Some of the new nations had received the Arian form of Christianity from the labours of Ulfilas, before they had set out on their wanderings ; others, like the Anglo-Saxons in Britain, conquered and settled as heathen. The Franks had been baptised, with Clovis their king, to orthodox Christianity : the monks of Columbanus taught the heathen on their borders, and the Frankish bishops, like Gregory of Tours, tried to consolidate their position in northern France by building outlying churches and chapels. When Gregory the Great began his pontificate, however, the Anglo-Saxons had driven British Christianity back into Brittany, Cornwall, Wales and Strathclyde ; and central Europe was heathen from the regions now known as Belgium, north-east France, and Alsace-Lorraine, across to where in the Balkans the east Roman emperors strove to protect Greek Christianity from the heathen invaders. The Christianity of the old Roman empire in the intermediate region, in the provinces of the Rhine and the Danube, had been wiped out : and even the

Christianity planted by Ulfilas in Roumania and the later Bulgaria had perished, or passed with the migrating Goths into western Europe. The conversion of the northern two-thirds of Europe was to be slow : that of Sweden was not begun till the ninth century, that of Norway not till the tenth.

The conversion of the Anglo-Saxons was begun by pope Gregory the Great from the south-eastern corner of England, and continued a little later by the Celtic monk Aidan, from the north-eastern ; the two missionary movements finally fused at the synod of Whitby, in 664. Gregory himself knew little of England except its heathenism ; he regarded the Frankish bishops as lacking in zeal in not attempting its conversion, and before the sending of his mission probably did not even know that British bishops existed in the west of the island. These latter can scarcely be blamed for failing to convert the invader, with whom they were still fighting. No certain frontier even was established between them, till a battle in 577 separated the Britons of Cornwall and Wales, and another as late as 607 those of Wales and Strathclyde. King Ethelbert of Kent, however, had by now married a Christian wife, the Frankish princess, Bertha, and allowed Liudhard her chaplain to celebrate the Christian rites in the old Roman church of S. Martin, in his royal city of Canterbury. Meanwhile in 595 Gregory was planning to buy Anglian slave boys, to be " given to God in the monasteries " and then sent on the English mission. In 596 he actually despatched a band of forty monks, to travel from Italy up the Rhone valley to Tours, Paris and England. The leader of the band was Augustine, who had been the " alumnus " of the bishop of Messina, (trained in his familia). He had then joined the monastery of S. Andrew on the Caelian, and become its prior ; he had at one time shared Gregory's private room and been his confidential secretary. He, like the other monks, was chosen by Gregory for his training in the regular life and his devotion. Gregory must have considered him the sort of man who could train up an episcopal familia of English boys, teach them to recite the divine scriptures in the office, assist in the administration of the Christian sacraments, finally, after long years of training, to reach the summit of the sacerdotium, and train up clergy of their own : all of which would be of more missionary value in the end than the immediate baptism of heathen multitudes. The charge often made against Augustine, that he proved lacking in statesmanship and breadth of view, is possibly true, and due to the narrowness of his training ; Gregory could probably have found ecclesiastics more urbane and statesmanlike among his seven deacons ; but it is not recorded that any of these were willing to go on a mission which involved lifelong banishment in a savage country. Of the monks who accompanied Augustine, Lawrence, who was to succeed him later at Canterbury, was a presbyter : it is, for various reasons, not likely that any others were as yet.

The missionary monks travelled over the Alps, and then, overcome by the difficulties, sent back Augustine to Rome. Gregory exhorted him to continue, strengthened his control over his followers by constituting him their abbot, and sent him back to Gaul. He rejoined his monks, received one or two presbyters from the Frankish king as interpreters, and the whole band landed at Ebbsfleet in Thanet in April 597. Ethelbert agreed to receive them in audience in the open air, and they walked to the meeting in procession, chanting a litany, and carrying a silver cross, and a picture of the crucifixion. They were given a residence " suitable to their rank " in Canterbury, and allowed to use the little old basilica of S. Martin with Liudhard. Here they remained, teaching those who came to them, and on 1 June, 597, Ethelbert was baptized in S. Martin's. In the autumn Augustine was consecrated bishop by Virgilius of Arles, the metropolitan and papal vicar of Gaul, and Bede tells us that on Christmas Day Augustine baptized 10,000 new converts, probably in the river. Augustine now set up his cathedral on the ruins of an old Roman church, and dedicated it " in the name of the holy Saviour, our God and Lord Jesus Christ." This earliest cathedral of Christchurch, Canterbury, was a basilica with apse and altar at either end, and a crypt or confession ; it was to be the church of the bishop's familia, and Ethelbert gave Augustine land for its endowment. Augustine must have ordained some of his monks, but have continued to live and worship with his whole familia at Christchurch for some years. Before his death, he had also rededicated a heathen temple, outside the city walls, to S. Pancras, and built a monastery near it, thus separating his monastic from his episcopal familia. Within the monastery Ethelbert built the church of SS. Peter and Paul, and here, though it was not finished at the time of his death, Augustine was finally buried. The foundation of an episcopal familia at Christchurch and the transfer of the Benedictine type of monachism to the monastery soon to be called S. Augustine's, was the real contribution of Augustine to the conversion of England.

For the settlement of certain problems Augustine again had recourse to Gregory. In 598 he sent his two chief followers, Lawrence the presbyter and Peter the monk, to ask further helpers and directions. After three years they returned, with Gregory's answers and monks who were to become the future bishops of London, Rochester, York, and an abbot of S. Augustine's. To the question, how the bishop should live with his clergy, and how he should divide the offerings of the faithful, Gregory answered by quoting the normal fourfold division practised on the continent : but pointed out that such division was superfluous in Augustine's own case, since as a monk he must live communally with his followers, after the manner of the primitive church. But any clerks in minor orders who wished to marry must be allowed to do so, and receive their stipends outside the community (as the council of Toledo, 531, directed more explicitly). This clause shows that Augustine was not seeking to establish a monastery of the Benedictine type at Christchurch, but to train a native clergy in a familia of the normal contemporary fashion. To the question whether, the faith being the same, different churches might have different customs, Gregory recommended Augustine to choose what was pious, religious and right from Roman or Gallic use, and accustom the minds of the English thereto. He also allowed Augustine, in his necessity, to consecrate bishops alone, committed the British bishops to his authority for teaching and guidance, and solved certain minor queries.

With these answers he sent Augustine certain books, sacred vessels and the pallium.

In his seven years' work in England, Augustine made one attempt to establish relations with the British bishops. These held the same faith, but had been out of touch with continental Christianity for 150 years while a wedge of heathen Saxons had isolated them. In certain points custom had changed, and the British now differed from continental practice in the use of an old cycle for determining the date of Easter, in the shape of the tonsure, and in the ritual of baptism. They were, moreover, unlikely to submit to the authority of the new bishop at Canterbury, one too who had been accepted by the hated Saxons. They came to a conference at "Augustine's Oak," but finding Augustine unbending in his claims, withdrew without arranging a concordat. In 604 the monk Mellitus converted and baptized the king of the east Saxons and was made bishop of London; the king built for him a basilica dedicated to S. Paul. Similarly, the monk Justus was made bishop and set up his familia in Rochester. In 604 both Augustine and Gregory died; but missionary work continued from Canterbury and the continent. Paulinus was made bishop and sent as chaplain to Ethelbert's daughter, when she married Edwin of Northumbria; in 627 he baptized Edwin and his thegns in a little wooden oratory at York. But five years later the heathen Penda of Mercia killed Edwin in battle, ravaged Northumbria, and wiped out Paulinus' work. In 631, Sigibert, who had learned Christianity while an exile in Gaul, became king of east Anglia: he asked Honorius of Canterbury for missionaries, and Honorius sent him Felix, who set up his cathedral in Dunwich, with a school of lectors after the Canterbury pattern, and Fursey, an Irish monk, who founded his monastery at Burgh Castle, in Suffolk. Wessex was converted by an Italian monk, Birinus, who was made bishop of Dorchester near Oxford.

The missions of the Celtic monks from Scotland began when Oswald of Northumbria, who had been baptized and educated at the monastery of Iona, won back Northumbria in 635. The Celtic monk sent in answer to his request to teach his subjects proved too stern, and the monks of Iona then chose the gentler Aidan to " give them at first the milk of easier doctrine," and gradually nourish them with the word of God. Aidan built his monastery, and set up his see, not in Oswald's city of Bamburgh, on its rocky Northumbrian headland, but on Lindisfarne, an island near by, only accessible at high tide. The monastery at Lindisfarne, a group of huts of rough stone or wood, surrounded by a rampart, became the centre of Celtic Christianity in the north ; Irish customs were followed, manuscripts were copied in the beautiful Irish handwriting and wonderfully illuminated, and a separate type of Northumbrian art arose, which was transmitted later to the two other great Northumbrian monasteries, Wearmouth and Jarrow. Aidan himself spent most of his time in preaching journeys, travelling on foot along the uplands of Northumbria, ascetic in his own life, generous to the poor, and gentle to all. In 642 however Penda defeated and slew Oswald in battle, and Aidan died before the old arch-heathen was himself defeated and killed by Oswy in 655. But Aidan's work was not wiped out as that of Paulinus had been, and Celtic Christianity spread, under the rule of Oswy, not only over Northumbria, but over Penda's old kingdom of Mercia. Cedd and three other Celtic monks had already been working in Mercia before Penda's death : Cedd was now sent off as bishop and chaplain to the king of the east Saxons, but Diuma, one of his followers, was ordained by Finan, bishop of Lindisfarne, as bishop of the midland Angles, and Mercia. The Celtic missionaries spread over England even more widely than the continental ones from the south : their small, rectangular churches, with a rectangular recess at the end for the altar, were easier to build than the apsidal basilicas of the south, and became the typical form for later English church-building. Though the Celtic cell church had no " confession " for the relics of the martyrs, yet the Celtic monks venerated the bodies of their saintly leaders as much as continental Christians. The head of Oswald, cut off in battle, was treasured at Lindisfarne, and when the Danes sacked that monastery later, Oswald's head and the body of S. Cuthbert were carried away by the monks as their most precious treasures, and rested finally in the new church of Durham.

The relation of the churches of Canterbury and Lindisfarne remained still unsettled in the mid-seventh century,
causing inconvenience by their variations of calendar.
The first native Englishman was made archbishop of
Canterbury in 653, a circumstance making reunion with
Lindisfarne easier. In 664 a great plague also made union
easier, by clearing away some of the older actors on the
scene. Besides the archbishop of Canterbury himself,
there died the king of Kent, the bishop of Lindisfarne, and
the Celtic abbots, Cedd, the brother of Chad, and Boisil of
Melrose. Among the Northumbrian priests, Wilfrid had
become the firmest advocate for the acceptance of the
Roman claims, and the subjection of Iona and Lindisfarne
to the metropolitan of Canterbury. He had studied at
Lindisfarne, Rome, and Lyons in Gaul, and in 661 had been
made abbot of Ripon by the influence of the son of Oswy
of Northumbria. In 664, Oswy convened a joint synod
of clerks, and it was held in the great double monastery of
Streoneshalch, (the later Whitby), ruled by the abbess
Hilda, a place only second to Lindisfarne in the training of
future bishops and abbots. The questions at variance
were debated by either side before the king, and Oswy
decided to range himself under the banner of Peter rather
than Columba. As a result, intercourse between the
English and continental churches was easier ; the Celtic
tribal, monastic episcopate was replaced by the continental, territorial one ; and five years later the pope sent
to England the great organiser of the English church, the
Greek monk Theodore.

Between 664 and 669 the see of Canterbury had remained vacant, and that of Lindisfarne was in dispute,
between Wilfrid, who had been elected bishop through
the influence of the prince, and Chad, who had been appointed by Oswy during the journey of Wilfrid to Gaul
for consecration. The task of the next archbishop of
Canterbury would not be easy. The pope had asked an
African monk, Hadrian, to undertake it ; but he had
excused himself in favour of Theodore, an older man,
" well instructed in secular and divine writings, as also in
Greek and Latin." Both finally came to England, and
proved themselves statesmen and men of affairs, as well as

scholars and good monks. Hadrian was made abbot of
S. Augustine's, and Theodore travelled round England, to
visit the petty kings, and obtain from each bishop an
acknowledgment of his authority. Wilfrid he established
at York, and Chad as bishop of Lichfield, for the kingdom
of Mercia. In 673 he summoned the first national synod
of English clergy to Hertford, and there and at a later
synod he obtained their consent to be ruled by the " things
of old canonically decreed by the fathers." Theodore's
great work was the increase of episcopal " parochiae " :
he began with six bishops under him, and ended with
fourteen. He divided the see of east Anglia, cut off three
new bishoprics from Wilfrid's see at York at the cost of a
protracted struggle, and three from Chad's see of Lichfield.
The kingdom of Wessex, with its single see of Dorchester,
was not divided till 705, but its division then was in accordance with Theodore's policy. The provision of these new
bishoprics entailed the supply of an endowment for each
new familia, one of the most important aspects of
Theodore's work, for the grants made for such endowment
before Theodore's time had been comparatively few and
small. The organisation of England as two provinces of
Canterbury and York was not accomplished till 735, under
bishop Egbert, whose care for his episcopal schools at York
made them widely famed. Gregory the Great had authorised Augustine to found two provinces each with six
suffragans under the metropolitans of London and York,
but this had never been carried out. The rivalries of the
kingdoms of Kent and of the east Saxons had made a
transfer of Augustine's see to London impracticable ; and
in the conversion of the north Lindisfarne had been more
important than York. The foundation of rural, presbyteral parishes, once attributed to archbishop Theodore,
was of later date. It is, however, possible that some of the
bodies spoken of by Bede, and mentioned in later charters
as "monasteries," may have originated as little bands
of clerks, living a communal life, like the presbyteral
familiae in France in the sixth century. The element
"minster," (monasterium), in place-names where no
Benedictine monastery is known to have existed. supports
this view.

E

The conversion of " Germany," the heathen borderlands of the Franks, was largely accomplished by missionaries from England.   When bishop Wilfrid of York was sailing to Rome to appeal against the division of his bishopric, he was shipwrecked on the coast of Friesland, or Holland ; he preached there for a winter, and baptized many of the chiefs and their followers.   The real conversion of the Rhine mouth, however, was due to another Northumbrian monk, Willibrord.   He had been from early childhood " entrusted by his father to the brothers of the church at Ripon," where he received the tonsure and made his monastic profession.   When he was twenty, led by the love of pilgrimage and study, he visited the monks of Ireland. In his thirty-third year he landed with eleven brothers near the " fort of Utrecht," to preach to the heathen. Pepin of Heristal, duke of the Franks, encouraged him, and allowed him to labour in the northern border of his dominions : after a journey to Rome the pope consecrated him archbishop, in November 695, that he might found a province for his new converts, and sent him back with pall, books and relics for his mission.   For his new see Pepin gave him Wiltaburg, near Utrecht.   But coming with Pepin's approval, he was looked on with disfavour by Radbod, the Frisian prince, and little real progress could be made till the question of the independence of the Frisians, or their subjection to the Franks, was settled. After building churches and monasteries, Willibrord passed on and preached the Christian faith to the Danes. Here his success was small : but he was allowed to take back thirty Danish boys with him, to baptize and train up as missionaries.   On his journey back he was shipwrecked on the "holy island," Heligoland, and had the temerity to baptize two persons in the holy springs.   For this sacrilege the Frisians attacked and all but slew him : one of his companions was slain, but Willibrord himself escaped to the Franks.   He continued his work in Frankish Friesland, and was helped by Pepin to found the cloister of Efternach in 706, and Süstern, shortly before Pepin's death, in 714. But the position of the church had always been insecure, and when Pepin died, Radbod rebelled, defeated Charles Martel in battle near Cologne, and regained all Frankish

Friesland. He burned the churches, destroyed the service of God, drove away the priests, and compelled Willibrord himself to retire from his see and live as abbot of Efternach. In 719, however, Radbod died, and his successor sought peace with Charles Martel, and put no more hindrances in the way of the conversion of his subjects. Willibrord regained his see of Utrecht, but was never able to ordain bishops for subordinate sees. For the last three years of his life he had as companion the young English missionary Boniface, whom he wished to ordain in his own lifetime and appoint as his successor. This however Boniface refused, and Willibrord, whom Bede described in 731 as living in " extreme old age, . . . after manifold conflicts . . . sighing with his whole mind for the reward of a heavenly recompense," died in November 739.

The work of Boniface, the apostle of Germany, can be known more fully than that of earlier missionaries, both from a life, written by Willibald the presbyter, one of his followers, and from Boniface's own letters. The son of a Wessex thegn, Boniface, or Winfrith, wished, said his biographer, from the age of four " to submit himself to the monastic yoke," from the day that certain presbyters and clerks came round preaching to the lay people, and were entertained by his father. The latter, indignant at this wish of his little son and heir, forbade him to leave home, and explained to him that at his tender years he would find the active life far more tolerable " than the contemplative life of the monastic militia." But when the child still " yearned after sacred letters," he took him at length to the monastery of Exeter,—probably a small house of clerks,—and commended him to the abbot. Here Boniface was made oblate monk, or boy lector, and remained for seven years, well trained in discipline, but without " magisterial " teaching. To obtain this, Boniface left Exeter, and joined another monastic house. Here he learned the classics, metre, and the threefold interpretation of scripture, and living under the rule of his abbot, he " persevered according to the definite form of a right constitution of the holy father, Benedict." He did not make his learning an excuse to seek ordination as presbyter before the due time, but when he was over thirty, being chosen to that office by the community, he was ordained priest " according to the rule of the canonical constitutions." He received the priesthood that he might give himself to works of mercy, *i.e.* not as chaplain to the community, but probably as a future missionary, " as far as he was able beneath regular monastic discipline."

For five or six years he was unable to fulfil his desire for pilgrimage : but in 716, with his abbot's consent, he went out to join Willibrord at Utrecht, sailing from the " market of Lundonwic." Here he found Radbod at war with Charles Martel and missionary work impossible ; he returned to England, and next year travelled direct to Rome, to receive the commission and blessing of pope Gregory II. After producing the commendatory letters given him by his bishop, Daniel of Winchester, he was received several times in audience by the pope, and given a letter authorising him " to hasten to any peoples that are held in the error of unbelief," preach among them the kingdom of God in the spirit of power and love and soberness, and administer to them the sacrament of baptism. He then travelled back through Lombardy, and on learning of the death of Radbod, joined Willibrord at Utrecht, and worked for three years with him. But in Friesland the faith may now be said to have been established, and Boniface himself prepared by knowledge of the local Teutonic language and customs for work among the untouched heathen. In 722 therefore he left Willibrord and visited Hesse and Thuringia, won over the chieftains, and baptized large numbers. He then journeyed to Rome, and in November 722 took an oath of obedience to Gregory II, and was consecrated bishop for his converts. He had as yet no see, but the day following his consecration the pope specified his commission, to " the races in the parts of Germany and on the east side of the Rhine, who . . . live in error, in the shadow of death." Boniface's fellow-bishops and presbyters were commanded " to provide things necessary for his journey, and give him companions, food, drink, and everything he requires." The pope wrote also commendatory letters to Charles Martel, to the Thuringian Christians, and to the heathen Old Saxons.

Boniface's work was henceforth of a double nature, and

made possible by a double protectorate. He was to lift the Frankish church from the state of barbarism and irregularity in which he found it to the due following of the sacred canons : and he was to evangelise, often at the peril of his life, the heathen beyond the Rhine. In this work his two protectors were the papacy and the Frankish princes, popes Gregory II and Zacharias on the one hand, and Charles Martel and Pepin the Short, his son, on the other. Boniface, as the product of the twofold conversion of England, by the Celtic and Roman monks, united in his work the fervour for personal journeys among the heathen of the Celtic monks, and the regard for the establishment of an ordered church, provision for the training of a native clergy, of the Italians. Work among the heathen, the establishment of a new church, observing the sacred precepts of the canons, was hindered by the ignorance and uncanonical behaviour of the neighbouring Frankish prelates. Boniface could not therefore neglect the condition of the Frankish church, the more so as his protectors, Charles Martel and Pepin, desired his help in its reform.

For the first ten years of his episcopate, Boniface was mainly occupied in preaching, and founding monasteries from which the neighbouring heathen might be taught. When he had hewn down the great " Thunderer's Oak," dedicated to Woden, in Hesse, his followers built on the spot a little wooden oratory, and this was later enlarged to be the church and monastery of Fritzlar, dedicated to the apostles Peter and Paul. Here he left an English monk as abbot, and in his charge the boy Sturm, to be abbot later of Boniface's most famous monastery of Fulda. This house was built to the south-east of Fritzlar, as an outpost for the evangelisation of Bavaria. After the district had been explored by Sturm, Boniface, Sturm and a band of monks cleared a space in the great beech forest, and built a church of stone, which they dedicated to the holy Saviour. For two years Sturm was sent by Boniface to Rome and Monte Cassino, that he might learn the observance of the Benedictine rule in its mother home, and when he returned Fulda grew under him to be the greatest abbey of Germany. Though Benedictine abbeys at this time, and later, were not intended for the education of laymen or secular clerks, yet in these newly-founded German abbeys, in a land where there were as yet no cathedral schools manned by secular clerks, there was usually a school for clerks as well as boy monks, or the two sets of boys may have been taught together. Besides monasteries for men, many of whom came out from England in response to Boniface's letters for helpers, he founded houses for women. One nun from the Dorset double monastery of Wimborne, Lioba, wrote to him between 732–5, begging him to remember his friendship with her father and mother, and his kinship with the latter : she was an only child, her parents were now dead, and " would that she might now have him in place of a brother." She sent him a " little present," that he might not forget her in their wide separa- tion, together with some Latin verses, " not in boldness, but wishing to exercise the rudiments of a slender talent." Lioba came out later and became the foundress of Boniface's nunnery of Bischofsheim, and the English nun Walpurga was set over another house. In 732 the pope created Boniface an archbishop without see, to strengthen his hands and enable him to consecrate his followers local bishops, and in 739, after another visit to Rome, Boniface consecrated four bishops for the church in Bavaria. In 741 he made three other of his monks bishops for the east Frankish church. He was now recognised as metropolitan for the bishops of Utrecht, the Rhine, and Germany beyond the Rhine. He was appointed to the see of Mainz by Pepin in 747, though the see itself was not definitely raised to metropolitan rank till 780.

The reform of the Frankish church was begun by Boniface in 741, when pope Zacharias made him his legate for the purpose. He received too the support of Pepin, later to be king of the Franks, whose youth had been spent in the royal monastery of S. Denis. Chief of the uncanonical abuses from which the Frankish church suffered was the rule of untrained, hastily ordained laymen as bishops and presbyters ; these often neglected to live apart from their wives, as the canons ordained, and were quite unfit to train up an episcopal familia. Laymen were also often in possession of the estates by which churches of monks or clerks should have been supported, and the divine service, for whose maintenance the endowments had been given, lapsed. With Pepin's support, Boniface presided over two synods of Frankish and German bishops, in 742 and 744, for the purpose of restoring the observance of the sacred canons : councils were to meet yearly, the canons about clerical marriage were to be enforced, irregular bishops and presbyters were to be deposed, and heathen customs were to be put away. The Frankish clergy were to be subjected to Boniface as metropolitan and the pope's legate.

The last two years of Boniface's life were passed in Friesland, the scene of his earliest mission, and here, in 753, he met his death. He and a band of converts awaiting confirmation at his hands were slain at Dokkum, by a band of heathen. The further conversion of the Germans was to be carried out by Pepin's son, at the point of the sword.

CHAPTER IV

THE CAROLINGIAN RENAISSANCE AND THE CHURCH

Chrodegang of Metz and the " vita canonica "—Effect in England
—Charles the Great and the Frankish church: tithe—Contemporary learning in Europe—Charles and learning—Charles's conquest and conversion of Saxony—Benedict of Aniane—Charles and the papacy

THE son of Pepin king of the Franks, patron of Boniface, was Charles the Great, who ruled from 768 till 814. He not only united under his rule all the Frankish dominions, but extended his realm by conquest over the Pyrenees into Spain, and over the unconquered Old Saxons and Slavs. The Lombards of north Italy acknowledged his sway, and the pope, after appealing to him for protection against them, crowned him emperor in S. Peter's on Christmas Day, in the year 800. His empire included so large a part of western Europe that his intervention in ecclesiastical affairs was of particular importance, for the measures taken were not only binding legally within the empire but affected by their example the lands without,—England and Christian Spain. The renaissance of letters which Charles the Great inspired marks the end of the dark ages.

This renaissance was prepared for and made possible by the canonical renaissance, or revival of interest in the canons of the church, under Boniface and Pepin, and particularly by the work of one of Boniface's disciples, the Frankish bishop Chrodegang of Metz, († 766). Boniface's concern was for the observance of all the canons: Chrodegang's the narrower and yet immense one of the observance of all those affecting the personal life of the clergy. Chrodegang founded with his own possessions, for he was the son of a great Frankish noble, two abbeys where the Benedictine rule was most strictly observed : and his admiration for monks could not but affect his conception of what the " vita canonica," the life of the secular clergy according to the canons, ought to be. In churches which had endowment for a familia of clergy, these should live in common, particularly in the case of the familia of a bishop ; in small, outlying churches such a life was, of course, impossible. Bishops should supply to the familia of their cathedral church sufficient for its common maintenance, and should build for it a cloister like those of Benedictine monasteries. This theory as to what was the " canonical " life for the clergy was not the view of Chrodegang alone, but probably of all the bishops appointed by Boniface. Rigobert of Reims, († 743), " restored the canonical religion to his clerks, and appointed them sufficient victuals and estates which he conferred on them, and he instituted a common chest for their use," as probably did other bishops. The notable point of Chrodegang's work was that he wrote a rule for the life and government of his family at Metz. This rule is of importance, because it gradually became the norm for the life of all cathedral and collegiate churches in Charles's empire : and in the council of Aix-la-Chapelle, held in 817, it was made solemnly binding upon them all. The version of Aix-la-Chapelle has a few additional chapters, and deals with life within the monastery and the cure of souls exercised by the clerks over their parochia, which was often that of the cathedral church, and always large. The canons were to range themselves, in church or refectory, in the lawful grades of their orders ; some of the canons would be " small children and youths " in the grade of lector or acolyte. Provosts and prelates must not admit more clerks than the endowment of their churches could support. Clerks might retain their own property, or receive the stipend for some office in the church ; those who had neither of these means of support must receive food and clothing in the congregation, and part of the alms ; rich and poor clerks must fare equally in the congregation. The archdeacon (still, at the time, a prominent officer of the cathedral as well as the diocese), or the provost, must train the clergy wisely and set a good example in his own life. None must enter the monastery save by the door of the cloister, and all must sleep in one dormitory. The clerks must say night office and the canonical hours, not pompously, or in a slovenly manner, but standing and chanting religiously. Lay people confess in Lent, and monks every Saturday; but canonical clerks must confess every third Saturday to the bishop or his deputy. Sick canons shall have houses appointed for them, and a specially appointed clerk to care for them. For parishioners there must be baptism, confirmation, confession, and preaching; every fortnight there must be a sermon, and it would be better if there were a careful sermon, according to what the common people can understand, on all feasts and Sundays. Prelates must provide a hospital for the poor, and the canons must gladly pay a tithe of all their alms and offerings towards it. Prelates must appoint fit brethren, not in the order of their entrance into the college, but of their merits, to rule the congregation in their place. The rulers of churches shall take heed that the children and youths committed to them to be brought up in the congregation shall be carefully and spiritually taught; they shall live in a common hall, and be in the charge of a brother of proven life. There were also many chapters about ecclesiastical seasons, offices, excommunications and penances.

This rule not only gives the most complete extant picture of life in a well-conducted cathedral in the Frankish empire, but it was influential in England. Archbishop Aethelhard of Canterbury in 805 gave a separate endowment to his familia at Christchurch, for their maintenance, and in 813 archbishop Wulfred built a common refectory and dormitory for them. That the familia there, founded to live communally by Augustine, had in the meantime adopted the continental practice of individual stipends is shown by Wulfred's clause, that the houses which the clerks have built for themselves they may keep, so long as they bequeath them only to members of the congregation, and not to outsiders. The rule of Chrodegang was translated into Anglo-Saxon: a catalogue of the Christchurch library indicates that the familia had a copy. Leofric, first bishop of Exeter, formally adopted the rule for his familia in 1050.

The reform of the church in Gaul, begun thus by Pepin, was carried further by Charles the Great and his ministers, in a series of royal capitularies and synodical canons. The Frankish kingship gained with Pepin a new sacred character and took upon itself, at the same time, the particular guidance and protection of the church. Charles's capitularies dealt equally with matters ecclesiastical and secular, and the " missi " whom he sent out from time to time to enforce them included generally a bishop and a lay noble. The clerks of the royal chapel, who attended Charles in his continuous journeys through his kingdom, formed the royal chancery, a department for the preparation of documents. Under the early Frankish kings its president had been a layman : under Charles, and later, its president was some great abbot or bishop. The boy lectors of the royal chapel, who travelled round with Charles except when he was on warlike campaigns, formed the nucleus of the famous " palace school." In this form, the palace school had existed under much earlier Frankish kings ; but the scholars had learned little but Latin, theology and the chant. Charles, however, appointed famous grammarians, like Peter of Pisa and Alcuin, to the care of the scholars, who now passed far beyond the rudiments of grammar to the study of the seven liberal arts ; he also allowed the children of nobles and other lay boys to share their studies. He cared equally for the supply of future defenders and statesmen of his empire, by the training in arms he provided for lay boys of his court, and the training of the young clerks to be the future bishops and abbots of his kingdom.

Charles's desire to reform the Frankish church dated from a visit to Rome in the Easter of 774, when he was honourably received by pope Hadrian I, spent a week visiting the shrines, churches and monuments of Rome, and was solemnly presented by Hadrian on his departure with a collection of the canons of the church. In a number of capitularies, drafted no doubt by his learned bishops and abbots, but enforced on his own authority, Charles during his reign defined the authority and provinces of metropolitans, confirmed the jurisdiction of bishops and abbots over their subjects, and ordered suits between clerks and other persons to be heard by the bishop and court jointly. By clauses which in many cases renewed old canons, he forbade the clergy to live with their wives after attaining to holy orders, to keep concubines, or to have any women, except certain relations, as servants or housekeepers. They must not frequent taverns, hunt, carry arms, meddle in worldly business, or transact as clerk that of the patron of their church. Nobles must not demand from bishops the sudden ordination of their own servants, when unsuitable, in order to appoint them to livings ; patrons must not usurp the estates of their churches, or oppress them ; builders of new churches on their estates must seek consecration from the bishop, and satisfy him that the new church will have sufficient endowment. Lay people must not work on Sunday, save to bury the dead, bring up the baggage of the army, or transport food.

" Tithe " had been paid in many cases for the support of the local churches since Pepin's time : Charles made the obligation to pay it legally binding and universal. The payment, now made in kind, consisted of a tenth part of the fruits of the earth, corn above all, wine, hay and the young of beasts. The obligation to tithe was laid upon the land, not upon any class of persons : all estates paid, even when their owners were Jews or women. Some bishops claimed it also on the produce of a handicraft, " each from his own art," but this obligation did not become binding,—probably because it could not be justified, like the tithe on land, from passages in the Old Testament. Payment was enforced on pain of excommunication. The country in this period was divided into rural parishes, (see p. 31), much larger than would be the case in England to-day ; tithe was paid, not to the chapels and oratories, but only to parish or " baptismal " churches, the church of a city, or of some large area. A capitulary of 818 allowed churches newly founded in " vills," (by private owners on their estates), to have the tithes from these same vills for their endowment, and during the next two centuries there was a good deal of quarrelling between the rectors of old, large parishes, and the priests of new churches within the old parish, as to the right to receive the tithe. A new church was fairly easily built, for a pious lord could call upon all the inhabitants of the village, coloni, serfs or freemen, to build it by forced labour ; churches were small, generally with only one altar, of timber and plaster, or if a more important building, of stone : the livelihood of the clerk or two who served it afterwards was the difficulty. Whereas before the Carolingian period this had depended completely on landed endowment and offerings, or the clerk had been paid a stipend by his bishop, after this period tithe became an equally important source of revenue.

The impetus Charles gave to learning affected the whole church in his empire. In Italy lay grammar masters had never ceased to teach for fees, but elsewhere in Europe the only schools were the household schools of boy lectors. The tradition of classical learning, of the seven liberal arts, was stronger in Italy than elsewhere. Apart from Italy, the best learning in Europe was to be found in the schools of Ireland, and still more, of England. The monastery of Jarrow had produced the greatest English scholar and historian before the Norman Conquest, the Venerable Bede († 735) ; for forty years he studied, taught, and wrote commentaries on the scriptures, treatises on natural history, grammar, history, and above all, the *Ecclesiastical History of the English Nation*. From Italy and England Charles chose the scholars who were to work in his empire : from Italy Peter of Pisa, Paul the Deacon, and cantors from the Roman school, to teach the cathedral schools of Metz and Soissons the Roman chant : from England his greatest scholar, Alcuin, some of his English students, and later, Clement the Scot. Alcuin had been educated at the school of York, by scholars trained by Bede, and he proved the ripest fruit of north-English scholarship ; between 781 and 796 he was a member of Charles's court, accompanying him on his journeys, and from 796 till his death in 804 he retired to teach the school in the monastery of S. Martin at Tours. He sought for no ecclesiastical preferment, he was not ordained above the rank of deacon, strife and hurry were to him, he said, " as smoke to sore eyes : " but under his influence not only the palace school of boys and youths profited, but Charles's court itself became an " academia," where Charles and his courtiers absorbed the seven liberal arts from Alcuin, by way of question and answer. In this enthusiastic circle, where the king himself delighted to propound questions on dogma and ritual to reluctant bishops, Frankish names were replaced by classical and biblical nicknames : Charles himself was " David," Alcuin " Flaccus," (Horace), Theodulf of Orleans " Pindar," Angelbert " Homer," and Charles's daughters " Lucia " and " Columba."

The influence of a learned court extended to the schools of bishops, abbots, and, finally, the presbyters of rural parishes. In 787 Charles addressed a capitulary to the abbot of Fulda, ordering that in all monasteries and bishops' houses there should be study, and " let those who can, teach." In 789 he enacted : " Let the ministers of God's altar . . . collect and associate with themselves children not only of servile condition, but free-born : and that there may be schools for reading-boys, let them learn psalms, notes, chants, the computus and grammar, in every monastery and bishop's house." Another capitulary of 805 referred to such schools, and ordered that all should learn rightly about the computus, that children should be sent to learn the art of medicine (presumably to some house in south Italy), and that all should use the Roman chant, as at Metz. Bishop Theodulf of Orleans went a stage further. He was a Visigoth who had travelled in Italy, a scholar, and a poet whose Latin hymn, *Gloria, laus, et honor* is still used ; he enjoined in his synod that priests who wished to send their relations for training to his cathedral school or to any of the great monasteries in his diocese, might do so freely. This would have applied to boys dedicated as oblates, or lectors : but in a clause following Theodulf tried to provide for the teaching of lay boys as day scholars, as they might have been taught in Italy. Priests in towns and villages should keep schools, and if any of the faithful wished to commend their little ones to them to learn letters, they should receive and teach them gladly for nothing. This canon is the high-water mark in educational activity in Charles's reign : it is not likely to have been widely observed, for through the disorders of the next century Charles's successors had the greatest difficulty in securing that even all bishops should maintain schools for lectors. It is a counsel of perfection and an aspiration rather than an index to normal prevailing conditions. It is found copied in a collection of " statuta " collected by the learned abbot, Aelfric of Eynsham, and in other collections of canons : but it is even less likely to have been observed in tenth century England than in the diocese of Orleans under Theodulf. The normal canonical duty of the presbyter with cure of souls was not to teach the children of his parishioners letters or grammar, but to administer to all the sacraments, and see that they knew the creed, (the " articles of the faith "), the ten commandments, and the Our Father, preferably in Latin, but failing that, in their mother tongue.

Two other points must be mentioned shortly in connexion with Charles's government of the Frankish church : his conquest of Saxony, and the attempt to organise the monasteries as a Benedictine " order," under himself and his successor, Louis the Pious. Between 772 and 776, Charles carried out in successive campaigns the conquest of Saxony : after this date his expeditions were rather punitory raids against conquered rebels. In 772 Charles advanced from the borders of the Hessian Franks, where Boniface and Sturm had laboured, to the Eresburg, a fortress just within the Saxon borders, where, within a holy wood, the Saxons congregated at certain seasons to honour the Irminsul. This was a tall pillar of wood, symbolic of the " all-sustaining earth tree, Igdrasil. Charles took the Eresburg, destroyed the Irminsul, and by 776 had taken the other Saxon fortresses, built his own, and carried off Saxon boys to be trained as missionaries. Rather later he issued a capitulary for the government of Saxony, as savage in its provisions for the conversion of the Saxons as his own treatment of them in warfare. Those who broke into or robbed a church were to be punished with death, as were those who ate meat in Lent, killed a bishop, priest or deacon, practised heathen rites, or burned their dead on pyres, or even those who omitted to be baptized. In time, however, the work of Sturm and the monks supplemented these savage prohibitions and enactments with teaching about the Christian faith.

It has been explained earlier that the Benedictine rule had been founded for a house, not an order, but that from the time of Boniface it had been regarded as the norm of monastic observance. Yet there must have been in Charles's reign many houses founded rather as houses of clerks, where the Benedictine rule had never been explicitly adopted, though recommended by various synods : these clerks seemed to strict Benedictines merely lax or worse than lax professors of their own rule. Moreover, in houses where the rule was adopted, Teutonic individualism prevented a rigid adherence to its tenets : the Roman ideal of discipline and uniformity was not yet grasped. Many a feudal lord retired, after a life of hard fighting, to a monastery, and finding the monotony of regular discipline irksome, saw no reason why he should observe it. Whereas S. Benedict's monastery had been a community possessing certain rights, especially that of the election of its own abbot, the Teutonic monasteries had become the property of the founder or his relatives. Charles himself was interested in the monasteries, but chiefly as centres of education. He sent to Monte Cassino, to have the rule copied and brought to him at Aix-la-Chapelle. But he did not allow one most important part of the rule to be observed, *i.e.* the free election of the abbot, save in the case of Fulda, and three other German monasteries. But during the latter part of his reign a second Benedict was being trained, first as a monk at Dijon, then as the founder of a small cell on his father's land at Aniane. Here the rule was kept in all its strictness, and the monks were occupied, not as Charlemagne wished them to be, in study, but in manual labour. By 813 Benedict's rendering of the rule was followed in all the Burgundian houses, and on Charlemagne's death, Louis the Pious called him to found a model monastery in the woods near Aix-la-Chapelle, and " set him over all the monasteries of his kingdom." In 817 a great council of abbots was held at Aix-la-Chapelle, which after discussing the rule with Benedict, drew up a set of customs, for the observance of the rule, which enjoined as a capitulary on all monasteries. It expressed

Benedict's desire for uniformity, his reaction from culture to asceticism. He then wrote the *Codex Regularum*, a collection of all the rules prior to S. Benedict of Nursia, and a commentary on the Benedictine rule, the *Concordia Regularum*. But the uniformity and reform he inaugurated was short lived, for the Scandinavian raiders in the ninth century were to destroy the peace of the monasteries.

In two matters the actions of Charles affected not merely the church within his empire, but the church at large : the title of the pope to his Italian patrimony, and the relation of the later medieval emperors to the papacy. The single empire did not remain hereditary among Charles's own descendants, but was divided. In 962 Otto I, king of the Germans, revived the imperial title, claiming to rule Germany and Italy, and this " Holy Roman Empire " was the supreme representative of the civil power in medieval Europe. For precedent and prestige it claimed descent from the empire of Charles the Great, and through him, from imperial Rome. The relations of Charles to the papacy and Christendom were therefore of importance.

The patrimony of S. Peter in Italy had received small, but no marked, accessions, since the days of Gregory the Great. Till 751 the eastern empire maintained its claim on Italy, for the exarch still ruled at Ravenna, with ever-narrowing lands. But in that year the Lombards took Ravenna, and the pope, the imperial representative in Rome, became the only representative of the empire in Italy. The Lombards, however, held most of the imperial possessions in the north, till Pepin and his Franks rescued pope Stephen II from imminent danger at their hands in 754. In return Pepin received a second anointing as king at the hands of Stephen, (see p. 87), and appears to have made Stephen a verbal promise to " restore the exarchate of Ravenna," or even to have made a written donation to the pope, not only of the old exarchate, but of the whole peninsula of Italy. That Pepin should thus have granted away Byzantine rights is possible, for the legend of a donation of Italy by the emperor Constantine to pope Sylvester was accepted as true by learned Frankish bishops at the time. Belief in this " Donation of Constantine " lies behind the donations of the Frankish kings to the papacy. Again in 774 the Lombards threatened Rome. Charles defeated them, was shown the written donation of Pepin, and confirmed it. From this time Ravenna and the surrounding districts formed part of the papal patrimony.

The imperial title was bestowed on Charles in return for help, not against the Lombards, but the pope's enemies in the city of Rome itself. Leo III was seized, severely treated, imprisoned and accused of various enormities. He escaped to France, and at Alcuin's suggestion, purged himself of the accusation by oath in a great assembly of Franks and Romans in S. Peter's. On Christmas Day, when Charles himself rose from prayer before the confession of S. Peter, Leo, after the Byzantine fashion, set a crown upon his head, and the assembled Romans hailed him as " the Augustus, crowned of God, the great and peace-bringing emperor of the Romans." A contemporary mosaic in the Lateran represents S. Peter presenting to pope Leo the pallium, and to Charles the banner of the imperial city, and expresses the coordinate nature of the powers divinely entrusted to each. Political thought in the middle ages postulated the unity of Christendom, in the spiritual and secular sphere, and was much occupied by the relation of the spiritual and temporal powers to each other. But in Charles's day no difficulty was felt at the encroachment of the secular power on the sphere of the spiritual. Not only did Charles rule the Frankish church, but he intervened in doctrinal controversy. The Adoptionist teachers in Spain taught that God the Son was " adopted," not eternally generated, by God the Father. Charles summoned synods to refute their heresy, presided over them, and condemned the Adoptionist leaders in the assembly of Frankfort, 794. Charles's share in the Iconoclastic controversy will be mentioned in Chapter VII : but it may be noticed here that the line he took was contrary to that of the pope. " This do we praise," wrote Alcuin, " as a wonderful and special divine gift : that thou dost endeavour to keep the church of God inwardly pure, and to protect it from the doctrine of the faithless, as to defend it outwardly against the plundering of the heathen."

CHAPTER V

RELATIONS OF EASTERN AND WESTERN CHURCHES TILL 1054

Byzantine art in the west—Veneration of the holy cross in the west—The Monothelete controversy—The Iconoclastic controversy —Greek missions : Cyril and Methodius—The schism of Photius— The schism of Michael Cerularius

WHILE Gregory the Great was ruling in the west, the eastern church had no one single ruler. The patriarchs of Antioch and Alexandria had greater and more unquestioned historical prestige, but the fortunes of the patriarch of Constantinople were of more importance to eastern Christians, because he ruled the church of the great eastern world capital. Since Constantine had presided over the council of Nicaea, a thirteenth apostle, the east Roman emperors had claimed a sacred character, and a large share in the rule of the church : the patriarchs of Constantinople were overshadowed by their presence, and rendered half superfluous by their activities. They did not, however, accept this complete subjection of the church to the state without a struggle : many of the doctrinal questions which agitated the eastern church drew their bitterness from the fact that the patriarch and the imperial court took different sides ; what appeared as doctrinal controversy was in reality a struggle for the independence of the patriarch and the Greek church. The great struggle over Iconoclasm, still in the future, was to partake of this character. The failure of the patriarchs gave Europe " one of the longest and most considerable experiments in a state-church that Christendom has ever seen." But though the subjection of the patriarch to the emperor helped to render the fortunes of the eastern church less splendid in these years than those of the western, yet eastern influences on the west between 600 and 800 were real and valuable. The east was the reservoir of civilisation, classical learning, and the primitive traditions of ecclesiastical discipline and Christian art. " The well-to-do classes in the west were as a rule illiterate, with the exception of ecclesiastics : among the well-to-do classes in the Byzantine world education was the rule, and education meant not merely reading, writing and arithmetic, but the study of ancient Greek grammar and the reading of classical authors."

The eastern empire and the eastern Church performed two services to Europe : they helped civilise and teach the newly-settled barbarians in the west, and they struggled with and eventually converted the barbarians who settled in the Balkans. The " dark ages " of barbarian invasion and settlement did not coincide in east and west. In the west the Germanic nations mainly conquered and settled between 400 and 600, while the eastern empire in the Balkans, by letting the Goths and other invaders pass through its territories, preserved its civilisation. The dark ages in the Balkans occurred between 600 and 800 when the Indo-Germanic Slavs, and the Mongol Avars and Bulgars, had settled in the Balkans themselves, and were to remain heathen till the ninth century. They destroyed monasteries and learning, and submerged the Latin-speaking provincials, until the eastern empire meant little more than Constantinople and a few walled cities, maintaining themselves in a barbarian flood. These " dark ages " in the Balkans were not to be lightened till the gradual conversion of the invaders, at the hands of Latin and orthodox missionaries, and mainly by the work of the Greek brothers, Cyril and Methodius, between 850 and 900. But even in this gloomy period Byzantine art, discipline and liturgy affected the west.

From the age of Justinian onwards, Byzantine (East Roman) churches and mosaics were built and used on the shores of the Adriatic, Italy, north Africa and Gaul. Churches and baptisteries were often of a circular plan, domed, and adorned with mosaics ; some octagonal churches were fitted with a circular dome, and sometimes the dome or domes were adopted as the roofs of basilican churches.   The chapel of Charles the Great at Aix-la-Chapelle was octagonal and dome-covered.   In Rome there are still several Byzantine remnants of the age of Justinian, particularly the choir enclosures of San Clemente.   Milan has a beautiful chapel with apsidal recesses and mosaics, one of which shows Christ and the twelve apostles.   Ravenna has a particularly large group of Byzantine buildings, churches, baptisteries and splendid mosaics ;   Lyons and Arles also had Byzantine buildings.   While the columns, capitals and basilican structure of many Byzantine buildings continued the Roman tradition, and the circular plan and domed roof were borrowed from Armenia and Mesopotamia, so the typical Byzantine figure and art forms go back to Egypt.   From the painted rolls and books of Alexandria were developed the types which became familiar in Byzantine paintings, and mosaics ; and from the Christian textiles found in Egypt was copied the favourite Byzantine imitation of jewelling.   Alexandrian codices with the text painted on pages of purple vellum supplied models for purple books painted at Constantinople, and later for others in famous western scriptoria.   The famous Byzantine ivory throne at Ravenna was probably made in Alexandria.

To this great school of Byzantine art belonged the Northumbrian art of the eighth century, though in this case it was fused with a strong Celtic tradition.   In 674 the Northumbrian monk, Benedict Biscop, was charged by Egfrith of Northumbria to build a monastery at Wearmouth.   He had already made three journeys to Rome, and when he found that native workmen were unable to build a stone church, he sent for continental masons who built him such a church " after the manner of the Romans, which he ever loved."   From Gaul he obtained altar vessels, vestments and glass-makers, who " not only did the work required of them but taught the English how to do it for themselves."   After a fourth journey to Rome, he brought back an " innumerable quantity of books and relics," and, to teach his English monks the chant, he even persuaded John, the arch-cantor of S. Peter's, to return with him. He brought back, too, pictures. stretched on canvas, to adorn his church after the Byzantine manner, scenes from the gospels and the apocalypse. " All who entered the church, even if ignorant of letters, whichever way they turned, might either contemplate the ever-lovely aspect of Christ and His saints, though only in a picture, or with watchful mind revere the grace of the Lord's incarnation, or else, having as it were the trial of the last judgment before their eyes, they might remember to examine themselves the more strictly." These Byzantine and Roman traditions were transferred in 682 to Benedict Biscop's second foundation of Jarrow. Here Bede wrote his *Ecclesiastical History*, and he tells us that Wilfrid's churches also were adorned with pictures of a series of biblical types and subjects : they too were brought from Rome. What Roman church paintings were like at the time can be seen from the walls of Sta Maria Antiqua, decorated by Greek artists in the Byzantine manner just at the time when Benedict Biscop was making his collections. During the second half of the seventh century Rome had become almost completely Byzantinised, and it was a result of this movement, and no mere chance, that the pope when asked to select an archbishop of Canterbury chose Theodore, a Greek from Tarsus.

The veneration of the cross, as the instrument of redemption, was a Byzantine devotion which spread gradually over the west. In the sixth century churches were not usually dedicated to Christ by name : in the west they were dedicated to the Saviour, in the east to (Christ as) the Holy Wisdom of God. The western dedication expressed the gratitude of man for redemption : in the east, since the discovery of the holy cross in Jerusalem by Helena (327), by a dedication to the Holy Cross. The mother of Constantine built the church of the Holy Sepulchre in Jerusalem to contain this most precious relic, which was set with gold and jewels, and regarded as having miraculous power from its contact with the Saviour's blood. The *adoratio crucis*, liturgical worship of the cross by kiss and genuflexion, was first practised at the dedication of the church of the Holy Sepulchre in 335, and by the beginning of the fifth century the ceremony

had reached Constantinople, where the emperor began a
three days' veneration by publicly kissing a symbolic cross.
The ceremony was described in the letter of a shipwrecked
monk to abbot Adamnan of Iona, and mentioned later by
Bede. In the western church the ceremony was practised in
the seventh century : the Persians had conquered Jerusalem
in 614, and carried off the relic of the cross from Jerusalem : but the eastern emperor Heraclius defeated them,
and restored the true cross to Jerusalem in great triumph.
The so-called *Sacramentarium* of Gregory the Great describes
the *adoratio crucis* at Rome, and its special place in the
ritual of Good Friday : the pope adored the Lord's cross,
and the bishops and congregation followed suit. The hymn
Pange, lingua, gloriosi proelium certaminis, ascribed to
Venantius Fortunatus, accompanied the ceremony :

Faithful cross, above all other one and only noble tree :
None in foliage, none in blossom, none in fruit thy peer
    may be :
Sweetest wood and sweetest iron, sweetest weight is hung on
    thee.

Bend thy boughs, O tree of glory : thy relaxing sinews
    bend ;
For a while the ancient rigour that thy birth bestowed,
    suspend,
And the king of heavenly beauty on thy bosom gently tend.

The practice reached Northumbria, possibly through Wilfrid
and Benedict Biscop, in the second half of the seventh
century, possibly at the beginning of the eighth. In 701
the pope, himself a Syrian, discovered a large relic of the
true cross in S. Peter's at Rome,—a discovery which
stimulated the devotion in the Latin Church. Ceolfrid,
abbot of Wearmouth, was in Rome that year : and the
setting up of the Ruthwell Cross in Northumbria can be
ascribed with great probability to this period. On its
shaft are carved sixteen lines of a beautiful Anglo-Saxon
poem, the *Dream of the Rood*, which curiously combines
Byzantine and old Saxon elements. The poet describes
his vision of the cross of Christ, invested with radiance,

adorned with gold and gems, yet still bathed in the
Saviour's blood, and then the cross itself speaks :

> It was long, long ago,
> Yet I recall—when, at the forest's edge
> I was hewn down, and from my stem removed.
> Resistless were the foes that seized me there . . .
> Then I beheld the master of mankind
> Approach with lordly courage as if he
> Would mount upon me, and I dared not bow
> Nor break, opposing the command of God,
> Although I saw earth tremble. . . .
> Then the young hero laid his garments by,
> He that was God almighty, strong and brave ;
> And boldly in the sight of all he mounted
> The lofty cross, for he would free mankind.
> Then as the man divine clasped me, I shook :
> Yet dared I not bow to the earth, nor fall
> Upon the ground, but I must needs stand fast.[1]

The claim the cross itself makes to worship is Byzantine ;
but the " young hero," the vassalage of the cross itself
to Christ, the admonition to every Christian to be a fearless
warrior under the gentle Leader of the Host, that he may
attain " the joy of heroes in the heavenly abode," the
death-wail raised by his friends for the " young hero,"
are purely Germanic.   The poem must have been one which
Bede tells us the followers of the Northumbrian Caedmon
continued to make after his death.   The sculptures on the
Ruthwell cross have affinities with those of the ivory throne
at Ravenna, and include those of the Crucifixion, Annuncia-
tion, and other scenes from the gospels, together with
Egyptian subjects like S. Paul and S. Anthony the hermits,
etc. : while some of the ornaments and symbols resemble
those of the illuminated Lindisfarne gospels. Other
Anglian crosses of the seventh and eighth centuries still
survive, like those of Bewcastle, and the cross of Acca
at Durham : while the Irish crosses were frequent, beautiful
and sculptured with a similar range of subjects.   Devotion

[1] See *Select Translations from Old English Poetry*, Cook and
Tinker, 1902, p. 94.

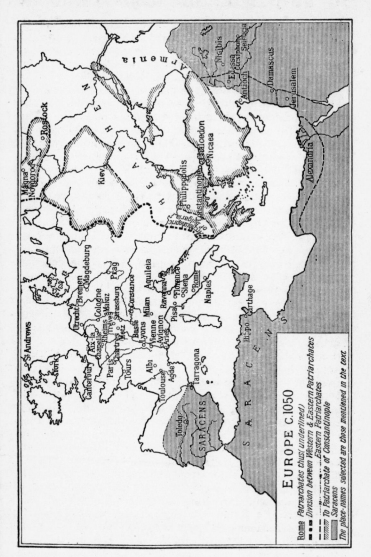

EUROPE C.1050

Rome *Patriarchates thus(underlined)*
▪▪▪▪ *Division between Western & Eastern Patriarchates*
////// *To Patriarchate of Constantinople*
········ *Eastern Patriarchates*
▨▨▨ *Saracens*

The place-names selected are those mentioned in the text

to the holy cross must have been popular in seventh
century England, and, indeed, over the whole continent
every layman as well as every ecclesiastic expressed in
this veneration of the cross his devotion to the passion
of Christ. It remained the normal Good Friday devotion
for lay people throughout the middle ages.

Two eastern doctrinal controversies reacted on the
west: those over Monotheletism and Iconoclasm. The
first resulted in a short schism between the churches of
Rome and Constantinople. The controversy over the
person of Christ had been decided by the council of Chalcedon: but the Nestorian and Monophysite churches had
been left in schism. While the eastern emperors were
at almost continuous warfare with the Persians, religious
disaffection in the border states was politically dangerous,
and this led Heraclius to encourage reunion. Cyrus,
patriarch of Alexandria, in the course of negotiations,
wrote to pope Honorius I, suggesting that the schismatics
might be reconciled if stumbling-blocks like the doctrine
of the two wills of Christ were removed: with this " Monothelete " position Honorius concurred. The doctrine of
" one will " was asserted by the patriarch of Constantinople
in a document known as the *Ekthesis*, (636), which Heraclius
signed. But the successors of Honorius rejected the
Ekthesis: Syria was lost to the Mahometan Arabs, Egypt
cut off by their invasion, and the question of Monotheletism
resolved itself into a contest between Rome and the
patriarchs of Constantinople, who continued to uphold
the doctrine of the " one will." In 646 the pope declared the patriarch deposed: but in 653 the emperor
sent an exarch to Rome, who arrested pope Martin I in
the Lateran church and brought him as a prisoner to
Constantinople, where after many indignities he died.
The schism lasted till 681, when, there being now through
the Arab conquests no strong motive for reunion with
the Monophysites, the emperor to end it deposed the
patriarch and had elected one who was willing to abandon
Monotheletism. Representatives of the conquered patriarchates of Antioch and Jerusalem were procured, and a
council calling itself oecumenical, and generally reckoned
as the sixth general council, met in the domed hall (trullus)

of the palace of Constantinople (681). The Monothelete leaders, including the dead pope Honorius, were condemned, the papal position accepted, and the schism ended.

The Iconoclastic controversy lasted during the years 726 to 842, and also led to a schism between east and west. The holy eikons were images or pictures cut in bas-relief : those who wished to abolish the veneration paid to them were the Iconoclasts, (image-breakers), and they termed those who opposed them Iconodules, (image-worshippers). Within the eastern empire itself the motives of the two parties were not simple, and the question became more complicated as involving the west. Within the Balkans the everlasting raids and attacks of Slavs, Avars, Bulgars, Persians, Saracens, etc., had been all but fatal to learning, tradition, civic sense, prudence and gravity ; the court had ceased to speak Latin and had adopted a barbarous Greek, Justinian's Latin *Code* was no longer understood, literature, poetry and sculpture were dead. Christianity had persisted, but among the masses of the population in an atmosphere of dense and savage superstition. Witchcraft, necromancy and magic were believed real powers, and miraculous powers were attributed, by the masses, not to the saint the image represented, but to the image itself. Superstitious practices followed. Moreover, Greek Christians in Syria were in contact with Islam, and the Koran forbade the use of images. The iconoclastic movement in Greece is now believed to have followed the prohibition of even the painted human figure by the caliph Yezid. In 723 he ordered the destruction of all images "whether in temples, churches or houses," and a campaign of destruction followed.

The attempt of the Isaurian dynasty of emperors to abolish image worship began with the Iconoclastic Edict of Leo III in 726. His motives included the real contempt for superstition felt by many of the educated classes, particularly the officers of the army, and the non-Balkan population of the empire; the desire to fight the monotheist Arabs by purifying the debased Christianity of Syria and the debateable provinces; and the desire to diminish the influence of the monks. These withdrew men in great numbers from the army, the public services and

agriculture at a time when the empire was hard pressed
for military defence, and cut down the receipts of the
imperial treasury through their immunity from taxation.
While the patriarchs had been subdued to the yoke of the
state, the monks continued to fight for the freedom of
the church to define matters of dogma and discipline.
As the supporters of devotion to the eikons, many of which
were situated in monasteries, and produced a considerable
revenue in offerings, a blow could be struck at them
through the campaign against images.   The results of the
edict of 726 were an immediate popular riot when the
soldiers destroyed the image of Christ above the entrance
to the palace, the proclamation of a rival emperor in Greece,
the denunciation of the edict by pope Gregory II, and a
rebellion in all the imperial cities of Italy.   In 730 Leo III
deposed the patriarch of Constantinople, seized part of
the papal patrimonies and placed the dioceses in Calabria,
Sicily, Crete and Illyricum, which had belonged to the
western patriarchate in its wider sense, under the patriarch
of Constantinople.   In the east Leo enforced his edict,
but he was too busy defeating the Arabs to be able to
enforce his decision on the pope.   The Iconoclasts acted
with even greater vigour and brutality under the next
emperor: "all beauty," says a contemporary, "disappeared
from the churches: "   " the emperor raged madly against
all that feared God."   Between 780 and 802, however,
the emperor was a boy, and the empress Irene, his mother,
a fervent image worshipper.   The second council of Nicaea,
787, made the veneration of images lawful by enacting
that *proskunesis* (reverence) might be paid them, but not
latria, (worship).   Relations between Rome and Constantinople were restored, till a fresh emperor renewed
the controversy in 815 by ordering the removal of the
images and deposing the patriarch, who refused to do so.
But there were no such violent persecutions of image-
worshippers and monks as in the eighth century, and the
decision of the council of Nicaea was reaffirmed in 842.
In this second phase of the great controversy, the Greek
church, led by the monks of the Studion, was really aspiring
to something more than the defence of images.   She aimed
at casting off the authority of the state, and finding her

most powerful ally in the pope, was willing, despite her former reluctance, to appeal to the pope against the emperor, and recognise the primacy of the Roman church.

The breach between the Iconoclast emperors and their Italian subjects had left the papacy with no protector against the Lombards except the Frankish kings, and contributed to the erection of the Frankish empire in 800 Charles the Great himself, however, took the opposite view on the Iconoclastic question to the pope : partly through misrenderings of the Greek canons of the council of Nicaea, he repudiated that council, had the " Caroline Books " written, probably by Alcuin, to controvert its decisions, and asked the pope, who had accepted them, to excommunicate the eastern emperor as a heretic. Pope Hadrian I, however, defended the Nicene canons, point by point, and though on bad terms with the eastern emperor over the question of the confiscation of his patrimony, (which was not formally annulled), did not proceed to excommunicate him.

The most notable missions of the Greek church were carried out in Moravia, a region in the ninth century extending along the south of the Danube across the Balkans. Part of this region had, as the provinces Noricum and Pannonia, been converted in the fourth century. The period of confusion and barbarian invasion which followed was marked by the labours of the missionary Severinus, († 482), who built a monastery near the modern Vienna. But his work was swept away, and Moravia became heathen, settled by Germanic and Slav tribes. The future apostles of the Slavs were two brothers, Constantine or Cyril, and Methodius. Methodius in youth was the Greek officer, or archon, of a Slav district in Macedonia or Thessaly. Constantine, the younger by about ten years, studied philosophy with the best masters in Constantinople, and was for a time librarian of S. Sophia. Both brothers eventually entered the monastery of Mount Olympus in Bithynia, till c. 863 they were sent on a journey to the land of the Chazars, (Moravia). The emperor had received an embassy from a Slav prince, asking for an able teacher to preach and instruct his subjects in the holy scriptures, for though Latin, Saracen and Jewish missionaries had reached them, they had not yet been converted to any faith. It seems clear that the Slav language was the key to the situation. The Slav prince, Rostislav, wished to remain as independent as possible, and while the adoption of Latin Christianity at the hands of priests from Salzburg or Passau would have linked Moravia with the Carolingian princes of the west, or the adoption of the Byzantine liturgy with the emperor at Constantinople, a new Slav Christianity might mean comparative independence for Moravia. The patriarch had advised the emperor to comply with the request, and as there was as yet no Slav script or alphabet, about two years were spent by Constantine in the production of a script for the south Slavonic tongue, from the contemporary Greek minuscules, helped out by certain Latin and Hebrew signs. He also translated the gospels and epistles for the mass before his departure, and later the psalms, Old Testament passages and hymns of the Greek breviary, (book of the canonical hours, the night and day offices). It is clear that Constantine must from the beginning have contemplated establishing Christianity in Moravia on the basis of a Slavonic liturgy, and the two brothers spent their first stay in Moravia largely in training a number of Slav youths in this liturgy. Constantine was the only priest of the mission, and it was soon necessary to seek ordination for his Slav pupils. Opposition to the Slav liturgy from the German missionaries had rendered application to Salzburg or Passau impossible : the church of Constantinople was torn by internal discord, and might also have raised difficulties. Constantine therefore came to Italy with his pupils, would appear to have made known his desires to the pope, and received from him an invitation to Rome just before his death in 867. Pope Hadrian II gave the Slavonic books his blessing, and priest's orders to Methodius, and, overruling the opposition of some Italian bishops to the Slavonic liturgy, he ordered one of them to ordain three of the Slav youths priests, and two lectors. Constantine died at Rome in 869, but Methodius returned to work in Moravia, with the papal blessing. When the pope created him bishop, however, he was accused by the Germans of exercising rights in another's diocese,

imprisoned for a year, and badly treated. The pope
eventually settled the question between him and the
bishop of Passau in his favour, proclaimed his orthodoxy,
and in 880 solemnly allowed the divine office and mass to
be said in Slavonic, provided the gospel at mass was read
first in Latin. A later pope, however, withdrew the permission to say mass in Slavonic, and even in Methodius's
lifetime the Latin liturgy triumphed in Moravia : but his
followers used it to evangelise Bulgaria, Serbia and Croatia,
and later, Russia, where its use became permanent. The
Magyars of Hungary were converted not to the Greek
church, but to Latin Christianity, by bishop Pilgrim of
Passau, about 971, and king Stephen, († 1038). Greek
Christianity began to spread in Russia soon after the first
expedition of the Russians against Constantinople in 860,
and by 945 Kiev was a bishop's see.

The relations between the eastern and western churches
were marked in the ensuing period chiefly by the temporary
schism connected with the patriarch Photius of Constantinople, and the permanent one inaugurated by the patriarch
Cerularius. There were two attitudes towards the pope
within the Greek church : that of the monks, and particularly Theodore of the Studion, who were willing to
admit the Roman primacy, and submit ecclesiastical difficulties to the pope for arbitration : and that of the higher
clergy, largely recruited from imperial officials, who viewed
the pope with suspicion as the enemy of the emperor. But
all alike refused to admit that the pope had any jurisdiction
over Constantinople : the eastern church held firmly by
the conception of autocephalous churches, in communion
with each other. The long break in the relations of Rome
and Constantinople during the Iconoclastic controversy
increased the independence of Constantinople.

The Photian schism lasted from 867 to 920. Ignatius,
the austere patriarch of Constantinople, offended the imperial court and was replaced by Photius, a renowned
lay teacher in the schools of Constantinople, in 858. Pope
Nicholas I held that the election of Photius was uncanonical,
and called upon him to resign : the question became one
of the jurisdiction of the pope over Constantinople. For
four years Photius hesitated : but when papal legates

arrived in the newly-founded Greek church of Bulgaria, he convoked a synod (867) which condemned the introduction of the Latin rites in that church, and the double procession of the Holy Ghost, (from both Father and Son). The same summer the emperor presided over a synod which made the schism formal by declaring the practices of the Roman church heretical, her interference at Constantinople unlawful, and pope Nicholas excommunicated. An oecumenical council was held in 870 to end the quarrel, but without success. Peace between Rome and Constantinople was, after many negotiations, restored in 920, and was real as regards the ordinary members of the churches for 134 years,—though the politics of the Byzantine emperors occasionally embittered the leaders.

The permanent schism occurred when two men of equal ability and determination occupied the sees of Rome and Constantinople,—Leo IX and Michael Cerularius. In 1024 the Greek emperor had sent an embassy to the worthless John XIX at Rome, asking that " with the consent of the Roman pope the church of Constantinople might be termed universal [oecumenical] within her sphere, as Rome was in the whole [church]." This demand for the recognition of the patriarch as " oecumenical " was one for the recognition of the *autocephalia*, independent rights, of the patriarch. John XIX might have been won over with presents ; but the influence of reformers at Rome forced him to repel the suggestion. Churches of the Latin rite were allowed, however, to continue in Constantinople, and Greek churches in Rome. But a real cause of schism existed in the rival jurisdictions of the Greek and Latin churches in south Italy ; the Greek province of Bari, with twelve suffragan bishops, was set over against the Latin church in Apulia. Cerularius' real motive for schism in 1054 was that an alliance was projected between the emperor and pope Leo IX to drive the Normans from Italy, an alliance which he feared might lead in an imperial transfer of the province of Bari to the pope. He therefore countenanced various attacks on Latin uses, especially the treatise of a Studite monk which condemned not merely the double procession of the Holy Ghost, but the use of unleavened bread for the eucharist, the Saturday

fast, and the celibacy of priests.   In 1053 Cerularius ordered
the closing of all the churches of the Latin rite in Constantinople : in 1054, in spite of the efforts of the emperor
for peace with Rome, the Roman legates at a council in
Constantinople excommunicated the patriarch and departed
in wrath.   Cerularius in turn anathematised them, with
a solemnity which showed he meant the schism to be
permanent, as indeed it remained.   For Cerularius the
schism was a great victory : he had defended the *autocephalia* of his church, and established his undisputed influence over the Slav world and the eastern patriarchates,
and this against the wish of the emperor.   But the severance of interests which ensued, at a time when the west
was emerging from barbarism, was unfortunate for the
Byzantine church : and it was the schism which half-
destroyed the effectiveness of the Crusades, and, by
rendering conciliation between the emperors of east and
west impossible, made possible the capture of Constantinople by the Turk in 1453.

CHAPTER VI

THE GROWTH OF PAPAL POWER, 604-1073

Factors in the growth of papal prestige till 604—Factors in the growth of papal power, 604-1073—The seventh and eighth century papacy—The ninth century : Nicholas I : the False Decretals—The tenth and eleventh century papacy

BETWEEN the death of Gregory I and the accession of Gregory VII the papacy underwent many vicissitudes, calamities as well as triumphs. Yet the general advance in papal power can be seen by comparing the position and claims of the first Gregory with those of his later namesake. Gregory I claimed the spiritual primacy which descended to the vicar of Christ, the successor of S. Peter, but he wrote to the emperor at Constantinople in humility as a subject. Gregory VII was to claim not merely supreme spiritual but supreme temporal power, to declare an emperor deposed, and to plunge Germany and Italy into war to enforce his will. With him the medieval conception of the papacy became fully shaped : later popes exceeded him in effective power, but they had no need to extend his statement of the papal claims. The period intermediate between these two popes was pre-eminently for the church that of the growth of the medieval papacy. The old conception of great autocephalous churches, united in the faith and in church order, has been explained in previous chapters : it was in this period to be completely lost in the west, where indeed, in view of the inclusion of the whole west in a single patriarchate, it had never been of great vitality. The relationship of metropolitan sees to the patriarchate of Rome had never included the Greek conception of autocephalia.

Several factors had raised the western patriarchate to the position it held at the beginning of the seventh century. All the patriarchates had centred in cities of world-wide importance, and naturally therefore in Rome, the central city of them all. In the earlier struggle of religions in the empire, all had sought to be represented in Rome by a strong community. Within the bounds of Christianity not only great orthodox leaders, but great heresiarchs had sought to establish an influence there. Then again, Rome gave her name to that ordered system of civilisation which marked off imperial citizens from barbarians ; and as in the time of Gregory I the Roman bishop took over the urgent and unfulfilled duties of empire, so by association he acquired the prestige of these inherited duties. The absence of a near and overshadowing lay power may be reckoned a third factor in the growth of papal power, and the influence of S. Augustine's *City of God* a fourth. In 410 Alaric and his Goths had sacked Rome, and the fate of the imperial city had seemed to contemporaries to mark the collapse of civilisation itself. S. Augustine had written his *City of God* to construct a new world polity for a new age, a Christian philosophy of history. The long training of the Jews, and the training in civilisation and humanity afforded by the Roman empire had, he claimed, been double lines of preparation for the " City of God," the Christian church. The new dispensation, heralded by the fall of pagan Rome, was no retrogression, but the crown and completion of the old. By stressing the providential character of the glories of pagan Rome, he implicitly witnessed to the commanding position prepared for the Christian church of the old city. His subject was the new Christendom, the Christian church, and not the rule of that church by any central power : the Roman empire itself in his day had for long ceased to be ruled from Rome : but the comparison between the Roman empire and the Christian church, once made, was to point towards an imperial position for the Roman patriarch.

Two other factors had already operated in the same direction : the position assigned to S. Peter in the gospels, and the record of the Roman patriarchate in doctrinal controversies. All medieval scholars believed, (and modern

scholarship has not refuted the claim), that S. Peter and
S. Paul both preached in Rome, and that the earliest
Christian community there profited by their apostolic
labours.   None of the other patriarchates could claim this
double link with the apostles, a link treasured because
apostolic foundation was regarded as guarantee for the
authenticity of the first preaching of the faith.   But the
claims of the church at Rome were based on more than
apostolic foundation.   They rested on the Lord's own words
to Peter : " Thou art Peter, and upon this rock I will
build my church, and the gates of hell shall not prevail
against it.   I will give unto thee the keys of the kingdom
of heaven, and whatsoever thou shalt bind on earth shall
be bound in heaven, and whatsoever thou shalt loose in
earth shall be loosed in heaven."   The bishop of Rome
as vicar of S. Peter was regarded as inheriting the divine
commission and the divine promise and was marked off
by them from the holders of other apostolic sees.   Finally,
the natural genius of the Roman church had been for the
practical pieties of rule and administration rather than for
research into the mysteries of the Christian faith.   Alexandria and Antioch, and, in the west, Carthage, had in the
first four centuries been greater as schools of theology than
Rome :   the statement of the faith in terms of Greek
philosophy had been worked out in the east rather than
the west.   As a consequence, the record of the Roman
church was remarkably free from heretical commitments.
The gravity, prudence and commonsense of the Roman
temper had prevented a hasty rush into controversy and
furthered a wise final decision.   The question whether
any Roman bishop ever took the ultimately wrong side
in a doctrinal dispute is one, naturally, hotly contested
between Protestant and Roman Catholic scholars, but
that by the beginning of the seventh century the Roman
church had in an impressive number of cases come down
on the ultimately right side is striking and indisputable.
This had contributed no little already to Roman prestige.

Five new factors increased papal power between 604 and
1073.   The first was the papal policy of balancing secular
rulers in Italy.   From the time of Gregory I the papacy
showed great skill in playing off its enemies one against

the other. For nearly two hundred years it could balance the Lombards against the representatives of the Greek emperor. Eventually the Lombards became too powerful in the north, and two Frankish kings were called in to subdue them. This might have left the papacy weak as against a Frankish emperor who controlled all north Italy, but the danger was averted by the break-up of the Frankish empire. In the eleventh century the Normans captured the greater part of south Italy and Sicily : here again, pope Nicholas II saw the wisdom of allying with them, and his successors balanced their new allies against the Greek cities of the south and the new western empire which centred in Germany.

Secondly, the growth of feudalism reacted on the contemporary conception of the hierarchy. As in the days of the Roman empire civil and ecclesiastical organisation had provided many analogies, so in the middle ages the ordering of secular society helped to produce analogous organisation in the church. In medieval society personal status and all duties, obligations and privileges were connected with the ownership of land. All land was regarded as belonging ultimately to the king, and mediately to a succession of greater and lesser tenants, who paid for their land by military service. The most solemn obligation of feudal society was the oath of homage and fidelity sworn by each tenant to his superior lord, and all the linked loyalties traced back to a final loyalty to the king. In medieval theory, though not in medieval practice, the final unity of society was provided for by the Holy Roman Emperor, who took precedence of kings. This conception of linked and delegated powers was easily applicable to the hierarchy. The subordination of priest to bishop and bishop to metropolitan was already there : feudal minds were ready to stress the subordination of the metropolitans to the pope, begun as early as the days of Gregory I, and to recognise them as enjoying their powers by his delegation.

Thirdly, the medieval papacy afforded a useful source of arbitration and appeal court for Europe. National feeling did not yet exist, justice was uncertain and dear, and appeal to the Roman curia was a convenience and advance in civilisation. When one of the main difficulties of kings was the control of their bishops, and one of the main dangers of bishops oppression by their kings, the papal court could at times be useful to both ; and useful also to less exalted litigants. Moreover, the papacy came forward eventually as guarantor of the canon (or ecclesiastical) law, and though the first compilation of canon law was not issued with the direct sanction of the pope, all later collections were so edited and issued. A great system of church law and church courts was built up, of which the papal authority and the papal curia were the keystones.

Fourthly, the growth of the territorial jurisdiction of the pope contributed somewhat to their power. In the days of Gregory I their estates had been merely the private patrimony of the Roman church. By those of Gregory VII they were much more. The Donations of Pepin and Charles had increased their extent, as had private legacies and benefactions. But the papacy now held these possessions not merely as private owner, but as temporal ruler. No great violence was done to contemporary feeling by this assumption of secular power by a spiritual ruler, for all over Europe certain bishops held palatine jurisdictions where their own law ran, and not the law of the lay ruler of the country. But the papal states were of peculiar importance to the pope for two reasons. By drawing a diagonal barrier across Italy they prevented the rise of any single strong Italian power, such as might overshadow and constrain the pope, and they afforded him revenue and a small army, necessary to his independence.

No attempt can be made to give an account of the fortunes of all the numerous medieval popes, for it was exceptional in the middle ages for a pope to reign more than five or six years, but the rise or decline in papal power in the succeeding centuries should be noted.

No seventh or eighth century pontificate can compare in importance with that of Gregory I. That of Martin I, who died in 655 as a prisoner of the emperor, shows the papacy in as weak a position as in the days of Justinian. But in three respects papal power increased in the west beyond the old canonical patriarchate. Whereas earlier the western churches had been practically independent, linked to Rome only by the veneration paid to the see of S. Peter, by the practice of pilgrimage, and by infrequent appeals, in the seventh and eighth centuries papal intervention was accepted in the normal church government of England, France and Germany. In England archbishop Theodore tightened up the connexion between Canterbury and the papacy, and in 787 two legates were sent from Rome on a general mission of reform. In Germany and France the work of Boniface rested upon papal support, familiarised recourse to Rome and increased veneration for the Holy See. In France the very title of the new Carolingian dynasty rested partly on papal confirmation. Pepin, Mayor of the Palace, already effective ruler of the Franks, sent to consult pope Zacharias on his right to assume the royal title. The pope sent word that the man who was in fact king should be so called, the Franks acclaimed him king, and in 751 Boniface blessed and anointed him. The papal blessing was quoted in later ages as precedent for the papal claim to make and unmake kings. Secondly, the latter part of the eighth century saw the birth of the papal states in the Donations of Pepin and Charles the Great, (see p. 65), while the so-called Donation of Constantine and the papal coronation of Charles gave a general sanction to the exercise of temporal power by the pope.

The ninth century brought danger to the papal patrimony from the Saracen raiders who infested the Mediterranean. They attacked Sardinia, took Palermo in 831, and also laid hands on Sicily, which had once been so valuable a part of the patrimony. Then they attacked south Italy, landed at Ostia in 846, came up the Tiber to Rome, and plundered the Roman churches. The Frankish emperor Lothar sent his son, afterwards Louis II, with a force of Franks to avenge these injuries. They defeated the Saracens, and even exacted reparations from them for the rebuilding of Rome, but the pope and Roman clergy were helpless under their immediate domination. The ninth century saw, however, one remarkable pontificate in that of Nicholas I, or the Great, (858–867). The Frankish empire, harried by the Norsemen, was now weak under Louis II, and Nicholas I found means, not only to reassert papal independence in Italy, but to intervene in the government of the Frankish church. He summoned the imperially-protected archbishop of Ravenna to Rome, excommunicated him in a Lateran synod when he refused to obey, and enforced absolute submission in spite of Louis' protection. When Lothar, the Carolingian prince of Lorraine, repudiated his innocent wife Teutberga, and obtained Louis' support, and the blessing of the bishops of Trèves and Cologne on a new marriage, Nicholas declared the said bishops deposed. Louis I and Lothar marched to Rome in support of the bishops and their decision, but Louis fell ill and submitted to Nicholas' will. With Hincmar, the most powerful and learned archbishop of Reims, Nicholas also contended ; Hincmar had to submit to the coronation of queen Teutberga, whom he had opposed, by a papal legate, and to receive back at Nicholas' command a bishop whom he had deposed. In the east, Nicholas supported the deposed patriarch Ignatius against Photius, (see p. 79), and the side he championed finally triumphed. But it was for the favourable reception given by Nicholas to the Pseudo-Isidorian or False Decretals that his pontificate was chiefly remarkable, both as a step in the building up of the canon law, and for the inclusion of unauthentic material in that body which went far to strengthen the papal position.

To understand the importance of the Pseudo-Isidorian Decretals the history of the early development of canon law should be remembered. There was no one, official, authorised collection of the canons of the church before the twelfth century. It had been from the council of Nicaea onwards a most sacred duty of every catholic bishop, eastern and western, to acquaint himself with the canons, and teach them to his familia : but while all accepted the canons of Nicaea and the subsequent general councils, local churches added canons from their own councils and those of neighbouring provinces without any special system. In the early centuries, texts were hard to procure. By the mid-sixth century, the Greek church, the African church, the Spanish church, the Gallican and the Roman church had formed their own collections. The African church had itself declined before the Vandals, but its canons of c. 390–420 had been embodied in the *Hispana*, the Spanish collection, and in the Gallican. Caesarius of Arles, († 542), had gathered into his *Statuta Ecclesiae Antiqua* these African canons, those of eastern councils, and certain papal letters. About 496 an eastern monk, Dionysius Exiguus, came to Rome and compiled two most important collections of canons : he translated a Greek collection of eastern canons, and he compiled the local canons of the Roman church. These consisted of the 39 decretals, or letters, of popes, dating from pope Siricius, († 398). The whole collection of Dionysius Exiguus remained the only official collection of the Roman church till the eleventh century. It was the one presented to Charles the Great by Hadrian I, and it was accepted by a council of Aix-la-Chapelle in 802, and became the official *Liber Canonum* of the Frankish church. It was indeed the most popular collection of canons in the whole church, except in England, where, though it was known, no one collection seems to have been generally used.

Between 847 and 852 the collection known as the False Decretals or the Pseudo-Isidore was produced in the Carolingian Empire, by an anonymous ecclesiastic of deep learning and skilled historical imagination, probably connected with the churches of Metz or Mainz. He wished to draw up a great collection of canons to strengthen the power of the harassed Carolingian bishop against the count, for the mid-ninth century was a time of extreme feudal violence, and as a Frank trained in the canonical traditions of Boniface, he looked to the papacy as a bulwark of defence against lay violence and irregularity. He took as the basis of his collection the old *Hispana* and he added to it a number of already existing apocryphal documents, and a series of letters of the earliest popes, from Clement to Damasus, († 384), inclusive. He thus filled up the gap before the decretals of Siricius, which were the first genuine ones in his collection. He also issued a collection of pseudo-capitularies, which stand to the secular Frankish law as the False Decretals to the canon law ; and a series of capitula ascribed to Angilram, bishop of Metz. He was not a forger in the modern sense. Contemporary custom allowed the keepers of records who were aware of the issue of some early chapter, letter, or privilege, to supply such a document, in as historically correct a form as possible : such documents were often needed in lawsuits, and were certainly produced, all over Europe. The author of the False Decretals, an artist in this particular line, used the old *Liber Pontificalis*, a very early and brief record of the pontificates of the Roman bishops, and supplied the letters he found mentioned therein, weaving in scraps from historical sources whenever possible. The whole collection he ascribed to " Isidore Mercator," who was taken by contemporaries to have been the learned Isidore, bishop of Seville. The most important feature of the collection was the antiquity it gave to certain later claims of the papacy. The pope was declared the sovereign lawgiver, without whose consent no provincial council might meet or pronounce valid decrees ; no bishop might be deposed without his intervention, and his decisions of themselves constituted law. While the Pseudo-Isidorian Decretals thus sought to give the bishop a protector as against his metropolitan or a lay ruler, they left the pope supreme head of the whole of Christendom. Knowledge of them spread from France to Rome. and Nicholas I accepted this teaching, and proclaimed it in all his letters and actions : " that which the pope has decided," he wrote, " is to be observed by all." The decretals soon won complete acceptance, and were used in later collections, including the *Decretum* of Gratian (see p. 140).

The tenth and first half of the eleventh century were for the papacy a period of obscurity and decline : the last half of the eleventh century one of recovery. The " cleansing of the papacy " by the emperor Henry III in 1046 marks the watershed. The violence of the invading Northmen had raised up a violent class of feudal nobles over Europe, and in the tenth and eleventh centuries civilisation and the church suffered from their wars and aggressions. The Italian church and the papacy suffered no less than the rest of Europe. The overshadowing power of the Roman nobles in their own city made the popes first weak and then debased.

The counts of Tusculum and the house of the Crescentii regarded the papacy as a desirable family possession, fought over the papal elections, and for some time procured

the election of undesirable popes. In 1046 a young
and scandalous member of the Tusculan house held the
papal chair, and when in disgust the Romans set up an
anti-pope, he sold the papal chair to yet a third claimant,
Gregory VI. In these straits an appeal was made to the
emperor Henry III to settle the matter. He came to
Rome, procured the deposition or resignation of the three
rivals, and nominated a most respectable German bishop
pope : he could scarcely have arranged the disputed
tenure of a German abbey with more promptitude and
less opposition. Peter Damiani, one of the most saintly
and zealous champions of reform, compared him to David,
and the Roman nobles to Goliath. As a result of this
" cleansing of the papacy," Henry himself nominated
from Germany the next three popes, whenever the papal
chair became vacant. His nominees were all German,
respectable and reforming : and a zeal for the Cluniac
ideals, (see p. 99), was imparted to Rome. In Germany
itself, where the abuses of lay control were worse than
elsewhere, Henry pursued a policy of reform, appointing
ecclesiastics himself, but appointing fit ones. The clerks
of his chapel were rewarded with bishoprics : but they
were the ablest bishops in the German church.

In three other ways the papacy was strengthened between
the cleansing of the papacy and the accession of Gregory
VII. The Norman raiders had secured their hold on the
south of Italy, and might have been as dangerous to the
papacy as the Lombards once were in the north ; after a
period of hostility and defeat, pope Nicholas II made a
formal alliance with Robert Guiscard and Richard of
Capua, in 1059. Robert he made " future duke " of Sicily,
hoping that he would drive out the Saracens. Secondly,
a canon passed at the Lateran synod of 1059 regulated
future papal elections : the old vague rights of the Roman
clergy and people to elect, which had made possible the
recent abuses of the Roman nobles, were defined in a
process by which the cardinal bishops chose, and the
cardinal priests and deacons " acceded to " their
choice. The question of imperial rights was passed over
in the vague phrase " saving the due honour and reverence " owed to the emperor : a right that was interpreted

henceforward as his right to be informed after the election. Though the provisions of this canon were frequently not followed, yet during the minority of Henry IV the consent of his mother the empress to a papal election was never asked. Thirdly, the election of Nicholas II in 1058 was the result and coping-stone of an alliance most valuable to the papacy, with Godfrey duke of Lorraine and his wife Beatrice, the heiress of Tuscany. Fourthly, the pope gained a valuable victory over Milan, the most independent see of Italy, and at the same time furthered the cause of reform and detached Milan from the imperial interest. In this see of S. Ambrose the practice of clerical marriage was stoutly maintained to be canonical ; but by an alliance with a set of ascetic reformers, known from the apostolic poverty of their clothes as the Patarini (rag-pickers), the papacy secured the submission of the archbishop and the condemnation of clerical marriage.

Thus when Gregory VII, the greatest of the early medieval popes, was elected to the papal throne in 1073, Rome was already reformed and powerful. She had taken over the leadership of a great reform movement from the abbey of Cluny, (see p. 99), and thus commanded the respect of the best elements in Christendom. She had freed herself from the power of the Roman nobles. She had asserted her jurisdiction over the metropolitans, her supremacy over councils. The abuses which remained unreformed in Christendom were now to bring her into conflict with the western emperor himself. The great struggle of Gregory VII's pontificate was to be not so much a quarrel over a particular abuse, as a vindication of the papal claim to world rule, for the reform of all abuses. The medieval papacy had reached maturity.

CHAPTER VII

CLUNY : HILDEBRAND : INVESTITURES

Lay control of ninth century churches—Foundation of Cluny—
Church in ninth century England—Dunstan and reform in England
—Cluniac influence towards reform of church at large—Career
of Hildebrand—Gregory VII and Henry IV—Gregory VII and
William I—Concordat of Bec—Concordat of Worms

THE greatest event of the tenth and eleventh centuries
was a reform movement, which began as an attempt
to co-ordinate and reform the monasteries, and ended
by remedying many abuses connected with the life of the
secular clergy and the laity. In the ninth and tenth centuries
Europe was given over to the harrying of the heathen
Vikings, or Norsemen : in England, for example, monasteries and bishops' churches were everywhere plundered
and destroyed. The Carolingian empire fared no better,
and ninth century synods show that in most dioceses
even bishops' schools could not be maintained. Whereas
the election of bishops, the priors or provosts of collegiate
churches, and of abbots, belonged canonically to the
chapter or the monks, in practice the king or some great
lord appointed his own nominee. In two ways the laity
had had, since the sixth century, their own canonical share
in the election of bishops and the appointment of presbyters
with cure of souls. The nobles shared with the cathedral
clergy the deliberations preceding the choice of a bishop,
and the common people signified their assent to his election,
when he was presented to them, by acclamation. Moreover, the founder of a church on his estates had canonically
the right of presenting a suitable candidate to the bishop
to serve his church. But in the ninth and tenth centuries

the feudal nobles went far beyond their canonical rights. Kings appointed to bishoprics and abbeys, and " invested " the recipients with ring and staff, the symbols not only of their temporal possessions, but of their spiritual office ; the new bishop or abbot did homage to the king, and swore fealty, like any other feudal tenant. Kings and nobles granted " benefices," (tenure for a term of years, sometimes one or three lives), out of church lands to their servants ; patrons often succeeded in treating the estates of their churches as their own, or in appropriating the tithes to their own use. The clergy were often untrained and hastily ordained : disregarding the canons, they married or lived with women. The old canonical arrangement of some preliminary years of matrimony before a late ordination to the diaconate was now impossible, as deacons might be ordained at twenty-one, and priests at twenty-five. The increase of small outlying churches had made more priests necessary. In the case of married clergy there was danger that church lands would become hereditary possessions. The bishop's office might become hereditary like that of the count. Churches were often actually left desolate, and the poor, like the clergy, were robbed of their endowment. A matricula was still maintained by some of the churches, and those enrolled on it for the reception of regular allowances were now exclusively the poor, and not the whole clergy of the church : but in these times of violence few churches had anything to distribute. Private warfare rendered the lot of the peasant, as of all but the highest clergy, a miserable one.

The movement for monastic reform originated with the foundation of the monastery of Cluny, in Burgundy. The pious duke William of Aquitaine, wishing to found a monastery, consulted the strictest monk he knew, abbot Bertho of Baume, who asked as the site of the new house the duke's favourite hunting-lodge of Cluny. The site was well chosen, for it lay near one of the pilgrim routes to Rome, and the highways of the Saône and Rhone ; in a land, moreover, where the Norsemen had not plundered. When William demurred to driving out his dogs, Bertho reminded him that God would reward him for monks, but not for dogs, and in 910 the duke signed the foundation charter. By a striking innovation, he allowed the monks freely to elect their own abbot, without interference from himself or any of his heirs. In return for a small tribute, the monks were to have the papal protection and guardianship, and be exempted from the jurisdiction of the local bishop.

The real founder of Cluny, however, was its second abbot, Odo, whose father had dedicated him to S. Martin and the service of the church in childhood, and then tried to make him a page at court. S. Martin, however, afflicted the boy with pains in the head, and the father recognised the sign that the boy ought to have received the tonsure. Reproaching S. Martin as a good hearer of prayers, but a sharp man of business in requiring the fulfilment of a promise, he let Odo become a clerk and canon of the fashionable community of S. Martin at Tours. This life proving not strict enough, Odo retired to one of great asceticism in a little cell near Tours. Later he heard with joy that S. Benedict's rule was strictly followed at Baume, and became a monk there, and master of the oblates' school. In 927 the Cluniac monks elected him their abbot, and he completed the building of their monastery. His great work was the extension of the reform to other houses, which were often affiliated to Cluny as to a parent house. The safeguard which Cluny introduced into the monastic system was this subjection of all subsequent daughter-houses to Cluny : such houses were not independent " abbeys," but " priories," whose priors were under the discipline of the abbot of Cluny. The greatest abbey of northern France, Fleury on the Loire, whither the bones of S. Benedict had been translated from Monte Cassino, had become relaxed ; and this house, too, Odo reformed, though it did not become a cell to Cluny. The monks, who had been expected by their bishop to murder Odo when he visited them, threw away their weapons, embraced his feet, and submitted to his ordinances. Odo's incessant almsgiving was one of the characteristics which struck his contemporaries most, and it was often a difficulty to those who had the financing of the monastery. John the prior of Cluny confessed that the sight often distressed him. " For though I had compassion on the poor, yet I was prior, and knowing the poverty of the monastery, and foreseeing the necessities of the brothers, I would point out that it was unjust to give all things thus indiscreetly away. I thought to act wisely, yet was I only wrapped in the mist of darkness." Another great abbot was Odilo, who, like Odo, began life as a canon in an aristocratic community, and then renounced his ancestral inheritance to become a novice at Cluny, not disdaining menial tasks, " the cleaning of lanterns, the scouring of floors, the care of the children." He was elected abbot c. 994. He both defended Cluny successfully from all attacks on her independence, from laymen and the diocesan bishop, receiving in this the support of the pope, and did much to make Cluny a home of learning, liturgy, and ecclesiastical art. Turning from the tradi- tion of agricultural simplicity, which had animated the observance of Benedict of Aniane, with which Cluny had been originally connected, he increased the time given to the singing of the divine office, and " marvellously adorned the cloisters with columns and marble brought from the farthest parts of the province." When in cheerful mood he compared himself to Caesar Augustus, in that he had found Cluny wood and left it marble. " He was the father of many monks . . . cherishing them all with one modera- tion and virtue of discretion, with maternal love and paternal care." Men sought the prayers of the monks of Cluny with such eagerness in his time, that in charity to the souls of the dead Odilo sanctioned an annual day of prayer for them, to be observed by all the houses under him on 2 November, the day following All Saints' Day. This observance of All Souls' Day by the private prayers, and public alms and masses, of the Cluniac monks, finally became general in the church.

The example of Cluny inspired monastic and clerical reform not only on the continent, but in England, where it was expressed in the work of Dunstan and Aethelwold. Before this, Alfred the Great had found his kingdom ravaged by the Danes, learning perishing, and the monas- teries destroyed. He had summoned to his court such scholars as he could obtain, Werfrith, whom he made bishop of Worcester, Grimbald, a monk of Corvey, John the Old Saxon, and Asser. He had maintained a palace school, provided that the young lay thegns as well as young clerks should be taught to read, at least in Anglo-Saxon, and even desired that adult ealdormen should learn their letters. He had drawn up a code of laws, beginning with the giving of the Mosaic law in Exodus, and the birthday of the Christian dispensation at Pentecost, and continuing with the early laws of Wessex, and such additions as he chose to make. Alfred also sought to advance the education of his clergy by translating the *Ecclesiastical History* of Bede, the universal history of Orosius, and above all, the *Shepherd's Book*, or *Cura Pastoralis*, of Gregory the Great. He was in touch with the continent and the papacy, (indeed, it is possible that when a child and a very younger son he received the tonsure from the pope, who made him his " bishop's son " at Rome), but though he admired continental monasticism, he can hardly be said to have revived it in England. He founded one monastery in his manor of Athelney, inviting foreign monks to begin the new foundation : and he planned the " New Minster " at Winchester, which was completed by his son. But the rule in both these houses was more probably that of canons than monks.

Desire for the revival of the Benedictine rule in England dates rather from the time of Oda, who, when he was made archbishop of Canterbury in 942, sent to Fleury for the monastic habit for himself, and shortly after sent his nephew Oswald to be trained as a novice there. Aelfheah, bishop of Winchester, 934–951, had the same reverence for monks, for he encouraged his young relative Dunstan to aspire to a monastic life. In 943 Dunstan was made abbot of Glastonbury, where he instituted a stricter monastic life, and trained his later helpers, especially Aethelwold, in spreading the Cluniac ideals in England. Aethelwold was made abbot of Abingdon in 950, and when he was made bishop of Winchester drove out the married canons of the Old Minster, and replaced them with monks. He reformed the great monasteries of the Danelaw, Ely, Medehamstead or Peterborough, and Thorney ; translated the Benedictine rule into English ; and drew up a customary for the English Benedictines, the *Regularis Concordia Anglicae Nationis*. This was partly founded on the

H

observance of Fleury and Ghent, houses reformed by the Cluniacs, and partly on the capitulary of Aix-la-Chapelle, 817. Aethelwold's motive was similar to that of Benedict of Aniane : uniformity, and stricter observance. Oswald was made bishop of Worcester, but proceeded more gently than Aethelwold : he founded a small monastery at Westbury-on-Trim, helped reform the great East Anglian house of Ramsey, used monks from Ramsey to reform Winchcombe, and finally brought monks from Winchcombe, and set them side by side with the [married ?] canons of his cathedral, hoping to change the character of his clergy gradually. The great " soke " granted by the king to Oswald, primarily as endowment, illustrates the contemporary tendency to regard bishops as great feudal lords. Within it the bishop of Worcester held the rights of jurisdiction which normally belonged to the crown ; he held three courts, instead of the normal hundred courts, for his tenants, and took the fees. The soke of the great abbey of Peterborough extended over eight hundreds in Northamptonshire : and the endowment of royal abbeys at this time frequently took the form of a grant of such " immunities " or " sokes," though generally on a smaller scale. Dunstan himself was archbishop of Canterbury from 960 till 988, and during the first part of that time the greatest ecclesiastical statesman of pre-Conquest England. His canons at Christchurch were probably of stricter life than those of other cathedrals : in any case, he made no attempt to eject them, and fill their places by Benedictine monks. He countenanced, however, the vigorous reforms of Aethelwold and Oswald ; he himself strove by synodal warnings and preaching to raise the level of the secular clergy generally, warning them against drunkenness and immorality. He had not merely fostered the tradition of learning at Glastonbury, but had himself practised various handicrafts : he now exhorted the parish clergy to learn crafts themselves, that they might teach their parishioners. It is a sign of the renaissance of learning at this period that Anglo-Saxon translations began to be made of the gospels ; Alfred the Great had not translated biblical books. The earliest vernacular translations which have come down to us, from the mid tenth century, are the interlinear verbal translations, or glosses on the gospels, the Lindisfarne gospels in old Northumbrian, and the Rushworth, in old Mercian ; besides a translation of the first fifty psalms. From Dunstan's time we have the West-Saxon gospels of Aelfric, monk of Bath, and a paraphrase on part of the Old Testament by another Aelfric, abbot of Eynsham, who also wrote a set of homilies on the Sunday gospels, prefacing most of them by a translation. It was usual to preach on the gospel if there was a sermon at mass, the ordinary Sunday service for lay-people ; but the only other part of the service in English was the " bidding prayer." In France in the next centuries it became usual to read a vernacular translation of the gospel at mass, immediately after the Latin : but there is no evidence for this in England.

The " Cluniac movement " helped to bring about a general reform in the church, though the leadership in that movement was contributed by the papacy, not by the abbot of Cluny. The Cluniacs influenced the church, however, in four ways. Their characteristic stand for the free election of their abbot and priors, independently of any secular control, was bound to react on the election of ordinary Benedictine abbots, and of bishops. Some of the latter would have been canonically elected by a chapter of canons, some even by a monastic chapter. Secondly, many Cluniac monks became bishops, and ruled dioceses. Thirdly, Cluniac abbots attended diocesan and provincial synods, and were on the side of reform, particularly that of enforcing the celibacy of the clergy in holy orders. Fourthly, Cluny took the lead, through her abbot, in a movement to mitigate the horrors of private warfare, and this promotion of peace made for the promotion of reform. In 989 a Burgundian council declared excommunicate those who attacked bishop, priest, deacon, or clerk, while at home or travelling : those who robbed a church ; those who stole any beast from the poor, or the tillers of the soil. Similar councils were held in all parts of France, oaths were taken to observe peace and justice, and after a time this " Peace of God " took under its protection clerks, pilgrims, women, children, labourers and the instruments of their work, monasteries and cemeteries.

These were to be undisturbed and in " perpetual peace." By an extension of the movement, the " Truce of God," first definitely mentioned in a council of 1017, nobles and princes swore to desist from all private warfare from noon on Saturday to prime on Monday. This would allow due reverence to be paid to the Lord's Day ; those who broke this " Truce of God " were cut off from the sacraments of the church and the society of the faithful in life : no priest might bury them, no man might pray for their soul. Those who swore to and observed the truce were assured of absolution from God, of the prayers of Mary and her choir of virgins, the defence of Michael and his angels, S. Peter, the chief of the apostles, and of all saints and faithful people then and for ever. In the institution of the " Truce of God " Odilo of Cluny took the leading part.

The ideals of Cluny, when championed by Gregory VII, were to lead to a bitter struggle between the empire and papacy for supremacy in world politics. This outcome was at first unforeseen, for two reasons. The early abbots of Cluny were traditionally friendly with the empire ; and they were no extremists in the difficult question of the appointment to and control of bishoprics and churches. Though the principle of treating ecclesiastical offices and benefices as private property was uncanonical and wrong, the chief obstacle to reform, and all too frequently accompanied by " simony," (obtaining of spiritual office by purchase or favour), yet the abbots of Cluny were willing to allow some lay share in elections, with the resultant control over the see, abbey, or cure. Secondly, the greatest of the Holy Roman emperors, Henry III (1039–1056), was a powerful champion of reform himself, and the friend of abbot Hugh of Cluny, who became the godfather of his son, Henry IV.

But while some rulers, like Henry III, and William I of England, used their powers to appoint good ecclesiastics, others abused their rights and appointed frankly bad ones, or kept the sees vacant for financial reasons. All abuses in the church came to seem connected with this question of lay control. Meanwhile, the future champion of reform, Hildebrand, had passed more than fifty years of his life in the service of various popes. He was the nephew of

8656

the abbot of S. Mary's on the Aventine, the Cluniac house in Rome. He himself, however, received the education of a clerk in the papal household, but left Rome in 1046, as the chaplain of the exiled and deposed pope Gregory VI. After three years in Germany he returned to Rome, and was made papal sub-deacon : he helped procure the election of Nicholas II, was made archdeacon, and from that time became an influential personage. Cardinal Humbert, however, and not Hildebrand, was the most extreme champion of reform, and the important Lateran canons of 1059 represent his views, and not the more moderate ones of Hildebrand. The laity were called in to assist in the campaign against clerical marriage,—already through the preaching of the Patarini they were in doubt as to the validity of the sacraments of married priests,—nomination to an ecclesiastical benefice obtained by money or " favour " was declared invalid, and the immunity of the clergy from lay jurisdiction was asserted. Hildebrand was no philosophical theorist : when sent as papal legate to preside over the synod which examined and condemned the views of Berengarius of Tours, he treated Berengarius with a leniency for which he was afterwards reproached. In theory he was not primarily interested : but he was interested in establishing on earth the " iustitia " (righteousness) of the psalms and the beatitudes. In fighting for " iustitia " he took up gradually more and more advanced theoretical positions, as he was driven in the struggle. He was elected pope himself in 1073, taking the title of Gregory VII, and in the struggle with Henry IV which took up most of his pontificate he advanced beyond his original position in two ways. In a synod of 1075 he issued the old decrees against simony and clerical marriage, and absolutely forbade the practice of lay investiture, the gift of ring and staff by a lay ruler to a bishop or abbot. This canon was difficult to observe when princes depended so much on the support of bishops, and when a distinction between the spiritual office and lay possessions of prelates had hardly been thought out : both were conferred in the words " Accipe ecclesiam." Secondly, as he found the emperor the greatest obstacle to the fulfilment of his ideals, he came to regard the empire, the secular power, not as co-ordinate and divinely inspired, but as subordinate to the spiritual, and finally even as the work of the devil. He conceived of society as a divinely governed feudal state, with Christ's vicar, S. Peter, as the supreme head. With S. Peter he identified his own office : blessed Peter, he said, was honoured, or suffered injury, in him, his servant : " while we sit in his seat and exercise his power, he himself receives the letters or speeches that are addressed to us."

The struggle of Henry IV and Gregory VII was marked by a dramatic incident. It was begun by Henry's disregard of the investiture canons and association with excommunicates : he proceeded to drive the Patarini from Milan, invest a new archbishop of that see, and in a council of Worms, 1076, declare Gregory no pope, but false monk, (Gregory had once acted as steward of a monastery, but had never been a monk).[1] Gregory answered by excommunicating and deposing Henry himself,—and the news made all men tremble. Henry's rebellious subjects in Saxony made it so clear that they would throw off the yoke of an excommunicate prince, that Henry was driven to circumvent them by submitting. Making a hasty winter journey into Lombardy, and finding Gregory at Canossa, one of the Alpine strongholds of the countess Matilda of Tuscany, he waited three days in the snow of the courtyard as a penitent, imploring release from excommunication. He had appealed from the statesman in Gregory to the priest, and on the fourth day, against the interests of the statesman, Gregory absolved him. But Gregory's allies, the Saxon rebels, were disgusted at conduct which, they told him, they considered playing fast and loose with them. In 1077 they elected a rival emperor, but sufficient of Henry's friends had returned to him to make their victory impossible. Gregory wished to act as arbitrator between the two emperors, and when neither party would accept his arbitration as mediator between them. But he had no sufficient worldly force behind him to back his claims ; the German bishops largely supported Henry, for they disliked reform, and they disliked Gregory's centralising policy. In their own words, " they disliked being ordered about like bailiffs." Civil war followed in

[1] See *War Gregor VII Mönch ?* Martens, W., 1891.

Germany from 1077 onwards ; Gregory again excommunicated and deposed Henry in 1080, and Henry answered by
making an anti-pope, whom he enthroned in Rome in
1084. Gregory, shut up in the castle of Sant' Angelo,
sent for help to Robert Guiscard : he came, took and laid
waste Rome, so that both Gregory and the anti-pope were
forced to leave the city. Gregory died the year following
at Salerno, still holding the promise of blessing to those
who suffer for righteousness' sake for comfort. " I have
loved righteousness, and hated iniquity : therefore I die
in exile." The issue of supremacy between pope and
emperor was left undecided : the struggle over investitures
was to continue for nearly fifty years.

It was decided between the English king and primate
by a local concordat before the general settlement between
pope and emperor. William I had been contemporary to
Gregory VII, but there was neither a struggle for supremacy
nor investitures in England in this reign. The relations
between William I and Gregory were friendly, though
both men were of resolute and unyielding temper. Gregory
was preoccupied with his struggle with the emperor ; he
was satisfied that William and his primate Lanfranc
would both further reform in England, as indeed, they
did ; and he had countenanced the conquest of England,
as an effort to get rid of the schismatic archbishop Stigand.
William laid down the modus vivendi between the English
crown and the papacy as a good Cluniac, firmly separating
matters temporal and spiritual. He refused to acknowledge Gregory as his temporal overlord, on the ground that
" his ancestors," the Anglo-Saxon kings, had never done
so ; but he never questioned the spiritual primacy of the
pope, and the duty of obedience. He invited papal legates
to come to England in 1070 and inaugurate the reform of
the English church; (Lanfranc was later appointed papal
legate). He promised that Peter's Pence, a small payment
from the laity, should be more promptly paid. But he
laid down certain safeguards for the royal power. No
archbishop was to receive the pall without his consent,—
this to avoid involving England in schism in days when
anti-popes were frequent. No tenant-in-chief was to be
excommunicated without his consent,—this to avoid

" excommunication by infection," such as the emperor had incurred. No papal bulls were to be received by any of his subjects without his consent, and no church councils were to be held, or canons passed, without his consent. These are the points mentioned by a chronicler : there was, of course, no formal agreement with the pope, but he seems tacitly to have accepted them. The last point, if not an overstatement, was highly uncanonical and contrary to the Cluniac spirit : but may have had reference to the difficult question of investitures, no solution for which had yet been thought out. Both William I and William II continued to invest their prelates without scruple on either side.

The question of lay investiture was raised in England by Anselm, at first the scholarly abbot of Bec in Normandy, and appointed archbishop of Canterbury by William II in 1093, during a sick-bed repentance. William had kept the see vacant four years to take its revenues, as he had others : when he recovered in body and relapsed in spirit there was manifold trouble between him and Anselm over his oppression of the church. At length Anselm set out to Rome to fetch his pall, and in 1099 was present at a synod which renewed the condemnation of lay investiture. By medieval theory those who were not present at a council were not, or were only doubtfully, bound by its provisions : henceforth Anselm could not in conscience give way on the point. Rufus died the next year, but though Henry I was far more righteous and moderate, Anselm could not do him the homage he demanded. After many negotiations and much correspondence with the pope a settlement was arranged with Henry at Bec in 1107. The election of prelates was to be freely made by the chapter : but in his presence, in his chapel. This satisfied the canons, but left the control of the election with the king. The bishop-elect was then to do homage for the temporalities of his see, after which the archbishop was to consecrate him, and invest him with the ring and staff, the symbols of the spiritualities.

The European question was settled on the same lines. By a curious settlement between Paschal II and the emperor Henry V, made while Paschal was in Henry's power in 1111 and afterwards repudiated, the pope nearly reduced the church to apostolic poverty : by the treaty, Henry was to renounce fealty and lay investiture, while the pope yielded the " temporalia " of the church but kept the " spiritualia." Actually, both sets of rights could have been reduced to the common denomination of hard cash, but the one affected mainly the bishops' revenues, the other the pope's. After protracted negotiations, the Concordat of Worms was signed in 1122, on much the same lines as that of Bec. The emperor renounced investiture by ring and staff, and promised canonical election ; the pope assented to election in the emperor's presence, to investiture with the " regalia " by touching the sceptre before consecration, and to the performance of homage and fealty. In practice, however, Henry V's power over the church fiefs was far less than Henry IV's had been, and he was willing to make these concessions, which were very similar to proposals Henry IV had refused. But though much ink had flowed, and pamphlets had fluttered abroad like leaves in a gale on the other question, the supremacy of pope or emperor, it remained undecided. And the private patronage of churches, so great a factor in the abuses against which the Cluniac reformers struggled, remains in many cases to this day.

CHAPTER VIII

THE CRUSADES AND THEIR EFFECT ON THE CHURCH

Nature and causes of the Crusades—The first four Crusades—Results : extension of Latin rite to kingdom of Jerusalem ; extension of Latin rite to Latin empire of Constantinople ; the military orders ; increased prestige of papacy ; increase of indulgences ; increase of eastern heresies ; the Albigensian Crusade ; general

THE Crusades were religious wars for the capture and defence of Jerusalem from the infidel, which succeeded in gaining the Holy City in 1099, and in holding it till 1187, and by which unsuccessful attempts were made to retake it later. As such, they could not be without results upon Christianity at large. Yet they were not only religious wars, but wars of frontier defence, between the civilisations of Europe and Asia ; their direct results were probably larger in the political and social sphere than in the religious. Though the Crusades affected mainly the twelfth and thirteenth centuries, their antecedents stretched much farther back.

Islam, the religion of surrender to God, had been founded by Mahomet, an Arab shepherd and prophet, who died in 632. His followers reckoned their era, not from his birth, but from his flight with a few followers from Mecca to Medina (a word meaning *the city* of the Prophet), in 622. His religion was an immense advance on the savage tribal cults of the nomads who in his day wandered and fought in the Arabian deserts and pastures, and traded in the coast towns of the Red Sea. It was derived from the " religion of Abraham," a monotheistic system practised by certain Arabs ; from Judaism ; and from a confused knowledge of Christianity gained orally by Mahomet; but the passion which inspired the religion came from Mahomet's long night watches, prayers and trances in the desert. The Koran is a collection of short sayings, the inspired utterances of the Prophet, strung together in no particular order: but while the earlier sayings are comparable in their exalted fervour to those of the Hebrew prophets, the later are a miscellaneous collection of Mahomet's borrowings from Judaism and Christianity, the " orders of the day " of a chieftain on a campaign, moral regulations for his followers, and even dispensations to Mahomet to evade his own earlier commands. The food supply of Arabia was strictly limited, and the population had earlier been kept stationary by child-exposure and tribal fighting: Mahomet forbade the first and gave an outlet to a growing population by leading his followers against the infidel. Islam became a religion of the sword. The caliphs, who ruled Islam after the Prophet's death, had by 652 conquered Syria, Egypt, Armenia and Persia, and by c. 750 north Africa, Spain and the Mediterranean islands: though they had been repelled from Gaul and Constantinople. The Arab civilisation of Persia, Egypt and Spain was at its zenith while the rest of Europe was fighting its way out of barbarism, and, through its commerce and intercourse with the old civilisations of the east, far more brilliant in learning and the arts.

Five circumstances contributed to the rise of the crusading movement in the eleventh century. Islam was now divided politically between the caliphs of Baghdad, Cairo and Cordova, and split into two religious sects: throughout the Crusades, Christian success depended largely on the divisions of Islam. Secondly, a stream of pilgrimage to the Holy Places had begun, especially after the land-route through Hungary became possible by the conversion of King Stephen. Free access by the pilgrims was threatened, however, by the rise of a new governing race in Islam: the fairly tolerant Arabs were displaced by the Turks, Mongols and barbarians from central Asia. They captured Baghdad by 1055, and immediately threatened the borders of the Greek empire. They defeated the Greek emperor in the pitched battle of Manzikert in 1071, and occupied Armenia and Syria. Next they advanced into Asia Minor and settled in Nicaea ; in 1078 they took Jerusalem, and in 1084 Antioch, the last Greek bulwark in Syria. They were now in possession of all the Holy Places, and neither showed veneration to Christian relics as the Arabs had done, nor allowed the pilgrims safe access to them. Thirdly, Europe had been trained to hate the Moslem by the long struggle in Spain and the Mediterranean : in Spain the Christians were now advancing, and in Sicily the Normans took Palermo in 1072. Fourthly, the Cluniac movement had fostered religious devotion ; and lastly, appeals from the Greek emperors for help led to the actual preparation of a Crusade. An eastern emperor had, it is true, appealed for help to Gregory VII, who had considered sending it : but he cannot be held the author of the crusading idea, as his plan, which did not materialise, was merely to send help to Constantinople. Urban II received fresh appeals from the emperor Alexius Comnenus. In 1095 Greek envoys came to Piacenza, and Urban, who was temporarily free from embarrassment from the western emperor, received them favourably. He conceived the idea, not of arranging to help in the recovery of the lost provinces of the Greek empire, but of taking the leadership of a united Christian effort to recover the Holy Places. In the years to come the Crusades were to be much hindered because the Greek emperors considered them expeditions to recover their lost territories, and the popes, as Christian efforts to take or hold Jerusalem. In addition, while fervent religious devotion was a mainspring of the crusading movement, especially in the early Crusades, there were other motives. Hard-headed kings were not unwilling that their turbulent nobles should perish in the Holy Land, taking with them their superfluous fighting men, and leaving their lands to defenceless minors. Crusaders desired to see the world, to fight, and to win personal glory. The merchants of Venice and Genoa did very good business over the transport of crusaders : and with those of other Italian towns profited by the increased trade with the east. But without the religious motive, the desire of the faithful liegemen of Christ to defend His honour against the followers of the Prophet, there could have been no

Crusades. The defence of the Byzantine empire from the Moslem would never have roused Europe to the necessary effort : it failed to do so in the fifteenth century.

The course of the Crusades must be passed over shortly. The first Crusade was preached by Urban II at the council of Clermont, 1095 : this was attended mainly by French bishops. In a famous speech Urban urged his plan on nobles and ecclesiastics : it would be a goodly thing to die in that city where Christ had died for them : let not love of any earthly possession detain them. Here they dwelt in lands narrow and infertile, devouring one another in war. As crusaders they should spoil their foes and return victorious, or dying in the attempt, win an everlasting reward. With shouts of " Deus vult," crowds pressed forward to take the crusader's oath, and bind upon their shoulders the crusader's badge, white linen crosses distributed by the pope. The pope appointed a French bishop his legate, and before the real Crusade could be organised, a number of popular Crusades started under various leaders, only to perish in Hungary or Asia Minor. " The whole world . . . desired to go to the tomb of our Lord in Jerusalem. . . . First of all went the meaner people, then the men of middle rank, and lastly, very many kings, counts, marquesses and bishops." No kings went on the first Crusade, however : it was led by great nobles like Godfrey of Boulogne, duke of Lorraine, Robert, duke of Normandy, and count Raymond of Toulouse. In 1097 the crusaders took Nicaea, and in 1099 Jerusalem itself. It was necessary to establish some government for the future defence of Jerusalem, and the route thither, through Antioch and Syria, which the Greek empire had been unable to defend : the clergy proposed a theocracy, but, after discussion and Godfrey of Boulogne's refusal of the title of king, he accepted that of prince and protector of the Holy Sepulchre. He died in 1100, however, and count Baldwin of Edessa was crowned first king of the Latin kingdom of Jerusalem.

The second Crusade was necessitated by the imminent danger to this kingdom from the Saracen rulers of Mosul, who saved Islam when its fortunes were at their lowest ebb. They conquered Mesopotamia, and then advanced against the Latins, capturing Edessa in 1144, at a time when the king of the Latins was a thirteen-year-old boy. Pope Eugenius III and S. Bernard (see p. 120) stirred up king Louis VII of France and the western emperor, Conrad III, to a Crusade. They started in 1147, but their journey was attended with disasters, some of which they attributed to the treachery of the Greek emperor ; they reached the famous gardens of Damascus, thick orchards whose narrow footpaths concealed ambushed Saracens, but even after clearing these, they failed to take the city, and the Crusade collapsed.

The third Crusade was occasioned by the loss of Jerusalem in 1187. Saladin, at first merely an unruly vassal of the emir of Damascus, succeeded in conquering all the emir's lands, and in reinspiring Islam and consolidating the Saracen power. In 1186 he proclaimed a holy war, and in October, 1187, Jerusalem was again in Saracen hands, and the Latin kingdom had received its death-blow. The emperor Frederick Barbarossa, the English king Richard I, and the French king Philip Augustus in 1189 attempted its recapture : but Barbarossa was drowned in Asia Minor. Philip Augustus returned, and Richard succeeded only in refortifying Acre after a long siege, and making a truce with Saladin.

The fourth Crusade was inspired by popular preachers, led by princes of the second rank, and mainly guided by the great pope Innocent III. A crusading army was gathered in 1201, to begin by attacking Egypt. The age of crusading zeal, however, was passed, and the army was diverted, first to attacking Venice's enemy, Zara, and then to capturing Constantinople itself in 1203, and sacking it in 1204, the claims of rival emperors affording an excuse. For the pillage of the city, and sacrilege and destruction of ancient churches, there could be no excuse.

Among the later Crusades directed towards the recovery of the Holy Land there were none as serious as the first four : but the Crusade of Frederick II in 1229 secured favourable terms for the access of pilgrims to Jerusalem : and that of S. Louis, king of France, in 1249–50 was notable rather for the purity of motive which inspired it than for its military leadership or success ; the French captured

Damietta, but were soon after forced to surrender, with the king himself. Edward I visited Palestine in 1270, and the council of Lyons, 1274, enjoined very heavy taxation on ecclesiastics for a Crusade to deliver the Holy Land, without effect. The English king, Henry V, died with the same wish on his lips : " Lord, Thou knowest mine intent hath been, and yet is, if I may live, to rebuild the walls of Jerusalem."

The most obvious result of the Crusades on the Church was the extension of the Latin rite in the east, at the expense of Byzantines and Moslems. The crusading state was a long narrow strip extending along the whole coast-line of Syria and Palestine ; this kingdom " of the Latins in Jerusalem " was organised as a feudal state, and supplied with a Latin hierarchy. Latin bishops were established in the conquered cities, following the divisions of the ancient oriental church. The hierarchy was headed by the patriarchs of Jerusalem and Antioch, the first with four archbishops and nine bishops under him, the latter with four archbishops and seven bishops. Abbeys, priories, and later friaries, of the Latin rite were also founded. The hierarchies of the Armenian, Syrian and Greek rites still subsisted, and while the rivalries of the Greek and Latin patriarchs were a frequent menace to unity in crusading counsels, Greek and Latin Christians seem to have lived together without acute differences. The different languages of the respective rites in fact made overlapping hierarchies practically inevitable. When the crusading state perished, the Latin bishops were driven from their sees, but successors were still consecrated to these sees, though, as they were " in partibus infidelium," they could not work there. They served the papacy in various ways, and frequently worked as suffragan bishops, in the modern sense. The registers of the archbishops of York, for instance, contain references to bishops of Chrysopolis or Philippopolis, who consecrated churches, ordained, confirmed, or otherwise did suffragan work for them, in return for fees.

A second result of the Crusades was the establishment of the military orders, particularly the knights Templar, and the Hospitallers, which attracted a continuous stream of knights to the Holy Land, apart from the great organised

Crusades. Europe was familiar with the old monastic orders, and the order of " Austin canons," or canons regular was, at the end of the eleventh century, undergoing a great revival : in the new military orders, the members were to take the religious vows of poverty, chastity and obedience, to live in houses definitely founded for the order, and to fight for the defence of Palestine. The Hospitallers were the earlier foundation : as early as c. 1023 the merchants of Amalfi founded a hospital at Jerusalem for poor and sick Latin pilgrims,—Europe was already studded with such hospitals (see p. 214). In the first Crusade the hospital became of immediate importance ; its master, Gerard, " during many years the devoted servant of the poor," obtained in 1113 a papal bull, confirming to the hospital all its endowments in Syria and western Europe, and granting it the special protection of the Holy See. In 1118 Gerard was succeeded by a knight from Dauphiné, within whose forty years' mastership the order of the Temple was founded. Following their example, he gave his own order a military organisation, by which they became the " Knights of the Hospital of S. John in Jerusalem." They were ruled by a grand master, and included knights, chaplains and serving brothers ; they had houses to serve as bases for the work in Palestine all over Europe, the head of each house being termed a commander or preceptor. When the Holy Land was lost, they settled in Rhodes, and later in Malta, and they fought the Saracen not only in Syria, but in Spain.

The Templars were founded by a Burgundian knight, Hugh de Payen, who joined with other knights to protect the poor pilgrims on the road to Jerusalem. In 1118 the king of the Latins assigned them a residence near the Temple of Solomon at Jerusalem, and in 1128 Hugh obtained from the pope the confirmation of the rule of his order. It had been drawn up in consultation with S. Bernard, and on the religious side had much in common with the Cistercian rule. S. Bernard describes the knights as living together without separate property, in one house, under one rule, avoiding idle words and immoderate laughter, and detesting those usual accompaniments of the knightly life, draughts and dice, hunting and hawking,

soothsayers, jesters, story-tellers and stage plays ; striving
to possess swift horses, but not gay trappings, thinking of
battle and victory, not of pomp and show. A hundred
years later a French chronicler could speak of them as
lions in war, lambs in the house : to the enemies of Christ
fierce and implacable, but to Christians kind and gracious ;
when summoned to arms, inquiring not the number of
their foes, but their position. The great red cross which
the knights wore on their white mantles has become the
chosen sign of modern ambulance work, for the Templars
continued to serve the pilgrims as well as fight. The
Templars had commanderies, or preceptories, throughout
Europe, as well as in Syria : their order accumulated such
valuable possessions that they acquired finally a bad name
for pride and avarice.

The Crusades, as a whole, had little effect on the architecture of the west, for the pointed arch of the new Gothic
architecture was not acquired from the east : but the
churches built for their preceptories by the Templars are
the exception. They were circular in plan, like the church
of the Holy Sepulchre in Jerusalem : the great Temple
church in London, and the Holy Sepulchre church in
Cambridge, were built on this plan. The word "Temple"
in English place names is derived from the endowments or
preceptory of the Templars in that spot (Temple Crossing,
Temple Cowley, Temple Coombe). Envy of the possessions
of the order finally led to its suppression in 1312. Among
the other military orders were the Teutonic Knights,
founded at the siege of Acre in 1190 by the German knights
who accompanied Frederick Barbarossa, and who removed
at the end of the thirteenth century, and devoted themselves to fighting and converting the heathen Prussians and
Lithuanians : the English knights of S. Thomas (à Becket)
at Acre : and the Spanish military orders devoted to driving
the Moor from Spain.

The kingdom of Jerusalem was not the only Latin state
set up in the east. As the result of the fourth Crusade,
the Greek dynasties were supplanted at Constantinople,
and a Latin empire set up there, which lasted from 1204
till 1261, when a Greek, Michael Palaeologus, was again
crowned emperor. Innocent III had condemned the

I

diversion of the Crusade from the Holy Land, and particularly the disgraceful plunder of churches and monasteries : but he was half reconciled when, after the count of Flanders had been crowned emperor, a Latin patriarch was enthroned in S. Sophia. The lands of the empire were shared out in fiefs among the crusaders, and the Venetians obtained the lion's share, including the church of S. Sophia. A Venetian, Thomas Morosini, was raised to the patriarchate, and became the head of the Latin church in the empire : but though the holders of crusading fiefs in many cases retained them after the fall of the Latin empire, the Latin church made no permanent impression on the Greek population.

The papacy gained greatly in prestige by its inspiration of the Crusades. Not only did Urban II send off the first Crusade, but the popes were throughout the period more anxious than any European potentate for the defence of the Holy Land : even when unity of Moslem command in the east had made Christian success practically impossible, they continued to urge the undertaking of fresh expeditions. They and not the emperors strove to unite Christendom against Islam, and their prestige grew accordingly. The new Latin patriarchates, the new military orders, were particularly under their protection. Dispensation from a crusader's oath could only be obtained from the pope, and this in the later crusading period afforded a considerable revenue. The sees of bishops who went as crusaders to Palestine were also under papal protection.

The practice of granting indulgences increased during the Crusades, and tended to increase the influence of the papacy : " plenary indulgences " could only be granted by the pope, and the first was granted in connexion with the first Crusade. The question of indulgences was so prominent at the Reformation that a word should be said of their origin and history. An indulgence was the remission of the temporal punishment, the canonical penance for sin. The church from the ages of persecution had taught that a penitent might be received back into communion after confession, the performance of a penance determined by the canons of councils, and absolution from the bishop. These canonical penances were heavy, including periods of anything up to twenty years, or even more, during which

the penitent wore a special dress, sat apart in church,
abstained from holy communion, and fasted a large proportion of the year on bread and water : those who had done
penance could not, in early days, ever be admitted to the
clerical militia. It was held that the guilt of sin was
forgiven the penitent through the merits of Christ : but the
performance of penance or " satisfaction " was a necessary
part of true penitence, a mark of its sincerity. If the
penitent died before performing his penance, it was held
that an opportunity was afforded him to do so in purgatory.
Purgatorial punishment as well as canonical penance on
earth was " temporal." By the ninth century, while the
whole canonical penance was still regarded as owing to
the outraged justice of God, it had become usual for bishops
to remit part of it in certain cases by applying the works
of satisfaction of the saints. The *Penitential* of archbishop
Egbert of York allowed a penitent to substitute the
recitation of fifty psalms kneeling for a day's fasting on
bread and water ; or for one year's fast on bread and
water, a mitigated fast, with the bestowal of twenty-six
shillings in alms. The commutation of penance for almsgiving was always liable to abuse : even earlier an English
synod had forbidden the hiring of substitutes for the
performance of penance. Bishops not only remitted parts
of the canonical penance themselves, after the fervent
performance of a part, but even gave the penitent letters
to other bishops authorising them to do so, if they thought
fit later. In the eleventh century bishops sometimes sent
penitents under heavy canonical sentence, as clerks for
murder, to the pope, to determine the relative remission
of the penance ; Alexander II († 1072) reduced a penance
from twenty-eight years to fourteen by mercy or " indulgence." Visits to the tombs of the apostles at Rome
were also already held as the equivalent of a certain amount
of canonical penance. But no complete remission of
canonical penance had been granted, till at the council of
Clermont Urban II decreed that : " Whoever out of pure
devotion, and not for the purpose of gaining honour or
money, shall go to Jerusalem to liberate the church of God,
let that journey be counted in lieu of all penance."
Similar plenary indulgences were granted for later Crusades :

S. Bernard preaching the second Crusade exhorted his
hearers to " Receive the sign of the cross, and thou shalt
likewise obtain the indulgence of all thou hast confessed
with a contrite heart." The remission of penance to a
crusader, who exposed his possessions to danger in his
absence and himself to hardship and death on the journey,
was no gentle exchange : but by the thirteenth century
the records of councils show that the grant of indulgences
was being abused. The fourth Lateran council, 1215, forbade bishops to give more than a year of indulgence, and
that only to those present when they consecrated a church :
on the anniversary of a dedication, those present, confessed
and contrite, might receive only forty days. It may be
repeated that an " indulgence of forty days," so frequently
met with in the middle ages, was not a remission of any
particular time in purgatory, but of the equivalent suffering
in purgatory to fasting forty days, a whole Lent, on bread
and water.

Various eastern heresies increased in Europe as a result
of the Crusades : it is scarcely possible to say that they
were introduced. Heresy of a Manichaean type, teaching
that two principles, good and evil, spirit and matter,
controlled the universe, persisted from the early centuries
in north Italy and Gaul : in the seventh century the
Paulicians of Asia Minor professed an especial reverence
for S. Paul, but were believed to be Manichaeans, and in
the tenth and eleventh centuries the Bogomiles (" friends
of God ") spread Manichaean heresy in Bulgaria. At the
end of the twelfth century a wave of Manichaean heresy
swept the south of France, through the teaching of the
Albigeois (see p. 224), and north Italy through the Cathari.
The Provençals who had made such devout crusaders may
have acquired a predisposition to such tenets in the east :
certainly the fact that these Manichaean heretics were
frequently known as *Bulgari* or *Boulgres* shows a connexion
with the Bogomiles : and equally certainly Provence and
Aquitaine were and had always been in close touch, along
the coast, with Moorish Spain. The word Cathari (katharoi)
is eastern, and was used generally both for French and
Italian heretics : their chief centre in France was the town
of Albi, and hence the name of Albigeois, given to the

French heretics. When the Cathari spread up the Rhine valley and into Germany, their name became " Ketzer," the ordinary word for heretic. The Cathari taught that God, the good principle of the world, had provided the New Testament, while Jehovah, the bad principle, was the creator of the material world, and author of the Old Testament. They distinguished between the two classes of " believers " and " perfect," or elders, who were initiated (or as the orthodox said, " hereticated "), by the sacrament of the *Consolamentum*. In this ceremony the gospel of S. John was laid on their heads, and their sins were forgiven : but as the rite could not be repeated, it came usually to be administered shortly before death. The perfect were expected to lead an austere life, renouncing animal food, marriage and property, all of which, as material, were evil. Sacraments, churches, the veneration of images, were equally evil. All authority, spiritual or secular, was rejected ; and suicide was practised as a religious rite, under the name of the *endura*, in the case of invalids who, after having received the *Consolamentum*, showed signs of recovery.

Cathari were known in the south of France in 1022, in Lombardy about 1032, and became numerous in Provence about 1200 ; count Raymond VI of Toulouse and other seigneurs joined them. After preliminary measures (see p. 158) to convert or extirpate them had failed, pope Innocent III inaugurated against them the Albigensian Crusade. The immediate cause was the refusal in 1207 of count Raymond to restore to orthodox use the churches he had seized, his excommunication, and the murder of the ecclesiastic who had pronounced the excommunication by one of his followers. Innocent released his subjects from their allegiance, placed his lands under an interdict, and adjured king Philip Augustus to march against these heretics " worse than Saracens." The French king supported and his nobles undertook the " Albigensian Crusade," which was to last for twenty years, although count Raymond himself submitted and did penance in 1209. The war profited the crusading counts, and brought the south under the real rule of the French king : but it failed as a means of conversion, and the mission of S. Dominic and a new

form of the Inquisition for heresy were used to supplement
it. One of the chief results of the Crusades was that, as
here, various wars for what was held to be a holy object
were proclaimed as Crusades, and preached as exercises
of piety. Perhaps the most notable of these was the war
maintained by Innocent III and his successors against the
emperor Frederick II and his successors in south Italy.

The result of the Crusades on the ordinary religion of
the town and countryside was not direct. Towns became
richer as trade with the east increased, and the medieval
merchant class were great builders of churches, and
generous in bestowing on them altar vessels and books,
tapestries and brocades for vestments, gold and silver to
cover the carved work of the shrines. Relics from the
east were brought back by returning crusaders. Many
hospitals were built for the increased number of lepers.
All were affected by the general widening of horizons.
Pilgrimage became a medieval habit, and the pilgrim or
man-at-arms returned from Palestine had strange tales
to tell to countrymen who had scarcely in their lives
left their native village. A few scholarly ecclesiastics
were kept in mind of the existence of the Greek church ;
Grosseteste, among them, was interested in primitive
Christianity, and translated in his investigations what he
believed the primitive Christian writings of Dionysius
the Areopagite. But through the establishment of the
Latin hierarchies, there was much less reaction of Greek
Christianity upon the west than might have been expected.

CHAPTER IX

TWELFTH CENTURY MONASTICISM: CISTER-CIANS; CARTHUSIANS: AUSTIN CANONS

Foundation of Cîteaux—S. Bernard—S. Bruno and the Carthusian order—S. Hugh of Lincoln—Cathedrals in tenth and eleventh centuries—Austin canons in twelfth century

THE twelfth century in Europe saw a great monastic revival, perhaps because by the mid-century it had attained a period of comparative peace. The raids of the Northmen, which had been such fatal enemies to monastic peace earlier, were over: the feudal forces which had been evolved in the struggle against them had made a stable civilisation possible. The investiture struggle came to an end, and cathedral schools flourished. The great order of Cluny had inspired a reform of Christendom, yet to some it now appeared itself in need of reform. In its desire for the due and splendid recitation of the praises of God it had departed far from primitive Benedictine simplicity and poverty. "We read the rule daily in chapter," zeal could say, "and we keep it not." Robert, abbot of Molême in Burgundy, and a few of his monks, were filled with the desire to keep the Benedictine rule in its original strictness and severity: when the other monks refused, they withdrew from Molême and founded in 1098 a new monastery at Cîteaux, (Cistercium), near Dijon. Building a small church and huts in the waste among the pools which gave the spot its name, they led for a time a struggling life, but the count of Burgundy built their cloister walls for them, and as they cleared the woods, gave them sheep from his demesne for the new pasture. They made their habits of the cheap undyed "blanket" woven from their own wool, instead of the dyed cloth of the black monks, and they made them straight and narrow. They would have no image or cross of gold or silver in their little church, no Cluniac marbles, nothing but the plainest of priestly vestments, none of the carvings and mouldings that made the late Cluniac churches so beautiful. They chanted the office plainly, but so beautifully that the duke of Burgundy loved to come and hear them. They dedicated their church to the Blessed Virgin, mother of the faithful and especial mother of monks. They rose at two for mattins, and for part of the year had but one meal a day, after vespers, and for the rest only two ; meat, fish, eggs, butter were forbidden them, and in spite of the hardness of their diet, they employed the hours allotted to work by the rule in agricultural labour of the severest kind. They were joined by Stephen Harding, an Englishman who was to become the second founder of Cîteaux : and when the duke of Burgundy died on the first Crusade, he ordered that he was to be brought back and buried in their chapel.

More famous than either Cistercian founder was Bernard of Fontaines, who joined the house in 1113. He was the younger son of a Burgundian noble, and destined for a learned career : but at the age of twenty-two, unsatisfied with this worldly life, " he began to meditate flight." As he was making his way in mental uncertainty to his brothers, who were besieging a castle with the duke of Burgundy, he turned aside and entered a wayside church, and there he prayed " with a great storm of tears, stretching out his hands to heaven, and pouring forth his heart like water in the presence of God his Lord : and from that day the intention of his heart remained firm." He did not enter Cîteaux alone, but with thirty companions he had persuaded to join him, including his uncle and some of his brothers. He spent his year of probation " in the cell of the novices," in such abstraction, and with such watchfulness over his eyes, that at the end of the year he did not know whether the ceiling were vaulted or plain, or whether the window had three lights or one. He worked like a peasant, slept in his habit like the others in the common dormitory, denied himself of even the meagre Cistercian fare, and prolonged his prayers and watches at night " beyond what was human." At the end of the year his health had completely broken down : but what did that matter, when the office of a monk was to do penance, to watch and suffer and fast and pray, not for his own salvation alone, but for the welfare of Christendom ? In a sense, S. Paul's words " I make up what is lacking in the sufferings of Christ " may be called the foundation text of monasticism : and it was the conception which dominated Bernard. As crowds of postulants came asking for admission to Cîteaux, it became necessary to found new houses : Bernard himself led out a band to Clairvaux, where he became abbot, and Clairvaux, with three other houses founded at this period, La Ferté, Pontigny, and Morimond, became the chief houses of the Cistercian order.

The personal attractiveness of Bernard made him extraordinarily beloved as abbot : none could withstand him. When he preached to seculars it was certain that some among his audience would hear the call to a monastic life, and ride back with him after the sermon to Clairvaux. " Mothers hid their sons from him, wives their husbands, and companions their friends." The novices he had once received he could not bear to let go : he had a long struggle with the abbot of Cluny over a young monk who, after trying the hardships of Clairvaux, returned to the moderate regimen of his mother house. He was not always stern, for he called the oaks and beeches, under whose shade he loved to meditate, " his friends, as if in joke." When his brother Gerard died, he was in the midst of a set of sermons to the brothers on the Song of Solomon, and though he began to comment on the verse for the day, he broke off to speak of his grief. " What have I to do with this Canticle, who am steeped in bitterness ? . . . I have dissembled till now, lest it should appear that faith was overcome by feeling. While others wept, I followed his body to the grave with unmoistened eyes ; I stood by, and dropped no tear till the burial of the dead was over. . . . Those who watched me wept, and wondered why I wept not also, for their pity was less for him than for me who had lost him. Would not even a heart of steel be moved, to see me the survivor of Gerard ? . . . He was

my brother by blood, but more than brother by religion.
. . . Yet in place of us, dearest brother, whom thou hast
not with thee to-day, what an exceeding multitude of
joys and blessings is thine ! Instead of me, thou hast
Christ ! . . . Because thou hast put on God, thou hast
not therefore laid aside all care for us, for : *He also careth
for us.* Thou hast discarded thine infirmities, but not
thine affections."

Bernard was able also to inspire his children to endure
the harsh Cistercian life, because he could train them to
find through prayer a quickened communion with Christ.
" I confess, though I say it in my foolishness, that the
Word has visited me, and even very often. But although
He has frequently entered into my soul, I have never at
any time been sensible of the precise moment of His coming.
I have felt that He was present ; I remember that He has
been with me : I have sometimes been able to have a
presentiment that He would come ; but never to feel
His coming or His departure. For by what means He has
made entrance or departure I know not." Most of the
Latin hymns attributed to S. Bernard are probably by
followers of his school, putting into verse the teaching on
the *Sermons on the Canticles* : the most beautiful, the
Dulcis Jesu Memoria, was translated into many vernaculars,
and carried devotion to the holy name of Jesus all over
Europe.

Jesu, the very thought of Thee with sweetness fills my
    breast :
But sweeter far Thy face to see, and in Thy presence rest.

    .   .   .   .   .

When once Thou visitest the heart, then truth begins to
    shine ;
Then earthly vanities depart, then kindles love divine.

In two other ways the Cistercian monachism that spread
over Europe exhibited new features. It was the Cistercians
who first made large use of lay brothers, *conversi* : in
S. Benedict's time the divine office had been said in the
Latin that was still the popular tongue, and the unlettered
could be professed as monks and taught the psalms by

heart. By S. Bernard's day monasticism had become an aristocratic, or at least middle-class institution, and it was not considered possible to teach peasants the divine office in Latin (though many of the monks themselves could scarcely read it). But by the Cistercians such devout peasants were allowed to be professed as *conversi*, to substitute a certain number of Paters and Aves for the office, and do agricultural work for the community. Secondly, a constitution was drawn up for the Cistercian order, the *Carta Caritatis*, which was meant to prevent relaxation. Each Cistercian house was subject to the diocesan bishop, but in addition its abbot was subject to the abbot of Cîteaux : and if the abbot of Cîteaux himself became lax, he was subject to the reproof and correction of the abbots of La Ferté, Clairvaux, Pontigny and Morimond. All Cistercian abbots had to meet once a year for a general chapter at Cîteaux,—except those from the more remote parts of western or northern Europe or the east, who came less often. The Cistercians began their foundations in Yorkshire (Rievaux, Fountains and the rest), in S. Bernard's own lifetime, and as elsewhere, flourished by turning the waste to agriculture and sheep-farming. But here as elsewhere, and in spite of the *Carta Caritatis*, wealth is supposed to have led to relaxation : though actually the relaxation seems to have been much worse when the houses were poor and debt-ridden after the Black Death.

S. Bernard not merely inspired his own order, but through mere belief in his courage, disinterestedness and devotion, he became a sort of censor to western Christendom, more respected than either pope or emperor. He helped draw up the rule of the Templars, and that of the English Gilbertines (see p. 129). He rebuked the laxity of the French royal abbey of S. Denis, interfered in the appointment of an immoral priest to a Spanish see, rebuked the French king when he expelled the bishop of Paris for putting regular canons into his cathedral, and drew various prelates to a more spiritual life. He was never afraid to rebuke kings or nobles on moral issues, or for cruelty to their peasants. He was called on to confute heretics, and to arbitrate in spiritual and secular disputes. He had an immense correspondence with men all over Europe, and even those nobles or heretics against whom he thundered seem never to have been able to withstand his attractiveness when he met them personally. He might have held any bishopric or the papacy itself ; but he preferred to remain merely a Cistercian abbot. Eugenius III was finally elected pope in 1145 merely as a Cistercian monk and the friend of S. Bernard, and for his guidance S. Bernard wrote the treatise *De Consideratione*. The most notable part of the book is his insistence that the popes are compelled to spend too much time determining lawsuits which ought never to have been brought before them, and in denouncing the loquacity and intrigues of the lawyers of the papal law-court, and the delays and injustice of some of its decisions. " The present fashion is plainly execrable and one which is unbecoming, I do not say to the church, but even to the market place." The system of indulgence and papal provision to benefices (see p. 186) is abused. " The ambitious, the grasping, the simoniacal, the sacrilegious, the adulterous, the incestuous, and all such like monsters of humanity flock to Rome, in order either to obtain or to keep ecclesiastical honours at the hands of the pope." A certain amount of S. Bernard's oratory can be discounted : medieval bishops frequently considered the lawyers of their own law-courts loquacious rascals, and passed statutes to try to circumvent them : but clearly the papal court was in need of reform.

The Carthusian order was founded a little before S. Bernard's, but was of such severity that it never spread as widely as the Cistercian. Its rarer houses, however, were among the few never accused of relaxation. Bruno, a German from Cologne, became scholasticus of the cathedral schools at Reims, where he taught the future Urban II. He left Reims to become a solitary in a wild spot near Grenoble, where a band of hermits gathered round him. These in 1084 he collected into the monastery of the Grande Chartreuse, called from the neighbouring village of Cartusia ; but he provided that they should, within the monastery, continue to live in separate cells, assembling only for night-office and mass, and a meal on certain feast days. Each brother prepared his own food, had his own garden, and said the day offices in his cell, though a certain amount of agriculture for the common benefit of the community was performed by the *conversi*. The life was one of great austerity, loneliness, and silence, the words " O beata solitudo : O sola beatudo " expressing the Carthusian ideal. S. Bruno died in 1101, having founded another house in Italy ; and " charterhouses " were gradually founded in all parts of Europe. The Carthusian order produced certain scholars, whose devotional treatises became widely popular ; Ludolphus of Saxony wrote the most widely read *Life of Christ* in the fourteenth century, and Denis the Carthusian, or Denis Rickel, wrote widely used mystical commentaries on the scriptures.

The most famous Carthusian in English history was S. Hugh, for the last part of his life bishop of Lincoln († 1200). He was the son of a Burgundian noble, who, when his wife died, retired with his little son to a small church near Grenoble, where they both became regular canons, and Hugh was trained in especial severity for the service of Christ. He was ordained deacon at nineteen, and placed by his prior in charge of a small church dependent on his community : but he now conceived the idea of joining the Grande Chartreuse, " built almost above the clouds and very near to God." A fellow canon dissuaded him : " How do you presume, O little son, to think of such a thing ? These men, whom you see live on the rocks, are harder than the rocks themselves : they have no pity on themselves, or on those who dwell with them. Their site is fearful, but their order is yet more fearful." His prior at length, however, let him go, and in 1160 he entered the Chartreuse, where he lived so devoutly that after ten years he was made procurator or steward. In 1175 his prior sent him, in answer to a request of Henry II of England, to build up the small charterhouse he had founded at Witham in Somerset. Here he was in constant intercourse with Henry, not failing when necessary to warn him of the wickedness of keeping bishoprics vacant, and in spite of his lack of deference Henry insisted in 1186 on getting him elected to the bishopric of Lincoln. Here he took with him monks from Witham, and lived in the same austerity and holiness, retiring every harvest time to his old priory to lead the life of an ordinary monk. He gave the deer from his parks to feed the poor, he procured learned clerks to serve his diocese, he opposed the king over matters of the oppression of the peasants and church discipline, and he would never confirm children brought to him on horseback, but always dismounted and laid his hands upon them. "He loved," says his biographer in some surprise, "not merely children, but even babies," and he had a curious attraction for animals; when he stayed at his manor of Stow a large and fierce wild swan would come, undeterred by the attendants, and stretch its head up into Hugh's sleeve at table.

One episode in his relations with the king well illustrates the belief of medieval laymen in the prayers of the monks; for Henry II was not a particularly pious king. Once when Henry was returning from France, he was very nearly shipwrecked by a storm. The ship tossed on the immense waves, and the ship's company, despairing of life, betook themselves to confession and prayer. "Then the king himself at length broke forth with these words, 'O,' he said, 'if that little Carthusian of mine, Hugo, were now pouring forth his private prayers, or if he were standing with his brethren, newly risen from their beds, and saying the night office, surely God would not have forgotten me for so long.'" Then he called upon God "Whom in truth the prior of Witham doth serve," to have pity on him through Hugo's prayers and merits: and without delay the clash of the tempest and the whirling of the wind subsided, the floods fell, a gentle breeze returned, all thanked the divine mercy, and the king in future held Hugo in the greatest veneration.

The twelfth century saw also a great revival of the canonical life for clerks, which was now associated more definitely than ever before with the name of S. Augustine, clerks who lived undei a rule being termed "Austin canons." The revival was not altogether a sudden one, or associated with any single reformer. Since the council of Aix-la-Chapelle in 817 there had been two tendencies in churches with endowments large enough to support more than a single clerk as priest, and particularly in cathedral churches. The stricter ecclesiastics of the ninth to the eleventh centuries wished to preserve the communal life safeguarded by the provisions of that council. This communal life was a safeguard to canonical celibacy, which the Cluniac party were trying to get enforced. While the Cluniacs were trying to reform the monasteries, a movement in Lorraine aimed especially at the canonical communal life for the clerks serving cathedrals and large churches, and this Lorraine movement spread to England in the period immediately preceding the Conquest. The Saxon Harold founded the church of Holy Cross at Waltham in 1061, on the model of the Lorraine reformers : it was to be served by seven canons and a provost, and Harold brought over a scholasticus from Utrecht cathedral to teach its young clerks.

The parallel tendency from 817 onwards was for chapters to divide up their endowment and allot " prebends " or portions to each canon's stall. The dignitaries of the church, the provost or dean, the scholasticus or chancellor, the treasurer and the precentor, had specially large prebends : and of course the division into prebends was preceded by, or marked, the break-up of the canonical, communal life. This was by no means a completely new arrangement : early bishops had frequently granted a particular piece of land or vineyard to one of their dignitaries in lieu of stipend : but the regular division of chapter property into prebends marked the failure of the movement begun by Chrodegang and made compulsory in 817. It was the final acceptance of this division as permissible, and therefore " canonical," on the continent by the middle of the eleventh century, that led to a revival of a stiffened form of the old canonical life. When it was recognised that such a communal life could not be safeguarded merely by appeal to the canons, founders of such churches began to safeguard it by drawing up their own constitutions or rule. One or two communities, therefore, including at first Prémontré, in the early twelfth century set out to keep the rule written by Augustine of Hippo for his clergy. (His authorship, long doubted, was established by Pierre Mandonnet in his *Saint Dominique* in 1937.) This austere rule, with its long disused form of the divine office, proved unworkable for clergy in northern Europe; but pope Gelasius II in 1118 allowed the community of Springirsbach to modify it, and others followed. The rule thus "decapitated" was widely used. At first these Austin canons did the pastoral work of their parish, and if they had small churches besides their mother church, sent out their own members (as S. Hugh was sent in his youth), to serve them. But gradually the monastic side of the life was stressed at the expense of the pastoral : superiors found it undesirable that canons should leave the dormitory in the middle of the night to take the sacraments to the sick, and the service of a small outlying cell was found similarly to unfit a canon for the strict regular life. Hence secular clerks were given a title to serve the outlying small churches : and while in many cases houses of Austin canons continued to serve large parishes, in others they had none. The regular life in some houses was so strict that the canons came to approximate more to Benedictine monks than clerks : but an Austin canon, however strict his house, was never enclosed, and was engaged in work like teaching, lecturing or writing, meant to promote pastoral work. A canon was essentially an ordained clerk and a monk essentially was not, though it had become usual by the twelfth century to give him priest's orders.

The Norman Conquest occurred in England just before the use of the " rule of S. Austin " had become general on the continent. Just before, the clergy of some bishops' familiae lived communally, in other cases separately. Giso, a Lotharingian and bishop of Wells, made his canons live communally, with dormitory, refectory and cloister : he lived till 1088. At Exeter Leofric's chapter was communal. Edward the Confessor had built a new abbey church at Westminster, for Benedictine monks. While in Lorraine the communal life was the ideal for large churches, energetic and practical Norman bishops favoured the new organisation of cathedral endowments in prebends, with dean, chancellor, treasurer and precentor as chief officers ; if a stricter life was desired, let the clergy of the cathedral be Benedictine monks. When Lanfranc was made archbishop of Canterbury the constitutions (unwritten) of the English cathedrals were gradually changed : some were organised with deans, on the new, prebendal plan (as Chichester, Exeter, Hereford, Lichfield, Lincoln, S. Paul's, Salisbury, Wells, York) ; the rest became Benedictine monasteries (as Canterbury, Bath, Coventry, Durham, Ely, Norwich, Rochester, Winchester, and Worcester). The diocese of Carlisle was not formed till 1133 and an existing house of Austin canons became the cathedral church. The earliest house of canons known to have adopted the " rule of S. Austin " in England was that of SS. John the Baptist and Botulph, Colchester, between 1093–1099. But a great number of quite small houses of clerks are known to have been founded to live " regularly " in the eleventh and early twelfth century, without adopting the " rule of S. Austin." Hospitals were generally served by a warden, and two or three clerks living the regular life : in the course of the twelfth century all these rather indefinite foundations came to profess, and to be regarded as having always professed, the rule of S. Austin. It was used by S. Gilbert of Sempringham, who founded an order in which most of the houses were double, for men and women. These worshipped in different parts of the same chapel, but led a separate life. The brothers acted as chaplains to the sisters and followed the rule of Austin canons : the sisters had a rule like that of Cistercian nuns.

On the continent various reformers founded specially famous houses, or orders, of Austin canons, adding to the rule of S. Austin their own constitutions. The abbey of S. Victor in Paris was especially learned and strict, and the Victorine canons produced scholars, like Richard and Hugh of S. Victor, to rival those of the cathedral schools of Notre Dame. The Premonstratensian canons were perhaps more widespread and well-known than any others. They were founded by Norbert of Xanten, who held a well-endowed and fashionable canonry in the (prebendalized) church of Cologne, and gave it up to become a mission preacher. In 1120 he founded in a forest not far from Laon a house of regular canons, calling the spot Prémontré (Pratum Monstratum) through its indication to him by an angel. As an admirer of S. Bernard, Norbert gave his canons a certain Cistercian character, and clothed them in the white Cistercian habit : but they preached, taught and heard confessions like the pastoral clergy. When

K

Norbert was made archbishop of Magdeburg in 1126, his secular chapter refused to be reformed, and he therefore founded a new house of Premonstratensians hard by. He was the friend of the emperor, and through his influence and their own holiness the Premonstratensians spread over western Europe, and did a great work in converting and civilising the Slavonic lands west of the Elbe. The houses professing the rule of S. Austin were collected by the pope into an order in 1339, and the rule was taken as the basis of new foundations by the military orders of the east, by S. Dominic, by the Austin friars (or Austin hermits), and S. Bridget of Sweden, who founded an order of double houses.

CHAPTER X

THE TWELFTH CENTURY RENAISSANCE: CANON LAW

Monastic and cathedral schools—Lay teaching in Italy—The
" universitas " at Bologna and Paris : Abelard—Medieval university
life—Twelfth century scholastic manuals—Civil and canon law at
Bologna—Gratian's *Decretum* and the *Corpus Juris Canonici*—
Henry II's struggle over the province of canon law

THE end of the twelfth century was marked by the
rise of the universities, an increased study of literature and the seven liberal arts, and the production
of universal manuals on all the different branches of knowledge ; the way was prepared for the co-ordination and
synthesis of theology, metaphysics and natural science in
the *Summa* of S. Thomas Aquinas. The characteristic new
development of the twelfth century in education was the
university : the characteristic new method for the attainment of truth was the rediscovered Aristotelian logic. The
church and her doctrines were directly affected by this
renaissance, for, except in Italy, all the scholars and teachers
were clerks, and interested in the various branches of
knowledge not only for their own sakes, but for the light
such knowledge threw on the interpretation of the scriptures,
theology, and the practical rule of the church.

Education between the Carolingian period and the end
of the twelfth century had been carried on by the monastic
and cathedral schools. The great monasteries—Luxeuil,
S. Gall Reichenau, Lorsch, Corbie, Fleury, S. Riquier,
Bobbio and Monte Cassino,—had been forbidden by the
council of Aix-la-Chapelle, 817, to have schools within
the monastery, other than those of oblate boys. But down

to the eleventh century monastic schools were probably even more famous than the cathedral schools : a scholasticus was appointed to teach the young oblates and novices, and when the monastery possessed a famous scholasticus, adult monks from other houses were sent to study under him. The children of wealthy and noble parents were also sent to board in the monastery, often with a servant or two, with the idea that they should there be instructed and enter the secular hierarchy. But this was by individual arrangement, which might be extended also to the sons of princes or nobles not destined for a clerical career, though the monasteries had no " schools " for lay boys. S. Gall had two distinct schools, for oblates and secular clerks, but this was not usual. The monastery of S. Riquier had three hundred monks and one hundred boy-monks in the habit, all taught together, but divided, like the monks, into three choirs. S. Riquier was built with a triple wall of enclosure connecting three churches, and the three choirs, each beginning the office when the other left off, made the psalmody continual.

The cathedral schools in the twelfth century eclipsed the monastic schools : many of them, of course, were the schools of regular canons, like that of S. Martin at Tours, and were at first predominantly " boarding schools." The young canons, and the boys boarded with them by payment to be " initiated into the clerkship and imbued with sacred letters," were the nucleus of the school. But even in Alcuin's time at Tours, and soon after at Reims, the magister scholarum or scholasticus began to teach also the " rural clerks " living in the neighbourhood : it was regarded as uncanonical to take fees for such teaching, and a ninth century cleric of Tours provided endowment for the scholasticus, lest he should be " occupied in the leisure of venal lecturing." From the ninth to the twelfth century the chief cathedral dignitary after the bishop and dean was the " magister scholarum " : but by 1150 he had begun to be called the " chancellor," to teach only theology and the seven liberal arts to the more advanced, and to delegate the teaching of the boys to a grammar master. But from his early connexion with the school the chancellor of the cathedral retained throughout the middle ages the control of education in the diocese. No master might teach in the diocese without his licence, no new grammar school might be opened without it. The licence to teach granted by the chancellor was the predecessor of a university degree. In the eleventh century, the most flourishing period of the cathedral schools, the greatest north of the Alps were those of Cologne, Laon, Paris, where William of Champeaux drew crowds of scholars to his lectures on logic, and above all, Chartres. Here a real enthusiasm for Latin literature pervaded the teaching, and the Platonist, Bernard Sylvester and his successor, William of Conches, made Chartres " the most abundant spring of letters in Gaul." Scholars, like John of Salisbury, trained in this classical tradition, could only lament when the new passion for logic diverted the enthusiasm of scholars. The classical renaissance of Chartres was frustrated by the logical renaissance at Paris.

Meanwhile in Italy conditions were different, and the difference was to be perpetuated in the character of the medieval universities north and south of the Alps. There were in Italy cathedral schools whose clerks taught and studied theology : there were also schools which consisted of the followers of lay " philosophers " (philosophy = " sapientia " = seven liberal arts). Peter Damiani and Lanfranc studied under such masters in their youth. Benedict, prior of Chiusa, was thus educated by his uncle : and " my philosophy," he says, " cost him 2,000 shillings." " Nine years have I studied grammar, . . . there are nine of us here who are scholars, and we study grammar together ; but I am much the most perfect in philosophy. I have two large houses full of books. I have not as yet read all of them, but I daily meditate upon them." Wippo († 1051), a Burgundian clerk, wrote a panegyric to the emperor Henry III, exhorting him to extend the Italian system of lay education to Germany : only in Germany was it thought unfitting for anyone to be educated, except by clerks. The city statutes of Bologna refer to grammar masters who taught children and " who call themselves clerks and have not the clerkship and tonsure." They desired, that is, the legal privilege of clerkship, though they were not clerks.

The Italian schools were the first to become universities. The word " universitas " was not at first used by itself, but in the phrase " universitas magistrorum et scholarium," and it was used to describe what was practically a gild of masters or scholars. The twelfth century term which corresponds best to our modern " university " was " studium generale." The schools of Salerno first rose to prominence, for the study of medicine. The tradition of Graeco-Roman science had persisted there, the Greek language was understood in south Italy and kept Salerno in touch with the Byzantine physicians, and Salerno may have gained some knowledge of Arabic medicine from Sicily. The schools had no connexion with episcopal schools, and women doctors were allowed to practise medicine. The first school where a " universitas " or gild was formed was that of Bologna, now and later the greatest European law-school. The gild here was that of scholars, largely adults and post-graduates from all parts of Europe. The masters, as mainly Italians and citizens of Bologna, were protected by their citizenship : it was the foreign students who needed to protect themselves by banding together. North of the Alps it was mainly the masters who were aliens (not citizens of the place where they taught), while the scholars were younger, and drawn chiefly from the locality : hence the transalpine universities (like Paris and Oxford) were universities of masters, not students. The universitas, formed at first for self-defence against the citizens or local authority, soon acquired the rule of all matters connected with the students and their life and studies.

It was natural that, while the first Italian university should be famous for the study of law and secular subjects, the first transalpine university, Paris, should rise to fame as the mistress of theology. Paris in the twelfth century was wealthy, and had several famous schools: the schools of the cathedral of Notre Dame, on the island in the Seine, and on the south bank the schools of the canons of S. Victor and of Ste. Geneviève. Paris cannot, however, be reckoned a university before Philip Augustus granted it a charter of privilege in 1200, or perhaps before its first grant of

papal statutes in 1215. The teaching of Peter Abelard
drew the crowds of scholars to Paris that made possible
the formation of a universitas later; the university was, in
fact, a gild of masters who taught this new concourse of
scholars. Abelard, the son of a Breton lord, had wandered,
like other medieval scholars, from school to school, seeking
particularly instruction in dialectic. (The seven liberal
arts were divided into two courses, the trivium and quadrivium, and dialectic was the third of the trivium.) He
studied under Roscelin at Loches, and then under William
of Champeaux at Paris. The old text-book on logic in the
hands of all medieval students was the *Eisagoge* of Porphyry,
but Aristotelian logic was studied, in Arabic translations, at
the schools of Cordova, and Latin translations of his works
were just beginning to be known. James, a clerk of Venice,
translated the unknown books of the *Organon* into Latin:
and in Abelard's time this " new logic " was just taking its
place as the foremost text-book. William of Champeaux,
archdeacon of Paris, had some fame as a teacher of dialectic,
though he lectured also on theology : Abelard challenged
his doctrine and was refused the licence to teach in Paris.
When William retired to the canons of S. Victor, Abelard
followed and again disputed with him ; and considering
himself now perfect in logic, went on to attend the lectures
of Anselm of Laon on theology. Here he again found his
teacher an " image of clay." He set up as a rival to Anselm,
and when forced to leave Laon by the cathedral authorities,
he returned and taught at Paris. The tragic ending of his
relations with Héloïse made him retire as a monk to S.
Denis, but here too he soon aroused enemies by proving
that the patron saint of the monastery was not Dionysius,
the friend of S. Paul. After an interval as abbot of a
Breton monastery, he returned to Paris, and lectured in
the schools of the canons of Ste. Geneviève : and it was
these lectures that drew such crowds of students to hear
him, that the schools of Paris thereupon developed into
a university.

Abelard's work was of great and varied importance to
philosophy and theology. He intoxicated the scholars
of his generation with a delight in logic, and the belief
that it might be used for the solution of all mysteries. In

particular, he applied its use to the problems of theology and metaphysics,—not without causing uneasiness to the more old-fashioned theologians. " A doctrine is not to be believed," he is reported to have said, "because God has said it, but because we are convinced by reason that it is so." Abelard was the true spiritual ancestor of the English bishop, who asserted later that " a syllogism well ruled is so strong and so mighty in all kinds of matters, that though all the angels of heaven would say that his conclusion were not true . . . yet we should leave the angels' saying, and trust more to the proof of the syllogism." Though Abelard claimed to be using the syllogism in defence of the faith, other theologians obscurely perceived that the method would destroy faith in the end, and that such matters as the being of God were not suitable for logical dissection and demonstration. Abelard's characteristic method, however, was to be of service both to theology and canon law : in the treatise which he chose to call, to the irritation of the orthodox, *Sic et Non* (*Yes and No*), he arranged side by side conflicting passages from the Fathers on various matters : he stated that he meant to resolve the difficulties thus exposed, but neglected to add such a solution to the treatise. To the orthodox he seemed to have merely sought occasion for scandal : but the method of comprehensively comparing authorities was soon adopted in theology by Peter Lombard, and in canon law by Gratian, with the greatest success.

England in the mid twelfth century was part of the Angevin empire, and the first English university, Oxford, was modelled on the studium of Paris. Oxford's central position in England conditioned the growth of a concourse of scholars in what was, in the twelfth century, a flourishing market town. It lay midway between Northampton and Southampton, midway between east and west, and it had the next stone bridge over the Thames up river from Staines. Towards the end of the twelfth century Oxford had already a concourse of scholars and in the thirteenth it became a universitas of masters. By 1257 this studium ranked as second only to Paris.

In Cambridge the canons of All Saints-in-the-Castle (afterwards at Barnwell), probably had some kind of school;

in 1209 a migration of scholars from Oxford joined them, or formed a new school, and by 1233 Cambridge was organised as a university, with a chancellor appointed by the bishop of Ely to grant degrees.

Student life in a medieval university was less organised, but much longer, than it is to-day. Students lodged as they could, and mainly with the masters or lecturers in hostels, before they were collected into colleges, and the present largest colleges of Oxford and Cambridge were generally formed by incorporating two or three smaller halls or hostels, through the munificence of some fifteenth or sixteenth century patron. Masters who took four or five students to board with them in their " chamber " generally had a large bed-chamber and bed for themselves, and truckle-beds for the students, pushed under theirs in the day ; the master himself had a quite small study for work. In the thirteenth and fourteenth centuries, however, pious or royal benefactors gave endowments and houses for the maintenance and lodging of masters and students. The course of study was long : the students normally came up at from thirteen to sixteen. They might have been well grounded in grammar or classics, but there were grammar masters at the university. For the first seven years all took the same course, that of the trivium and quadrivium, and if their funds held out as long, and they had heard the requisite lectures and maintained the necessary disputations, they became bachelors and masters of arts. The mastership was the licence to teach : now granted by the chancellor of the university. Civil and canon law, medicine and theology were "post-graduate" courses ; a student passing through the arts course, taking his B.D., and proceeding (after lecturing on the Bible and theology for some years himself,) to his doctorate of divinity (S.T.P. = *sacrae theologiae professor*), could scarcely reach this summit before he was thirty ; his course would have taken at least fourteen years. Those who obtained only the mastership of arts, however, would get a comfortable benefice : most ordinands were not graduates of universities. A large proportion of those who graduated in universities did not do parochial work : they became clerks in royal or noble houses, and formed the civil service of the kingdom.

A notable result of the twelfth century renaissance was the composition of comprehensive manuals on different aspects of knowledge. Jacobus de Voragine, bishop of Genoa, made a great collection of all the lives of the saints, the *Legenda Aurea*. A saint's " legend " was the account of his life and miracles which was read in the nine lessons of Mattins, (night office), before his feast day : as the ecclesiastical day began with vespers the evening before, the reading of the *legenda* was part of the festival office. The commonest commentary or gloss on the Bible had hitherto been the ninth century gloss of Walafrid Strabo, the *Glosa Ordinaria* : Anselm of Laon now composed a *Glosa Interlinearis* which became equally popular. Two harmonies of the Latin gospels were produced : that of Victor of Capua, which made use of Tatian's *Diatessaron*, had not been widely known, but the *Unum ex Quattuor* of the Englishman, Clement of Llanthony, and that of Zachary Chrysopolitanus, a magister scholarum of Besançon, were now acquired by every monastic, cathedral and college library. Peter Comestor (the devourer) summarised world history as he knew it in the *Historia Scholastica* : his main source for the pre-Christian era was the Bible, but he inserted information about personages like Herod and Augustus, and used patristic and secular sources to bring the history down to his own day.   In his *Speculum Historiale* Vincent of Beauvais was to provide the other medieval text-book of general history, carrying it down to 1243.   The *Sentences* of Peter Lombard († 1160), formed the stock manual of theology, used even after S. Thomas had surpassed it with his *Catena Aurea*.   Peter Lombard was educated partly at Bologna, and afterwards at Reims, and by the canons of S. Victor.   He was also one of Abelard's pupils, and used his method, though more timidly, in his *Sententiae Patrum*, a collection of the opinions of the Fathers on theological points.   It dealt with Christian doctrine at large, but was especially important as crystallizing the doctrine of the sacramental system, and definitely accepting seven sacraments.

Among the results of the twelfth century renaissance for the church, the codification of the canon law rivalled in importance the application of logic to theology.   The renaissance in Italy centred in the outburst of legal studies at Bologna. To some extent knowledge of Roman law in Italy had never died out. Justinian's *Corpus* was studied in the famous law-school of Rome, which was removed in 1084 to Ravenna; at Pavia there was a law-school of Lombard law. Ravenna had been a famous law-school from the seventh century: in the eleventh it was strongly imperial in sympathy, and opposed the Cluniac reformers on the question of the marriage of priests. `Bologna in the eleventh century was still a school of philosophy or "arts"; but the teaching of Irnerius and others gained it the first place as a school of law. Irnerius, at first in the service of the countess Matilda, lectured on the *Corpus Juris Romani*, and was later employed by Henry V: though both papalists and imperialists welcomed the increased study of the civil or Roman law, the civil lawyers and the university of Bologna found themselves drawn by their studies strongly to the imperial side. Bologna produced most of the arguments and treatises for the emperors in the struggle with the papacy: but Bologna trained also in Honorius II and Alexander III popes ready to oppose them. It was also the revived study of civil law at Bologna that prompted a study of the law of the church, and the codification of her canons by Gratian.

Between the issue of the Pseudo-Isidorian decretals and the work of Gratian about forty collections of canons are known to have been made in the western church, none of which became official. Hildebrand encouraged the study of the canons, and several collections were made to aid the holy see in the investiture struggle. A famous intermediate collection was that of Ives of Chartres, the greatest canonist before Gratian. Gratian himself was a monk of the monastery of S. Felix at Bologna, who taught canon law and produced the *Decretum* about 1148. Its full name was the *Concordantia Discordantium Canonum*, and in it Gratian resolved the various disparities. But the importance of the work lay in the fact that he quoted all his authorities in full in the text, so that for later students his work was primarily a collection of authorities, arranged subject by subject, instead of in a roughly chronological order, under the councils or popes which issued them.

It soon became the sole manual, both for teaching and practice in the courts ; in the universities all canonists taught from it, and glossed and commented upon it. Yet the authority of the *Decretum* was not official, but only that of custom and precedent. From the authority of usage and from the fact that it was cited, corrected and edited by later popes, it was always reckoned the first part of the *Corpus Juris Canonici*. The second part of this *Corpus* was formed by the *Decretals* of Gregory IX, collected in 1230 at his order by the Dominican, Raymond of Peñaforte, which brought the canon law up-to-date by drawing from the letters of popes later than the *Decretum*. The third part was the *Liber Sextus*, or *Sext*, of Boniface VIII, issued in 1298, and two supplementary collections not of papal but private authority were also finally included (the *Extravagantes*). " Canon law " in the middle ages, the law which was binding on church courts all over western Europe, was this *Corpus*, and not, from the twelfth century, any local body of canons. The enactments of national or provincial synods were held to be not binding if they clashed with it, and to have only a local, explanatory force for the national or local church : such canons were not quoted as authoritative in the church courts. Theoretical uniformity existed alongside widespread disregard in many points by the lay potentates.

A result of the legal renaissance at Bologna was that all over Europe civilians and canonists were eager to claim the whole province of law for themselves, and arrogate as large a proportion of cases as possible to the secular or church courts, as the case might be. In the twelfth century secular law was largely unwritten customary law, only defined in small measure by royal edicts or statutes. There was a large borderland between secular and church cases, which either side might seize. This was one of the large causes which lay behind the struggle of the English Henry II and Becket over the trial of criminous clerks : the other was that the rise of the universities, and increase of grammar schools, made clerks, and those entitled to benefit of clergy, much more numerous than they had been a hundred years earlier. There was a great increase of scholars who were legally clerks, and yet, judging from the numbers of those entered in later bishops' registers as having received the tonsure, can scarcely all have been episcopally shorn. Many of these scholar clerks had no intention of proceeding to orders, at any rate holy orders, and were probably also more disorderly in conduct than the older race of clerks in minor orders, mainly occupied in humble work about the churches. The *Decretum*, and far earlier councils, had laid down that clerks should not plead before any secular court ; a clerk who had committed a crime must purge himself (produce a varying number of witnesses ready to swear that they believed that his defence was true), in the bishop's court. By this process a criminous clerk was more likely to escape than a layman was to escape the sheriff, and even if the compurgation failed, the clerk was punished only by imprisonment when the layman would have been hanged. It was the aim of Henry II to make his legal system equal the best continental model, to suppress over-strong subjects, including church-men if necessary, and to assert the competence of the royal law-courts as widely as possible, especially as regards the punishment of clerks. His favourite Thomas à Becket, however, had been trained in the archbishop of Canter-bury's household, and sent by him to study for a time at Bologna, among the enthusiasm of the new canonists. It was unfortunate for Henry, for when royal favour had promoted Becket to Canterbury there were two enthusiastic lawyers in England, each eager for the expansion of their own legal system. At the council of Westminster, 1163, Henry, aggrieved at some cases of clerical underpunish-ment, demanded that clerks found guilty by the church courts should be handed over to the secular courts. Becket opposed this, on the general canonical ground that laymen might not judge clerks, and because the process suggested would involve two trials and two punishments for the same offence : " not even God judges the same matter twice." The king pleaded, however, the " ancient custom of the realm," alluding perhaps to the pre-Conquest period, when spiritual and secular cases were tried together by bishop and ealdorman in the shire-court. In the constitutions of Clarendon, 1164, a string of clauses re-stricted canonical jurisdiction and privilege. Among

other clauses, disputes over advowsons must be settled
in the king's court : the beneficed clergy might not leave
the realm without the king's consent : the appeal from
the archdeacon's court lay through bishop's and archbishop's finally to the king (a clause never observed) :
and clerks accused of crime must be brought before the
king's court to prove their clerkship, then be tried in
the bishop's court, with a royal official there to watch the
case (an extremely uncanonical provision) : and if found
guilty, be degraded and handed over to the secular arm
for punishment. (Degradation and subsequent punishment were allowed in the *Decretum.*)

To these constitutions Becket would not consent, and
particularly to the clause about criminous clerks, which
he claimed still involved two trials. At the council of
Northampton the barons supported the king, but refusing
to hear their judgment as that of " lords of the palace,
lay persons, secular persons," Becket appealed to Rome.
Peace was arranged between him and Henry, and he
returned in 1170, amid popular rejoicings. But Henry
heard with exasperation that he had excommunicated
the bishops who had assisted the archbishop of York in
the coronation of the king's son,—an infringement on the
rights of Canterbury : and the king's exasperation inspired
four knights to ride to Canterbury and murder Becket.
An immense revulsion followed against his murderers and
the king who had inspired them : in 1173 Becket was
canonized in response to genuine popular demand, and
the next year Henry himself did penance at his tomb.
Churches were dedicated to S. Thomas of Canterbury all
over England and even in France, and the shrine of the
martyr became the most popular place of pilgrimage in
England, eclipsing even those of the Confessor at Westminster and S. Swithun at Winchester. The widespread
popularity may partly be ascribed to Becket's dramatic
death, but it is also an indication that, however reasonable
Henry's plans may have seemed to the barons and the
royal lawyers, they were popularly regarded as an aggression
against God and His church. In course of time the royal
lawyers, however, devised formulae by which much of
Henry's method for the punishment of criminous clerks
was adopted.

CHAPTER XI

INNOCENT III

Character and aims of Innocent III—His imperial policy—His Italian policy—Innocent and the national kings—Result of his policy in England—His spiritual policy—The fourth Lateran council

THE pontificate of Innocent III, 1198–1216, may be taken as the most splendid period in the history of the medieval papacy. Gregory VII, Innocent III and Boniface VIII stand out as the three popes who stated most clearly the claims of the papacy both in spiritual matters and secular : but Innocent III alone made good the claim. He not only ruled the church, but he was a greater force in the secular politics of Europe than either emperor or national king. This end he achieved partly fortuitously, through a long schism in the empire, but also largely through devotion, ambition and ability. He belonged to a noble Roman house, and in his youth studied theology at Paris and law at Bologna, attaining distinction as a canonist and a writer. His uncle, pope Clement III, made him a cardinal before he was thirty, and at thirty-seven years of age, in January 1198, he was elected pope. One of the most brilliant of the Hohenstaufen emperors, Henry VI, had died four months previously : he had inherited and made his power real in Sicily and south Italy, as well as Germany, but he died leaving only a three-year-old child to succeed him. The Hohenstaufen dynasty, and Henry VI in particular, had dreamed of making their temporal sovereignty of Europe as real as their local rule in Germany : but the heir to their dreams of empire was Innocent III. The two aims dearest to his heart were those which he put forward when summoning

the great council of 1215, the recovery of the Holy Land
and the reform of the church, both rather spiritual than
temporal ambitions : but like Gregory VII he found that
temporal world power was needed to achieve spiritual
reform, and he was more successful than any other pope
in attaining it. In his temporal policy the points of greatest
importance were his relations with the young emperor,
Frederick II, with the national kings, and his success in
building up the papal estates into a real Italian principality. His spiritual achievements included the launching
of the fourth Crusade , the war against heresy, especially
the Albigensian ; the patronage of the new orders of
friars ; increased papal control of elections and appointments to benefices ; and the great reforming council known
as the fourth Lateran, 1215.

Innocent stated the claims of the spiritual power to
supremacy over the temporal in famous and unfaltering
language. " The sacerdotium is the sun, the regnum is
the moon. Kings rule over their respective kingdoms,
but Peter rules over the whole earth. The sacerdotium
came by divine creation, the regnum by man's cunning,"
—with a reference to theocracy and kingship in the Old
Testament. " The Lord Jesus Christ has set up one ruler
over all things as His universal vicar, and as all things
in heaven, earth and hell bow the knee to Christ, so should
all obey Christ's vicar, that there be one flock and one
shepherd."   " No king can reign rightly unless he devoutly
serve Christ's vicar."   " Princes have power in earth,
priests over the soul. As much as the soul is worthier than
the body, so much worthier is the priesthood than the
monarchy." In spite of these claims, the papal power, as
an international tribunal in a violent age, was actually
seriously threatened, if not during the minority of
Frederick II, at least for the future. The Hohenstaufen
had ruled Germany and north Italy : they had inherited
Sicily and south Italy through marriage : if Frederick or
his successors succeeded in making their rule real in both
portions of their empire, the papacy would be in the
position of a nut in the nut-crackers. Hence the supreme
importance to Innocent of avoiding such a contingency
and strengthening the papal states in central Italy. The

decreased prestige of the papacy in the fourteenth century, during the papal residence at Avignon and consequent domination by French interests, shows that Innocent feared no imaginary danger. Even to-day, when great wealth is possible apart from landed property, the modern Roman papacy suffers as an international power because, through its delicate relations with the kingdom of Italy, only Italians are in fact elected as popes. It was far more vital then, in the twelfth century, than now, that if the papacy were to remain international, it should not be over-shadowed by any one national ruler, and that the papal states should therefore be developed into an independent temporal principality. The papal states were involved by the international ideal, at a time when the old small local counties, duchies and principalities of Europe were being welded into the modern national kingdoms. But the policy inaugurated by Innocent had unfortunate results. Earlier popes had fought kings and emperors for a spiritual ideal : later popes, for their temporal possessions. And while an able pope like Innocent was countering a real danger of the union of Germany and Sicily, later popes pursued the fatal feud with the Hohenstaufen when the danger was no longer real. Attempts to finance these wars involved far heavier taxation of local churches than ever before, and produced, in England at least, the first national anti-papal feeling. Englishmen, on the whole, had sided with Becket against Henry II : they sided with Stephen Langton and the pope against John : but the attempt in the thirteenth century to render England the milch cow of the papacy to support papal wars against Frederick II and his successors aroused national opposition. And England was not the only country where funds were raised, in spite of opposition, for these ends.

In detail, Innocent's imperial policy consisted, from 1198 till 1210, in an attempt to arbitrate between the claims of two adult relations of Henry VI to the empire, and to get the candidate he favoured generally accepted. This involved ten years' civil war in Germany, and by 1210 Innocent had found his candidate ungrateful, and threatening, when he should rule Germany, to put forward the Hohenstaufen claim to Sicily as well. Innocent therefore

L

declared him deposed, and accepted the young Frederick, who had been his ward since his mother's death, as the emperor Frederick II. Innocent exacted from him a promise that he would not attempt to unite the German with the Sicilian lands, a promise which was not kept. Frederick defeated his enemy and established his position as emperor by the battle of Bouvines, 1212 ; he was thenceforward strong in Sicily and south Italy, and weak in Germany. The excellent education Innocent had afforded him, and Frederick's own ability and disposition, made him one of the most remarkable of the emperors, half oriental sultan, half renaissance despot. He drew from western civilisation his skill in war, in the seven liberal arts, as a linguist, a poet, hunter, physician, surgeon, as ruler of the highly-developed Norman curia in Sicily, together with his nominal religion, as a persecutor of heretics and even a crusader : his morals, his belief in astrologers and his fatalism were more akin to those of his Arab subjects. He kept dromedaries and elephants, and a harem of wives at Lucera, entering their expenses in the public accounts of the realm : when on Crusade, he visited the mosque of Omar and the church of the Holy Sepulchre at Jerusalem with equal zeal : he was suspected of being an atheist. His curious character added to the political bitterness with which Innocent's successors regarded him.

Innocent's guardianship of Frederick was useful to his Italian policy for the greater part of his pontificate. The countess Matilda of Tuscany had left her inheritance to the papacy a hundred years before, but Innocent was the first to secure real papal control of it, and provide for its administration. He became the patron of the league of Tuscan cities, and the ally of certain Lombard cities, aiming all the time at converting alliance into allegiance. He restored Spoleto to papal rule, and in the Romagna and the Campagna he drove out the petty German nobility, and established Italian rule. He made himself supreme in Rome itself : the prefect of the city, hitherto the delegate of the emperor, now became his own nominee and vassal, and the chief senator, head of the municipality or commune, became also his servant.

Innocent had also extraordinary success in his dealings with the kings of Europe, Portugal, Aragon and England becoming his feudal fiefs. The Norman kings of Sicily had been the first to recognise themselves as the vassals of the papacy, and Portugal had followed suit. The king of Portugal now tried to repudiate the earlier submission, but was forced by Innocent to accept it. The king of Aragon went in 1204 to Rome, was solemnly crowned by Innocent, and received investiture of his kingdom from him. Innocent's quarrel with John of England was due generally to John's practice of keeping bishoprics vacant and wasting church lands, and particularly to the difficulty over the Canterbury election. In 1205 the archbishop died, and as in all monastic cathedrals, the right to elect the new archbishop lay with the chapter of Benedictine monks. The younger monks, with certain irregularities, elected their sub-prior ; the elder were persuaded by John, also irregularly, to elect the bishop of Norwich. Delegations from each side appealed to Rome and Innocent quashed both elections, and, with very doubtful canonical right, ordered the Canterbury monks to make a fresh election in Rome. Under his influence they chose Stephen Langton, a cardinal, and John refused to accept him. To enforce his claims Innocent placed England under an interdict in 1208 : churches were closed, and sacraments could only be administered privately to the sick and dying. John in return seized church lands, and most bishops had to flee the realm. In 1209 Innocent excommunicated him personally : but excommunication was only an effective weapon against an unsupported individual. In 1212 he declared John deposed, and invited the French king, Philip Augustus, to invade England. This proved effective. John made his submission to Pandulf, the papal legate : the dramatic success of Canossa was repeated. John promised to accept Stephen Langton, to restore church property and compensate for damages : and he then proceeded to buy an active papal alliance, by resigning the crown of England, and receiving his kingdom back as a papal fief. In 1214 he granted a charter to the English church, promising freedom of elections, and conceding all the demands of the English bishops from the crown. When Magna Carta was granted next year, the grievances of churchmen had been already redressed.

Innocent himself died in 1216, but a word should be said as to the after-results of his policy in England. What were the results of the triumph of the papacy over John ? The permanent gain was relatively small. The indignity of the position was not felt at the time : Matthew Paris, the historian of the Benedictine house of S. Albans, was the first to notice it, in the next reign. On John's death, the young Henry III was crowned and supported for nine years almost entirely by papal influence : Gualo, the papal legate, became the official colleague of the regent, from 1216–1218, and his successor Pandulf from 1218–1221. The legate Otho was received in England from 1237–1240, and Ottobon from 1265–1268. In elections, papal influence increased. Innocent refused to receive the candidate whom the York chapter elected at the Lateran council of 1215, and had a fresh candidate, acceptable to himself, elected at Rome. In 1228 the pope set aside the rival candidates of king and chapter at Canterbury, and nominated without an election ; in 1231 he declared three successive elections at Canterbury irregular, and persuaded the monks to elect Edmund Rich. In both cases his candidates were superior to those who would have been elected without him. The permanent loss from the continuation of Innocent's policy probably, however, outweighed the gain. A legacy of English hostility was raised up by the mission of a papal legate to claim a tithe of clerical property for a Crusade against Frederick II, and by the sudden access of papal appointments to benefices (provisions). Bishops were given lists of papal nominees, and forbidden to fill the benefices in the diocese with Englishmen till these had been " provided " for ; in 1231 there were riots all over England against beneficed aliens. The interference of papal legates with the government was unpopular, but the main source of anti-papal feeling was financial. The tribute of 1,000 marks per annum which John had promised was not long paid, but the legates were always asking for money, and often got it. In 1229 the clergy paid a tithe, in 1240 the legate Otho asked for a fifth of all goods, clerical and lay, in 1246 the pope asked for half the ecclesiastical revenues of the country, and in 1250 Henry III took the crusader's oath, and was allowed to tax the clergy for a Crusade. Annates (see p. 186) were first paid at the end of Henry III's reign. The general result was bitter fiscal hatred of the papacy and of foreigners.

With the powerful king, Philip Augustus of France, Innocent quarrelled on purely moral grounds. Philip repudiated his wife the day after his marriage, and persuaded a synod of French bishops to hunt up a remote kinship between them, and declare the marriage void. The queen appealed to Rome, and Philip married another lady. Innocent ordered him to recall his lawful wife, placed France under an interdict in 1201, and after a long struggle procured the restoration of the queen.

By patronising both the Franciscan and Dominican friars Innocent associated the papacy with the new spiritual forces in the church (see p. 155), and not merely with the extension of papal domination. By his crusading zeal, a Latin hierarchy was established at Constantinople, and the leadership of the crusading movement regained for the papacy. By his zeal against heresy (see p. 236) and by the Albigensian Crusade, the unity of Christendom was preserved in the west, though the use of the term " Crusade " for a war other than for the Holy Land ended by degrading the crusading ideal. By the policy of centralisation, Innocent aroused the hostility of local churches, but often secured the appointment of superior and more learned clergy. He claimed the right to " provide " to any benefice held in plurality for six months : the sole right to translate bishops to other sees : and in the cases of disputed elections, the right to reject both candidates and nominate himself. But it was above all by his great reform council of 1215 that he rendered best service to the church.

In April 1213 he sent out a circular summoning the whole clergy, and lay rulers or their representatives, to a council to open in Rome on All Saints' day, 1215. Archbishops, bishops, abbots, priors, the heads of the Cistercians, Premonstratensians, Hospitallers, Templars, and other religious orders, were summoned in person : it would suffice if archbishops left two bishops in each province. Kings (not being excommunicate) and rulers were summoned in person or by representative : the Lombard and Tuscan communes by representative. Absence would entail canonical penalties. There might be obstacles : but " we should never set sail if we waited to embark till the sea was waveless." The circular stated the aim of the council, the recovery of the Holy Places, and the reform of the church : the council must root out heresy, strengthen faith, reform manners, repress tyranny and establish peace and liberty. The intermediate two years must be used for preparation, and legates would be sent everywhere to incite Christians to take the cross, and to gather funds for a Crusade. All the spring and summer of 1215 crowds poured along the roads to Rome. Though scarcely with the completeness that Innocent had ordered, yet in enormous numbers the episcopate of Europe collected in Rome. At the first session of the council in the basilica of S. John on the Lateran the aged archbishop of Amalfi slipped and was trodden under foot, and he was not the only ecclesiastic during the council to be crushed to death in the crowd. Four hundred and twelve bishops were present, including the Latin patriarchs of Constantinople and Jerusalem, and more than eight hundred abbots and priors : the Greek bishops, alienated by the new Latin hierarchies in the east, and the long schism, did not appear. Three days of full session were held, and a multitude of small informal sessions and conversations. The bishop of Liège took advantage of the summons to lay potentates to make clear the lay dignities which he also held : he appeared the first day robed as count, in scarlet tunic and green hat, the second as duke, in a green, sleeved cape, and the third as bishop, in a mitre. He asked an Italian bishop the population of his diocese, and was told " about a thousand " : " In mine," he rejoined, " I have more than a hundred thousand." At the first session Innocent preached, and traced the evils of Christianity to the shortcomings of the clergy : reform was necessary. An edict was issued in preparation for a Crusade, and the council discussed in semi-public sessions and accepted in full session, at Innocent's hands, a list of canons embodying the reform desired.

Heresy was dealt with first. To a profession of faith
following closely on the creed, clauses were added protecting
the sacraments of the altar and baptism, and adding that
married persons might attain to eternal blessedness as
well as the celibate—this against the Cathari and Albigeois.
The teaching of abbot Joachim of Flora, and a pantheist,
was condemned—the latter "not as heresy, but as insanity."
Those condemned for heresy must be handed over to the
secular arm for punishment, and their goods confiscated.
Secular lords who neglected to purge their dominions of
heresy after ecclesiastical monition should be excommunicated by the metropolitan. If they remained obstinate,
the pope should absolve their subjects from the oath of
fealty. (Procedure already adopted in the Albigensian
crusade.) The canon concluded by ordering all archbishops and bishops, personally or through their archdeacons, to hold an inquisition at least once a year in their
see, if suspicion of heresy had arisen: they should travel
round and compel witnesses on oath to disclose any knowledge they possessed of heretics or "secret conventicles."
The bishop should then summon the accused, and unless
they cleared themselves by compurgation, or if after purga-
tion they relapsed, they should be canonically punished.
If they refused to take an oath (this against the Waldenses,
see p. 227), they should be deemed heretics. The punishment by the secular arm was left vague, beyond confiscation
of goods and loss of civil rights.

Greek Christianity was then declared subordinate to
Latin : "that there may be one fold and one shepherd."
An appeal from all the patriarchates lay to the Roman see.

Provincial councils were ordered to be held yearly by
metropolitans, the "canonical rules" read aloud, and
abuses corrected. The abuses of cathedral canons should
be corrected as formerly by their own chapter. Cities
whose population had different tongues and rites must
have the same bishop, who should appoint suitable persons
to perform the said rites in the said tongues, (this with
reference to the east). Since the food of the word of God
was necessary to salvation, and many bishops were
hindered from preaching, by the size of their diocese, or
other causes, (not to mention defect of learning, which in

them was altogether scandalous, and for the future not to be tolerated), bishops should appoint suitable men as preachers and confessors in their diocese. The third Lateran council (1179) had ordered that each cathedral church should confer a prebend on a master, to teach the clerks of that church and other poor scholars freely : this had been by no means observed in many churches, and it was ordered that in cathedral churches, and others which had the means, a master should be chosen by the bishop and chapter : metropolitan churches should also have a theologian, to teach the priests and others theology and those things which pertained to the cure of souls. Each master should have a prebend : he need not be a canon, but he must have sufficient to continue teaching.

Bishops must visit monasteries under their care to correct abuses, and prevent seculars from oppressing them. No new orders might be founded : patrons who wished to found new houses must subject them to recognised rules.

Clerks must shun incontinence, drunkenness, hunting and sorceries : they might not engage in secular business, haunt taverns, play dice, or similar games. They should wear the tonsure, and clothes neither too long nor too short, neither in red nor green cloth, nor adorned with superfluous ornaments.

Prebends must not become hereditary, nor the sons of canons receive a benefice in their father's church. Bishops should demand no fee for instituting cures, and the sacraments must be given without payment. The provision of the third Lateran about benefices held in plurality having been evaded, it was ordered that two benefices with cure of soul should not be held together, and the same person should not hold two " dignities " in one church.

Priests must not sell relics, or show them for money, or lightly receive new ones for reverence. Bishops must see that the faithful were not abused by false legends or documents produced " for the sake of filthy lucre." The right of bishops to grant indulgences was limited. Everyone who had come to years of discretion should confess all his sins at least once a year to his own priest, fulfil the penance he received, and receive the sacrament of the eucharist at least at Easter, (unless by the counsel of his own priest he refrained for a time) : otherwise let him be excommunicate. If anyone wished to confess to another priest, he must first obtain the leave of his own priest to do so. The stress in this canon at the time was on yearly confession to the parish priest, who could thus be responsible that none of his flock were tainted by heresy. Confession at least annually had been customary for hundreds of years. The necessity for members to confess to their parish priests was pleaded by a parliament of Henry IV of England as an excuse for dissolution before Easter.

With these and a string of canons dealing with the details of discipline and administration, the greatest general council of the medieval church closed its labours. A Greek version of the canons was prepared, but won no acceptance in the east.

CHAPTER XII

THE FRIARS

Antecedents of the friar movement—Francis of Assisi—Dominic de Guzman—The friars and holy poverty—The friars in England—Work of friars : social, pastoral, educational—Friars' missions

RELIGIOUS enthusiasm in the twelfth century had produced a monastic renaissance : in the thirteenth century it led to the work of the friars (fratres or brothers). They exercised an immense influence on popular religion, social conditions, and finally, the universities and learning. The reasons for their appearance and success at this stage of Christian history are of interest. Religious enthusiasm and the character of S. Francis, whom the middle ages considered the most perfect Christian since Christ, do not fully account for it, although they gave the movement its peculiar grace and character. Four other circumstances determined their success. First, the friars' movement was democratic compared to the monastic. The monks' life about 1200 was held to be the most perfect life, yet a certain contrast was perceptible between the lives of the monks and those of the early Christians : not the contrast that a modern mind would find first, between an enclosed life, and one lived in the world, but that between the socially great and the humble. The monks belonged to the upper classes and had upper class sympathies. Even the Cistercians were thriving agricultural communities. Yet the apostles and first Christians had been fishermen and peasants. The personnel of the friars was relatively democratic : their leaders might be of the merchant class, or even noble, but the rank and file were men of no patrimony. Secondly, the parochial system (see p. 204) at the time failed to reach the poor of the towns ; it had been designed for the country and left largely untouched the slums that clustered outside the walls of a medieval century town. Moreover, many of the country clergy were drawn from the peasant class, and had little learning or specific training. Thirdly, the remedy of lay preaching and lay missions was always distrusted in the middle ages, because the mass of the people could not read or write, and illiterate lay preachers tended to produce erratic heresy. For this reason, canon law forbade laymen to preach, or teach the faith. Fourthly the friars owed the papal approval of their rules to the statesmanship of Innocent III, although they were in these early days mainly laymen, not clerks, and nevertheless preached. He dealt skilfully with them, because he had just failed to deal skilfully enough with the Waldensians, who from being a sort of devout gild of lay people within the church, had developed into proscribed heretics (see p. 227). His experience with the Waldensians lent him patience and imagination in dealing with the early friars : and possibly lent them also to S. Francis in his dealings with the hierarchy.

The inspiration of the whole movement came from Francis of Assisi (1182–1226). John Bernardone was the son of a rich cloth-merchant of Assisi, one of the little hill towns of Tuscany, and nicknamed Francis, or the Frenchman, for his friendship with that race, or his fondness for the French " romances," the troubadours' songs of chivalry, war and love. There is something in common, in any case, between the perception of the glow, colour and adventure of life in the romances, and the attitude to religion which John Bernardone was to make known later as typically " Franciscan." His father gave him plenty of money, and was content that his son's gaiety and attractiveness should render him popular with the young Tuscan nobles, and that he should make them his companions. Like S. Bernard, however, Francis underwent a sudden conversion : on recovery from an illness he meditated how he could change his life and find that of " perfection." Attributing his silence and reflectiveness to desire for a wife, his friends questioned him, saying : " Francis, art

thou going to take a wife ? " But he would answer : " I
will marry a nobler and a fairer bride than ever you saw,
who shall surpass all others in beauty and excel them in
wisdom." The bride of whom he dreamed was the Lady
Poverty : he gave up his possessions, renounced his inheritance, attached himself to an old priest, and lived just
outside his native town a life of prayer and poverty.
Gradually he collected a band of followers to lead the same
life. They had no settled home, but went about in the
little Tuscan hill cities, working on the harvest or wherever
casual work was offered them, sleeping in the open, or in
the shelters of the lepers whom they nursed. They found
all nature friendly and beautiful : all animals, depending
as they did on heaven for subsistence, their friends and
kin : Francis preached one famous sermon to his " little
sisters the birds." At first they were all laymen, but
sometimes they preached : they nursed the sick : they
said the divine office : they lived hardly : they spent
nights in prayer : and with it all they were so merry and
joyful, they earned the nickname of " joculatores domini,"
(God's jesters). To Francis, the supreme motive for himself and his followers was expressed in the old saying, " to
follow naked the naked Christ " : to renounce all things
and never to have individually or corporately any money
or possessions. Those who thus embraced holy poverty
could pray, as one of Francis's friends heard him pray
during a whole night, using only the words : " Deus meus,
et omnia." Complete poverty, Francis taught, made
possible gaiety of spirit : his brothers need have no cares,
for God Himself would provide for their wants by alms.
The stress laid upon mendicancy by the friars goes back to
this providential and sacred character of alms : and to
Francis's teaching, that only those who had themselves
stood barefooted in the market-place, asking for alms,
could have real compassion on the poor.

In 1209 Francis and eleven companions travelled to
Rome, and asked Innocent III to confirm their rule of
absolute poverty, and devotion to good works, and after
some hesitation Innocent gave a verbal approbation.
They were to be known as the " fratres minores," wear a
dark grey habit, and go barefoot. They then returned to

Assisi, and Francis spent the rest of his life after this pattern, gradually arranging the groups of men who joined him into an order. The preservation of the complete Franciscan poverty in an order, however organised, was and has always been the great difficulty in the Franciscan ideal. In 1217 Francis had to divide his followers within Italy itself into provinces, appointing a " minister " over each. At the head of each friary was a " father guardian," and within the province the friaries were grouped in " custodies." In his wish to distinguish his brothers from the old religious orders, Francis avoided all the usual monastic terms. He worked not only at building up the order in Italy, but throughout Europe : he himself travelled through Europe, preaching and collecting followers, and even pleading for Christianity before the sultan of Egypt, and he sent off bands of missionary friars to all parts. In 1220 he returned to Italy, gave up the post of minister general of the order, and appointed brother Elias of Cortona. In 1223 the fixed rule which he had long been drawing up for his friars was confirmed by pope Honorius III, and at other times he also drew up a rule for his friend S. Clare and her " Minoresses," and for the Franciscan third order, or tertiaries. The Minoresses, like the brothers, were to have no corporate possessions, and live on alms, but they were, like all the monastic orders for women at the time, strictly enclosed. The tertiaries kept their own property and lived a life of good works in the world, and acted as the " spiritual friends " of the brothers, receiving money gifts on their behalf and expending them for their benefit. Francis was nearly blind by this time, from tears and prayer, and his followers observed with awe that his hands and feet and side had received the stigmata, or wound prints of the passion of Christ. He died in 1226, leaving as his testament to his followers an entreaty to follow strictly his love of holy poverty.

The founder of the other great order of friars was Dominic de Guzman (1170–1221), the son of a Castilian noble, of fiery Spanish zeal and valour : Spanish Christianity had long been tempered by the age-long struggle with the Moors. He became a canon regular of the cathedral of Osma, near his birthplace, and was then sent to Provence to help convert the Albigensians. The connexion between Spain and Provence was always close, and the Provençal language akin both to French and Spanish. He settled in Toulouse with a band of followers, and remained there teaching and preaching throughout the Albigensian Crusade. He was impressed with the connexion between an ignorant clergy and the spread of heresy, and the need of a clergy able, above all, to preach. He tried to get the rule of his followers recognised by the Lateran council of 1215, but that council was even then legislating against the foundation of new orders. By the advice of pope Honorius III, Dominic adopted the old rule of S. Austin as the basis of his rule, and called his brothers the " Friars Preacher of Toulouse." On his return his friars increased and daughter houses were established in many places, including the convent of the Jacobins in Paris, and a house in Rome which Dominic founded by the help of Francis's patron, cardinal Hugolino. With him also he discussed the final form of their rule, and through him he met Francis, and admired his vision of a life of complete poverty. In 1220 the Dominican rule was confirmed, based, like that of all canons regular, on the Augustinian rule, but embodying in its constitutions the Franciscan directions as to mendicancy and absolute corporate poverty. In 1221 Dominic died, at the university of Bologna, where he was buried, and in 1234 he was canonized.

The Friars Preacher, like the Friars Minor, spread over Europe, and in missions to heathen countries ; they wore a white habit and black scapular. To their contemporaries they were the " watch-dogs of the Lord," sent out to run down heresy and ignorance : for was not a frater Dominicanus a " domini canis " ? The Dominican ideal differed from the Franciscan, and at first the work of the two orders differed widely. Francis delighted that a friar should not even have a breviary as his own : Dominic desired books for his followers, and in his rule made study a most binding duty. The Dominicans studied that they might preach themselves : they kept theology and arts schools for their own brothers : they allowed secular clerks to attend the lectures in their houses, and they became finally some of the foremost divinity lecturers at the universities. But almost from the first the two orders tended to assimilate : the Franciscans found it needful to train their own young friars, and soon became also a learned order.

Francis's contention that his friaries should be completely unendowed was extremely difficult to carry out in a world-wide order. He and his early followers might live on casual earnings and alms, but the countryside could scarcely support a great number of friars in this way. The early friars had often come as adults, of good education : the later friars were often recruited as youths who needed education and training, and it was almost impossible to support houses for them on casual alms received in kind. But the friars made great efforts to retain their principle of mendicancy. No friar might receive or touch money, or take it from place to place, or have a servant to carry it. Even Francis had allowed money alms given to the friars to be received by a proctor or " amicus spiritualis," but alms so given belonged to the donor till they were actually received in kind, and the friars could not sue a defaulting proctor for them. As they could not bind themselves to pay debts, they could not borrow money. In time, however, the early, loose arrangement about the " spiritual friends " came to be held unworkable. In 1283 the pope allowed all friaries to appoint proctors to represent them in the law-courts, and to enforce the payment of legacies, and the proctors soon became merely the friars' legal officials, appointed by them and dependent on them. The question of holy poverty caused a split in the Franciscan order itself : as early as 1239 there was trouble over the worldliness of the government of brother Elias, and he was deposed. The friars who contended most strictly for Francis's own teaching about poverty, and the avoidance of endowments, were known as the Spirituals or the Fraticelli, and, for their refusal to accept the papal ruling as to the order, were cast out from it, and finally excommunicated as heretics ; the party willing to accept the arrangements which organisation as an order involved were known as the " Conventuals."

The first friars to reach England were the Dominicans, who were welcomed by archbishop Stephen Langton and his brother, and founded a friary at Oxford. Their houses spread all over England, and there was one Dominican nunnery, at Dartford. The Franciscans came in 1224, nine friars, four of whom were clerks and five laymen, led by brother Agnellus of Pisa, a deacon. Four of them only were Englishmen, among them William of Nottingham, later a famous scholar and provincial of the order. One or two of them, however, had known Francis himself. Their friaries spread quickly and by 1230 they had houses at Canterbury, London, Oxford, Northampton, Norwich, Worcester, Hereford, Salisbury, Nottingham, King's Lynn, Leicester, Lincoln, Cambridge, Stamford, Bristol and Gloucester. In the next ten years they founded twenty more. Usually some benefactor or benefactors of the friars gave a site to the corporation of the town, who held it for their use : sometimes the town itself bestowed it on them. The sites were often undesirable, on marshy and unhealthy ground, and in the " slums : " the houses and the chapels which the friars built were of the plainest. Grosseteste, the patron of the Franciscans at Oxford, remonstrated with them for building on land liable to flooding.

The work of the friars in the thirteenth and following centuries was social, pastoral, educational and missionary. They continued to tend the lepers and the sick, a practice which stimulated the study of medicine within their orders. In the frequent medieval pestilences they gained especial honour for their work among the sick and dying.

Their pastoral work was even more important, though it soon raised difficulties between them and the parochial clergy. The latter lived a life of great monotony and isolation, almost without books (which were enormously expensive, compared to their stipends), and without much intercourse with each other, except for the diocesan synod. Even when worthy, they must often have been dull. The friars in any case soon surpassed them in popularity. They were better educated, specially trained to preach, in touch with other friars and the books of their convent, and at first, at least, under the spell of a greater zeal for holiness. Preaching manuals were written for them, supplying them with skeleton discourses and startling anecdotes, like the

Dormi Secure ("Sleep soundly," because your sermon is here all ready), the *Speculum Laicorum*, the *Contes Moralisés* of Nicole Bozon, which supplied material from a mixture of natural history and moral fable : the *Liber Exemplorum*, which supplied discourses on the life and passion of Christ, and on a neatly arranged, alphabetical list of subjects, beginning, "Accidia : Advocates : Avarice : Baptism : Charity : Clerics, evil : Carnal thoughts : Confusion : Conjugium . . ." The friars did not disdain the use of humour, and even rhyme and stories, in their sermons (a fact which Wycliffe cast up against them later) : and they used the homely incidents of common life as illustrations. "Now I imagine," runs a sermon in one of the manuals, "our whole life to be like a fair, for as in a fair there is a great concourse of people, and great paraphernalia and trinkets, merchandise of various kinds, and lots of booths : and yet in a short time it will all be taken away and removed elsewhere, and all the expense will have gone for nothing, unless one has been clever in buying or selling, and in the place itself nothing remains, except more filth than elsewhere : so it is in our life." Till 1300 the mendicants were allowed to preach at any time in their own churches, and while travelling : but in this year, through the difficulties raised by the secular clergy, they were restrained from preaching at a time when the prelate of the district was preaching himself.

By the same bull they were ordered, instead of hearing confessions generally, to send certain brothers to the bishop, that they might become his licensed penitentiaries. Brother Geoffrey of Salisbury heard confessions with such gentleness and pity, that if his penitents "did not show fitting signs of sorrow he would weep and groan, until they too began to weep, as happened to a nobleman, sir Alexander de Bissingbourne. He had confessed his sins as though he were telling a story, but brother Geoffrey wept so bitterly that at last the nobleman wept too." The friars were no less popular as confessors than preachers : sometimes for the best reasons, sometimes because it was pleasanter to confess to a friar who would perhaps never return than to one's parish priest.

In two respects the friars had considerable literary as

M

apart from scholastic influence. They wrote manuals of devotion in the vernacular, as well as vernacular paraphrases and glossed translations of the gospels and other biblical books : and they produced some notable religious poetry. Finest among the Franciscan might be mentioned Francis's *Canticle of the Sun ;* Thomas of Celano's *Dies Irae,* and the mystic, Jacopone da Todi's, *Stabat Mater Dolorosa ;* and among the Dominican the hymns of Thomas Aquinas.

The educational work of the friars was no less important. The English Minorites had a school for young friars in each house, and a school of liberal arts and theology in each custody : secular clerks would thus attend the friars' lectures in seven towns, as well as the cathedral school. The Blackfriars' convent in London was a famous theology school. Thomas Aquinas states in his writings that the regulations of the third and fourth Lateran councils failed to provide teaching for the secular clergy, and that the friars then stepped in and filled the gap. Scholars who would have gravitated to the universities, not content with the opportunities of the cathedral school, were content as friars to stay and teach in the various custodies. The friars too had houses at all the universities, and famous ones at Paris, Oxford, Cambridge, and Bologna. They had a prolonged struggle with the university authorities to obtain permission for their members to read theology without taking the preliminary arts course, (ground they might cover in their own custodies), a permission which they finally attained. The most famous of the Franciscan scholars included Bonaventura, a great doctor, mystic, and general of the order : philosophers and theologians like Alexander of Hales, William of Okham and Duns Scotus ; the Norman Hebraïst, Nicholas of Lyra : the scientist, Roger Bacon, and the English archbishop Peckham. The Paris Dominicans obtained special repute for their work on the holy scriptures. The lack of an authoritative text of the Vulgate was a perennial medieval difficulty : copyists' variations occurred in all manuscripts, and made even the recognition of different schools of texts difficult. In the early century the " stationers " or booksellers of Paris adopted a uniform text, unfortunately a

bad one, and the university of Paris accepted it. Various
schools drew up " correctories " to remedy the defects
from Hebrew and Greek sources, and that of the Dominican
cardinal Hugh of S. Cher became the most famous, and
known as the *Paris Correctory.* It was accepted as
authoritative by a Dominican general chapter, and remained so for thirty years : but it was rejected by another
in 1256, and fresh Dominican editions issued from the
Jacobin convent, the Paris house of studies. The work of
Hugh of S. Cher was of immense importance for medieval
study of the Latin scriptures : for it included, beside his
relatively unsuccessful correctory, a set of commentaries
on all the books of the Bible, and the first concordance to
the Vulgate. This made possible a comparative study of
scripture, and has remained the foundation of all con-
cordances to the Vulgate since.

The foreign missions of the friars were a most stirring
and notable part of their work. In 1219 Francis himself
sent off friars to Spain, Hungary and the east, and the
Dominican work also soon spread beyond Provence.
Dominicans and Franciscans both desired to promote the
study of oriental languages in the universities, to further
the conversion of Saracens and others. The Franciscan
tertiary, Ramon Lull, founded a school for his community
in Majorca, where Arabic and Chaldean were studied. He
preached and disputed with the Saracens, induced the
council of Vienne, 1311, to pass a canon enjoining the
universities to appoint masters for oriental languages, and
was himself stoned to death by the Saracens in Tunis in
1315. The Franciscans worked from 1220 onwards in
Morocco, Libya, Tunis and Algiers, many of them meeting
death on their travels, and at the hands of the heathen.
They preached, and founded convents and houses for
pilgrims, in the Holy Land and Egypt : in 1291 two
Franciscans sailed round Africa with Genoese merchants,
and in the fifteenth century they preached in Cape Verde,
Guinea, and the Congo. They preached on the heathen
borders of Europe, Lithuania, Poland and Prussia, and in
the borderlands where the Greek church already struggled
with the heathen or the Turk : Armenia, Bulgaria, and
round the Black Sea and the Caspian. The work was not

done without many martyrdoms, and most adventurous of all were the Franciscan and Dominican missions to Asia. They passed along merchant routes through Armenia and central Asia to Persia, India, Sumatra, Java, Borneo, Thibet and China; as early as 1245 Innocent IV sent a Franciscan mission to the Great Khan of Tartary, and the friars continued to work in the far east till the rise of the hostile Ming dynasty in 1368.

One of the most wonderful of the Franciscan missions was that of brother John of Monte Corvino to Khanbalig, or Peking. He was born in south Italy, was at some time in the service of the emperor Frederick II, became a friar, and was sent about 1280 with a band of missionaries to the east. He returned with letters from the Khan of Persia in 1289, and was at once sent back by the pope. This time, after prodigious journeys, he reached the court of the Tartar (Mongol-Chinese) Khan of Khanbalig,— in modern terms, emperor of Peking, where he lived and worked till his death, c. 1329. In 1307 he wrote to the friars' minister general, describing his work and asking for further help : the letter was carried by Venetian merchants, who delivered it to a friar preacher travelling in the east. The letter stated that in 1291 John left the land of the Persians and came to India, travelling with a certain friar preacher, who died there. After thirteen months John proceeded further to Cathay, the land of the Great Khan, to whom he presented a papal letter urging him to adopt Christianity : " but he had grown old in idolatry." There were already Nestorians in China, " men who bear the Christian name, but deviate very far from the Christian religion : " they resented John's coming, and hindered his work. " I was alone," said John in the letter, " in this pilgrimage, without confession, for eleven years, till there came to me brother Arnold, a German of the province of Cologne, last year. I have built a church in the city of Khanbalig, where the king has his chief residence : this I completed six years ago . . . I have baptized there, as I reckon, up to this time about 6,000 persons ; and I am often engaged in baptizing. Also I have bought, one after another, forty boys, the sons of pagans, aged between seven and eleven years, who so far knew no religion. And I have baptized

them and taught them to read Latin, and our ritual ; and
I have written for them thirty psalters with hymn-books,
and two breviaries, with which eleven boys now say our
office, and attend service, and take their weekly turn in
the convent, whether I am present or not. . . . And the
emperor is greatly delighted at their chanting. I strike
the bells at all the hours, and with this congregation of
babes and sucklings I perform divine service : but we sing
by ear, because we have no service-books with the notes."
After describing the difficulties of the route to Khanbalig,
John begged the minister to show his letter to the pope,
and to send him books. " Now I am building another
church, so as to distribute the boys in more places than
one. I am now old and grey, more from toil and trouble
than from age, for I am fifty-eight years old. I know the
Tartar language and writing, and I have now translated
into that language and writing the whole New Testament and the psalter : . . . which I keep and read and
preach from openly, as it were in testimony of the law of
Christ. . . . And whilst [the aforesaid king George] was
alive, mass used to be celebrated in his church, according
to the Latin rite, in the Tartar character and language,
both the words of the canon and the prefaces." The
letter was read to the pope, and he ordered seven other
friars minor to be consecrated bishops to journey to John
in Khanbalig, and consecrate him their archbishop ; the
boys John had trained would form a native clergy. Three
friars survived the journey and accomplished their mission,
and the friars worked in Peking till a change of dynasty
brought about the murder of the survivors in 1362.

CHAPTER XIII

THE SCHOLASTIC PHILOSOPHY: S. THOMAS AQUINAS

The question of universals—Realists and nominalists—Eriugena and extreme realism—Roscelin and extreme nominalism—Anselm and Abelard—S. Thomas Aquinas: life and work—Thomist philo-. sophy and theology—Feast of Corpus Christi

SCHOLASTIC philosophy has by some historians been used as a term to cover all the conflicting philosophies, taught in the schools or universities, of the middle ages. By others it is used as the equivalent of Thomism, the philosophy of S. Thomas Aquinas. More strictly, it should be used of the philosophy which was taught by a group of leading western philosophers, from Anselm of Canterbury to Thomas Aquinas and William of Okham, who all used the same fundamental theories while adding their individual contributions to the whole structure. In the terms of their own day, and in opposition to the rival schools of philosophy which faced them, they were all "moderate realists."

Before the beginning of the medieval period eastern and western thinkers had built up a Christian philosophy, by coordinating deductions as to the nature of the universe from the revealed scriptures with the Greek philosophies. The teaching of Plato was particularly attractive to Christian thinkers, and passed into the medieval heritage through two channels: through the Neo-Platonists, Plotinus, Porphyry and the pseudo-Dionysius, and through S. Augustine. Till the twelfth century Aristotle was neglected and largely unknown. The Platonic metaphysic, or doctrine of Ideas, was handed on both by the

pseudo-Dionysius and S. Augustine, as supplying an
answer to questions raised by passages in the scriptures,
but about which the scriptures afforded no comprehensive,
systematic information.   The particular form under which
medieval philosophers speculated about existence was the
question of "universals," universal ideas, and was determined by a text in Porphyry's introduction to Aristotelian logic (the *Eisagoge*) : " do *genera* and *species* exist
in nature, or do they consist in mere products of the
intellect ? " (sive subsistant, sive in nudis intellectibus
posita sint ?) Had universals, universal ideas, that is, an
objective existence, or did they exist merely in the mind
of the thinker ?   What was the relation of thought to the
object of thought ?   Was humanity objectively real, or
were there only men ?   Plato had taught and early
medieval thinkers had held that the ideal was the real, the
underlying substance : that the universal (as humanity)
was real in a sense that the particular (individual man)
was not : was this valid ?   To the answering of this
question, and the correlation of all knowledge or theories
about the universe to the answer given, medieval philosophers directed their energies.   Their solutions were
important for the history of the church, because throughout
the medieval period the truth of the Christian revelation
was not questioned ; primary theological doctrines were
held as data, and the bearing of theology on philosophy,
and vice versa, was very close.   Philosophical discussion
often involved theological points : and the teaching of
medieval theology on such matters as the nature and being
of God, the change in the sacramental species in the
eucharist, etc., was given in terms of the current secular
conceptions about universals.

The two main schools of thought about the problem of
universals were those of the realists and the nominalists,
though there were numerous grades and shades of difference
within each school : the tendency was for each to define
its position more subtly, and in a manner less open to
attack, as time went on.   The realists held with Plato
that universals were real : the nominalists held that
universal ideas were " mere names " and that only the
individual was real.

The greatest thinker of the early middle ages was Johannes Scotus Eriugena, an Irishman, and the greatest scholar at the palace school of the ninth century emperor, Charles the Bald. The Byzantine emperor had presented to Charles the Greek works of the pseudo-Dionysius, and John the Scot translated and annotated them. His own treatises show that he absorbed Neo-Platonism from this work, and became rather pantheist than Christian in the process, though his philosophy presented a rough accommodation of the two systems. God, he taught, was the one divine substance, Who by a series of substantial emanations gave birth to all things. All contingent beings were "mere blossomings of the divine substance, theophanies." Everywhere at bottom was the single, all-pervading substance, and material visible individuals differed from one another only in "accidents" (things perceived by the senses). By the outflowing of the godhead into all life, the genus existed before the species, and the species before the individual; by which teaching he can be classed as an extreme realist. He reconciled his philosophy with the Christian revelation by explaining that the cosmic absorption of all things into the bosom of God, to which fatal necessity tended, would be effected by the redemption of man through Christ. All medieval pantheists tended to draw inspiration from Scotus, and his works were solemnly censured in 1225. Nevertheless, his teaching was used by certain orthodox theologians, particularly Odo of Tournai († 1113) in his teaching on original sin. Since all men formed but one substance, he taught, one specific reality, the fall of Adam and Eve vitiated the entire human substance, the souls of all.

As early as the eleventh century the realist philosophy was being used by theologians to explain the words of institution quoted in the canon of the mass : *This is My body : This is My blood*. By the consecration, the realists taught, the underlying substance, the reality of the bread and wine, was changed according to Christ's words to His body and blood, while the accidents of the bread and wine, that which was perceived by the senses, (touch, taste, sight, smell), remained unchanged. Nothing new or exceptional was predicated of the nature of the bread and wine : all things had substance and accidents. The doctrine merely explained the change in terms of the current philosophy of those centuries. Berengarius, the scholasticus of Tours, denied however that the accidents could remain without the underlying support of the substance, and particularly the teaching of this philosophy in the gospels. Lanfranc and other theologians disputed with him and he was at length condemned by four synods.

The early method of theological debate had been by the collection of authoritative passages in the scriptures, the Fathers and the councils bearing on the point at issue. Lanfranc himself, however, was the first to use the Porphyrian logic of the schools in theological controversy : " he blamed not the art of disputation but its perverse use by those who disputed." The increased use of dialectic led to the foundation of the great rival school of medieval philosophy, that of the nominalists. Roscelin, a monk of Compiègne, and the rival in the schools of Lanfranc, Anselm of Canterbury and Ives of Chartres, asserted that universals were mere words : " he was the first in our time," said a contemporary, " to teach the doctrine of words " (names, voices). His nominalism led him to a crude tritheism in theology. Only the individual was real : therefore there was no unity in the Christian godhead. If God was one, then the Father and the Holy Spirit would have become incarnate with the Son. The three divine persons were three independent beings, like three angels, and if custom allowed it, we might speak of three gods. In spite of the *Quicunque Vult*, he taught that there were three substances in the godhead : a position which followed from a philosophy that taught that only the individual had substance, was real. Roscelin disowned his views after a controversy with Anselm in 1093.

Anselm himself, the greatest theologian of the eleventh century, was a realist in philosophy. He studied with grammarians in Italy, and under Lanfranc at the abbey of Bec in Normandy. He became monk and finally abbot of Bec in 1078, and archbishop of Canterbury in 1093. Following on Lanfranc's footsteps in theology as well as active work, he made some use of logic to build up a philosophical system more in accordance with Christian theology than the extreme realism of Scotus and his followers. His formula, *Crede ut intelligas*, implied that faith should precede reason, but be " perfected and completed by a rational study of the contents of revelation." His treatises, the *Proslogium* and the *Monologium*, contain proofs of the existence of God, dissertations on the divine attributes, on creation, and on the "exemplarism " which was the Augustinian form of the Platonic doctrine of Ideas. This is presupposed in his famous ontological argument for the existence of God. (Ontology is the science of being, or reality). Since perfection is an attribute of being, the idea of " that which there can be no greater," God, must exist, in substance and reality, and not as a bare intellectual concept, (et in intellectu et in re). The argument attracted a generation of realists, but it implied that the human mind could only conceive " ideas " which already had an objective existence in reality, and was rejected by the later scholastics as confounding the subjective and objective orders. Truth Anselm defined as " the rectitude of what is accessible to intelligence alone : " things were true when they were " in conformity with the destination revealed by their essence." He refuted Roscelin's tritheism with the contention that " he who does not perceive how many men may be in species one man, how can he understand how many persons, each of which is perfect God, may be one God ? " He explained original sin by the teaching of Odo of Tournai, and adopted the theories of S. Augustine on evil and predestination. He defined freedom of the will as " the power of preserving the rectitude of the will for the sake of rectitude itself." In the treatise, *Cur Deus Homo*, he explained the Christian doctrine of the incarnation and the atonement as the means whereby an infinite satisfaction was made to the justice of God : none but the God-man could have made it.

A far abler enemy to realism than Roscelin was Peter Abelard, equipped as he was with the new Aristotelian logic. The subtler doctrine which he taught is generally classed as conceptualism. The individual being only had substantial existence : universals, genera, species were not substantial, not real. But we possess abstract universal concepts : we represent to ourselves elements common to different things and conceive these elements as *distributively* real in an indefinite multitude of individuals of the same species. There was, it would seem, some relation between the individuals of a species : the whole universe need not be regarded finally as a mass of unrelated atoms : but in so far as Abelard admitted the relationship, not only in the subjective concept, but in the objective world, he was admitting virtually the reality of the species, a universal. So far his work was a step towards Thomism. His didactic method was also to prove a bulwark of orthodoxy later ; the systematic arrangement of authorities of the *Sic et Non*, mentioned earlier, was really an outgrowth of the old pre-logical method of theological disputation. In spite of the opposition which he aroused, Abelard's work inspired an immense advance in both methods of theological proof, logical reasoning, and the quotation of authority. The secret of the distrust he inspired and his eventual condemnation for heresy was his own combative disposition, and the distrust which was felt for Aristotle himself, as pagan. Abelard's outstanding mental ability made him delight to demolish established systems and teachers of reputation. He held formally that man cannot demonstrate the mysteries of the faith, but only perceive or believe them. Nevertheless he plunged into disputation about the nature of God, declaring that the existence of the blessed Trinity was accessible to reason. The Greeks, he found, had by reason attained to some knowledge of this doctrine, and supported his contention by reference to the Neo-Platonic teaching about God, the νοῦς and the world soul. He joined with Anselm in condemning Roscelin's tritheism, and then proceeded to teach a doctrine which was eventually condemned also. Each of the three divine persons did not constitute the whole divine essence, but one modality or attribute of the godhead,—power, wisdom, and goodness respectively. This and other errors of Abelard were attacked by S. Bernard and condemned at the council of Sens, 1141. S. Bernard and the school of the canons of S. Victor were the arch-opponents of Abelard's excursions into theology ; S. Bernard also secured the condemnation of certain tenets of Gilbert de la Porrée, Abelard's most brilliant follower, and bishop of Poitiers 1142-54. But

these condemnations of academic heresies in the middle
ages generally took years to fall, and did not render suspect
the other works of the condemned teachers : the commentaries on the scriptures both of Berengarius of Tours
and Gilbert de la Porrée were in all academic libraries.

Just as the philosophy of Abelard and his contemporaries
in the twelfth century had been conditioned by the discovery
of Aristotle's treatise on logic, so the philosophy of S.
Thomas Aquinas and his followers was conditioned by the
discovery of the other works of Aristotle, which meant
largely a rediscovery of the Greek view of natural science
and ethics. Thomas of Aquino, a village between Rome
and Monte Cassino, belonged to the family of the counts of
that name, and as a child was sent with his tutor and
servants to the monastery of Monte Cassino. He pursued
his studies at the studium of Naples, and against the
wishes of his family he entered the order of S. Dominic
there in 1243. He was sent to work under the greatest
Dominican master, Albert of Cologne, with whom he spent
some years both at Cologne and Paris. In 1252 he was
called to teach at Paris, and till his death in 1274, at the
early age of forty-eight, he spent his time teaching, writing,
upholding the rights of the mendicant orders, and living a
life of great personal holiness under the Dominican rule,
in Paris, various towns in Italy, and at the papal university
of Rome (studium curiae). In 1272, at the height of his
fame, and in spite of the regrets of all the university of
Paris, he was recalled by his superiors to organise a
studium generale at Naples. He died on the way to the
general council of Lyons, 1274, at which he had been
commanded by the pope to assist. He was a profound
student, endowed with the encyclopedic knowledge at
which all contemporary scholars aimed, with an orderly
and synthetic mind, and a massive sobriety of judgment.
The thirteenth century is the century of the scholastic
philosophy par excellence, and it was dominated by the
work of Thomas, and his master, Albert. Thomas's
numerous treatises, among them especially the *Summa
contra Gentiles* and the *Summa Theologica* (the third part
of which was left unfinished at his death), mark its
climax.

In many special ways the scholastic work of Thomas had been prepared for and made possible. The universities, as has been said earlier, had codified, summarised and expounded the various branches of knowledge : grammars and manuals had been written, and medieval knowledge made surer and more accessible. The concordance of Hugh of S. Cher and the work of the Dominicans had provided an apparatus for the comparison of scriptural passages. The position of moderate realism had been half-worked out by philosophers subsequent to Abelard : Simon of Tournai († 1192) had taught that while similarity of essences exists in the objective order, and an abstract, universal concept in the subjective order, yet that things really possess the natures apprehended by the process of abstraction. John of Salisbury had reached the same position, and proceeded from it to a further study of psychology. The fourth Crusade and the fall of Constantinople allowed Byzantine learning to make its contribution to western philosophy, and with it came an increased interest in Jewish, Armenian and Syrian thought. Arabian philosophy had long flourished at Baghdad and Cordova, and was now to influence the west. Orthodox Moslem philosophers had already made their peace with Aristotle, especially in the person of Averrhoës, whose work was much studied in the west : but the Arabian conception of Aristotelianism was partly vitiated by the number of languages intervening between Aristotle and the Arabic translations, (Syriac and sometimes Hebrew). The Jewish philosopher Moses Maimonides († 1204) had further effected a reconciliation of Aristotle and Jewish philosophy, via the Arabic version of Averrhoës, and his works also were read in the west. Finally, in the time of Albert of Cologne and Thomas, Latin translations of Aristotle were being made directly from the Greek, partly as a result of the setting up of the Latin empire at Constantinople in 1204. Robert Grosseteste, lecturer at Paris and Oxford and later bishop of Lincoln, wrote a commentary on Aristotle's physics and ethics, the latter possibly with a translation. Italian and Sicilian philosophers translated certain Aristotelian works directly from Greek into Latin, and an even larger number of Latin translations made their way into Europe via the

Arabic versions of Cordova. It is not impossible that Thomas himself had some acquaintance with Greek, which was still a commercial language in south Italy : but he requested a fellow Dominican and oriental scholar, William of Moerbeke, to make him either a complete translation of Aristotle's works, or a revised translation of certain portions of them.

Albert of Cologne began the work of " reconstructing Aristotle for the use of the Latins," a work for which he was prepared by a knowledge of Jewish and Arabian Aristotelianism greater than that of his contemporaries. He wrote a free paraphrase of all Aristotle's works, which was meant to be a work of popularisation, and in it he distinguished the thought of Aristotle from that of his Jewish and Arabian commentators. He was interested in the natural sciences of his day, zoology, botany, geography, astronomy, alchemy and medicine, and recommended exact observation for the attainment of truth in this direction. But his mind was compendious rather than profound or original : he placed within reach of the medieval savant the previously acquired treasures of human knowledge : but he formed no definite, organic system of philosophy. He prepared the way for his disciple Thomas.

The merits of Thomas as a teacher, his brilliance of thought expressed in clear, simple, precise and scientific language, were perpetuated in the method of his two summae, and other treatises. His style was orderly, free from glosses and digressions, and every detail was fitted in so as to become subservient to the main truths he was establishing. His work appeared to contemporaries to be so original as to be revolutionary : its interest lay not in its appropriation of Aristotelian logical doctrines, but the whole Greek view of the natural sciences as embodied in Aristotle's non-logical works : " the enthusiasm of the thirteenth century for Aristotle was prompted by the very same spirit as the protests of Galileo against the Aristotelian traditionalists of the seventeenth century." [1] The originality of Thomas's work can be maintained, moreover, permanently, since it involved the substitution of

[1] *St Thomas Aquinas as a Philosopher*, A. E. Taylor, p. 9

Aristotelianism for Platonism as the specifically Christian philosophy. Nor can Thomas fairly be said to have accepted Aristotle uncritically and as an absolute authority : in his refutation of the Averrhoïsts, he contended that the question at issue was not what Aristotle personally meant to say, but whether what he said was true. He rejected, moreover, the ontological argument for the existence of God, which most of his contemporaries accepted : he differed from them by teaching that philosophy, apart from revelation, would lead to the belief that the world was created *ab aeterno :* he differed from Aristotle in not rejecting the Platonic Ideas as " empty words : " and while he accepted the Aristotelian astronomy with its machinery of rotating spheres because " it saves the appearances," he would not allow that this machinery was real, because " appearances may equally well be saved by some other theory yet to be put forward." Unlike his later followers, Thomas would have remained undisturbed by the discoveries of Galileo.

Thomism teaches that philosophy and theology are independent sciences within their own sphere. The criterion of distinction between the two sciences is not their subject matter, but the manner in which they deal with that subject matter. Philosophy examines the natural order by the light of reason : theology the supernatural order as revealed in the word of God. " The study of dogma rests on authority : the rational study of the universe on scientific demonstration." The existence of a divine revelation does not fall within the province of philosophy : it was a thesis which all medieval European thinkers granted. Consequently, in matters common to both sciences, philosophy cannot contradict theology. There can, however, be no opposition between the two, because granted the truth of divine revelation, it will never be opposed by philosophical truth : truth cannot contradict truth. Human reason can demonstrate several of the truths contained in the divine revelation, and even in the case of the mysteries which it accepts, can show that the supra-rational is not anti-rational.

To the Thomists, as to Aristotle, philosophy, sapientia, is a synthetic knowledge of nature. In their view the special sciences, the sciences of observation (astronomy, botany, etc.), come first in an ascending hierarchy of knowledge : above them come the speculative sciences, physics, mathematics, metaphysics. Among the speculative sciences are included history (including biblical history), ethics, and education. Philosophy, finally, is in the crowning sense the unified study of the whole of nature.

The *Summa Theologica* is divided into three parts, which treat respectively of God, of man, and of Christ as God and man. The first part deals with God's existence, nature and attributes, and of the Holy Trinity : God is the prime mover, the first cause, from Whom all things come, and the final cause, to Whom they must return. The second deals with man as fallen and capable of redemption, and of human behaviour, virtues and vices, law and grace. The third deals with Christ the Redeemer, opening up a way for man's journey back to God.

Thomist theology is demonstrated by Thomist metaphysic, founded on Aristotle. Scotus Eriugena, we have seen, had reduced his categories of being to one, the universal substance : he was a monist, a pantheist. Aristotle had defined ten categories of being ; dividing all being, and beings, first into two categories, substance and accident, he had proceeded to divide the accident into nine categories (quantity, quality, relation, time, etc.). This classification was statical : but he has also adopted a dynamic classification, based on the change or flux of being, the distinction between potentiality and act. That which changes had within itself the potentiality to be changed to that which it now actually is : potentiality may be classed as imperfection and non-being, but not as mere nothingness ; passage from the potential to the actual state is motion or movement. Thomism holds most firmly to the distinction between potentiality and act, essence and existence. God alone is pure act, the prime mover, with no admixture of potentiality (imperfection) whatever : in Him alone essence is identified with existence. Everything created contains both potentiality and act : it exists in a state of imperfection, it is changed and " becomes." " Potentiality which is really distinct from act can never become act unless it be reduced to act by something which is in act." Pure potentiality is substance without accidents ; a " thing " has one set of accidents now, it may have other accidents when it is changed : substance is therefore " in potentiality to the accidents which are its acts or perfections." The Thomist doctrine of transubstantiation demonstrates the real (substantial in the contemporary sense) presence of the body and blood of Christ in the eucharistic species by the use of this metaphysic, and the doctrine as to the nature of dimensive quantity which is part of it. Transubstantiation, the change of substance and retention of the accidents of bread and wine, had long been accepted by theologians, a miracle accredited by Christ's promise : the Thomist doctrine of transubstantiation expressed the change in the subtler Aristotelian metaphysic.

The distinction between potentiality and act also forms the basis of the Thomist psychology, and doctrine of the sacraments. The faculties of intellect and will are in a state of potentiality, are passive, towards their objects, thought and choice ; God pre-moves the intellect to the act of thought, and the will to the act of choice. The sacraments are instrumental causes of grace, producing grace in the soul : the soul is a potentiality, and grace is the act.

The work of Thomas was monumental for theologians, philosophers, and the learned generally, but its effect was to extend to popular religion. The twelfth century had witnessed great attacks on the sacraments from various heresies (see p. 227); the thirteenth century reacted in an increased expression of reverence, especially to the sacrament of the altar. The institution of the feast of Corpus Christi allowed the expression of a joy in the sacrament which had been out of keeping on the anniversary of its institution in holy week : the feast was kept first in the diocese of Liège, and in 1264 Urban IV, an ex-archdeacon of Liège, made the festival of general obligation for the first Thursday after Trinity Sunday. The new office for the festival was written by Thomas Aquinas himself.

Thomas the saint and poet is rather apt to be neglected for the study of Thomas the philosopher and theologian : but in both respects he was remarkable. Several of his Latin hymns, especially those written with reference to

N

Corpus Christi, became the heritage of catholic Christendom. The *Pange, lingua, gloriosi corporis mysterium*, with
its verse beginning, *Tantum ergo sacramentum* : the hymn
containing the *O salutaris hostia*, and the *Adoro te devote,
latens deiias*, expressed for popular devotion the doctrines
of the schools. Manuals of devotion for lay-people contained frequently verse prayers inspired by them, like the
fourteenth century

> Welcome, Lord, in form of bread !
> In Thee is both life and death,
>   Jesus is Thy name.
> Thou that art in Trinity,
> Have Thou mercy Lord of me,
>   And shield Thou me from shame.

CHAPTER XIV

THE AVIGNON POPES: THE CURIA: AND THE SCHISM

Boniface VIII and *Unam Sanctam*—Clement V—John XXII—
Results of Avignon papacy: general political—Results of Avignon
papacy: general administrative—Results of Avignon papacy:
organisation of curia—The Great Schism

THE twelfth and thirteenth century popes had struggled, not unsuccessfully, with the Hohenstaufen emperors: their successors were to find the national kings of Europe enemies as dangerous. The delimitation of the boundary between secular and spiritual jurisdictions had always been difficult, and it was likely to be more difficult. The power of the national kings, considered in relation to the spiritual claims of the papacy, was more compact and less vulnerable than that of the emperors had proved. It was more difficult to construct a society in which secular power should be national and spiritual power international, than one where both had been, at least in theory, international. This fact lies behind the weakness of the papacy in the fourteenth, fifteenth and sixteenth centuries, and accounts for the divisions of western Christendom at the Reformation.

The failure of pope Boniface VIII (1294–1303) to perceive this change in European politics accounts for the dramatic character of his pontificate, the contrast between his claims and his weakness. The claims he made for the papal power were as wide and as unfaltering as those of Gregory VII and Innocent III ; he was a canonist himself, and stated with particular boldness the claim to be the sole source and depositary of canon law. All law, he said, was locked within his breast. In the bull *Unam Sanctam* he laid down that the Christian faith taught that the head of the one, holy, catholic and apostolic church was Christ and His vicar Peter, " in whose power are the two swords, spiritual and temporal. For when the apostles said. Here are two swords (that is, in the church), the Lord replied not : It is too many : but : It is enough." " Either therefore is in the power of the church, the spiritual and the temporal. But the latter is to be used on behalf of the church, the former by the church : the former by the hand of the priest, the latter by that of kings and knights, but at the bidding and by the for-bearance of the priest. . . . For the temporal power ought to be subject to the spiritual power. . . . For as truth itself testifies, it belongs to the spiritual power to institute the earthly power, and if it be not good, to judge it. . . . Whoever therefore resisteth this power ordained by God, resisteth the ordinance of God. . . . Therefore we declare, state, define and pronounce that for every human creature to be subject to the Roman pope is altogether necessary for salvation." The claims which Boniface made so clearly and so definitely about the temporal power were a source of difficulty to later canonists : but certain irregularities in his election rendered it possible to argue that they were not binding on the whole church.

Boniface came into conflict chiefly with Edward I of England and Philip IV of France, whom as rivals for the English possessions in France he might, with prudence, have been able to play off against each other. Both resented, however, the bull *Clericis Laicos*, which in 1296 forbade the clergy to pay taxes to the secular power. Edward I, in particular need of funds, was trying to collect large sums, from both clergy and laity. He replied by outlawing the clergy, and Philip by prohibiting the export of money from France, which cut off French contributions to Rome : as a result Boniface had to recede from the position he had taken up, in the bull *Etsi de Statu*. Boniface then claimed Scotland as a papal fief, and forbade its invasion by Edward. In return, Edward summoned to Lincoln a parliament which forbade him to answer to the pope for any of his temporal rights. The pope's relations with both Edward and Philip continued hostile, and in 1302 he defined the papal claims in the *Unam Sanctam*. Philip then sent his servant, Nogaret, to seize Boniface, and Nogaret in company with the head of the Colonna family, a personal enemy of Boniface, surprised him at Anagni. The palace was stormed and plundered, Boniface's life threatened by the Colonna, and his person imprisoned for three days. A month later he died : and even Dante, his political enemy, wrote that when the fleur-de-lys entered Anagni, Christ, in His vicar, was made captive and mocked a second time. The pope who succeeded Boniface attempted at first to conciliate Philip : but at length he found it necessary to issue a bull against those who had taken part in the outrage at Anagni : and four weeks later he died—contemporaries said, by French poison. It was eleven months before a successor could be elected.

Even then the papacy was so much under French influence that for seventy years it resided beyond the Alps. The first of these Avignon popes was Clement V (1305–1313), who was chosen by the cardinals as likely to be anti-French, as he was a Gascon noble subject to Edward I. Actually, however, Philip bought him over. He was crowned at Lyons ; his first act was to make twelve French cardinals and one English one, and he never ventured into Italy. His pontificate was one long struggle to avoid making concessions to Philip which should prove fatal to the papal position later : and for this reason he sacrificed almost everything to French demands, rather than explicitly condemn the acts of Boniface VIII. He fixed his residence at Avignon in 1309, and though Avignon was in Provence, and not yet technically a French town, he and his successors, who lived there till 1378, were very much in the power of the French kings. In particular, Clement sacrificed the Templars to the greed of Philip to avoid the condemnation of Boniface : the Templars had outlived their usefulness, their lands were coveted by the secular rulers, and they were rumoured to have imbibed strange heresies from the east : but the form of their trial, and the burning of the Grand Master and sixty-nine of the Templars for fabulous crimes and heresies, was a rank injustice. But by this policy of complaisance, Clement got the question of Boniface referred to the council of Vienne, 1311, which exonerated his memory.

The papal residence at Avignon was a great scandal to the church. It was compared by the Spiritual Franciscans or Fraticelli to the captivity of Israel in Babylon, and the denunciations of Babylon in the Apocalypse supplied them with strictures against the papal court, rich and splendid and well-organised like the courts of the English and French kings. To contemporaries, Rome, the see of S. Peter, containing as it did the tomb of the apostles, was the natural centre of Christendom. Rome, it was felt, was an international city: the pope's own city: the successor of S. Peter should dwell in Rome, as he had in the past. The actual difficulties of residence in Rome, among the turbulent Roman nobility whom no king held in check, were realised more by the papal curia than Christendom at large.

The residence at Avignon was a special grievance to England, for it coincided with the first part of the Hundred Years' War. English clerics could not get promotion to the cardinalate, even when this was requested by the king: French cardinals abounded. Justice between Englishmen and Frenchmen at the court of Avignon was not likely to be evenhanded. The anti-papal movement in Henry III's reign had been financial: it now became political as well. National feeling was anti-French, and necessarily hostile to French influence over the papacy. Money collected for the papacy in England benefited France. The papal right to provide to English benefices played into French hands, and was especially resented. In 1351 parliament passed the great statute of Provisors, denying the papal right to provide to English benefices: and as this was not effective, it supplemented the measure with the statute of Praemunire, 1353. The latter forbade appeals to Rome, but was passed particularly to prevent suits about provided aliens from being taken to Avignon. Both statutes had to be repeated later, which shows that they were not successful. All this anti-French, anti-papal political and financial grievance lay behind the Wycliffite movement at the end of the fourteenth century, and

Wycliffe's championship by John of Gaunt. Wycliffe desired real spiritual reform (see p. 229) : but he was used to voice anti-French interests particularly in three ways. He declared as a theologian against the English obligation to pay the tribute promised by John : he declared against papal provisions, and the whole system of canon law by which the papal right to provide was buttressed ; and he denounced the temporalities of the church, and asserted the duty of the state to bring about disendowment. This was a most useful doctrine when funds were needed for the French war : and though Englishmen were not convinced by Wycliffe of the uselessness of episcopal or monastic endowments in general, they were ready to disendow the " alien priories," which sent money out of England to their mother houses in France. The alien priories were usually Cluniac houses, and such of them as did not make expensive bargains with the king for protection were dissolved in Henry V's reign.

After a two years' interregnum, a Frenchman succeeded at Avignon as John XXII (1316–1334). The French royal house was closely connected with the house of Anjou, which ruled in Naples and opposed the imperial (Ghibelline) leaders in Italy : John XXII, a canonist and theologian, trained in youth by the Dominicans, was the firm ally of the Angevin Robert of Naples. He claimed to decide a disputed election in the empire, and in 1327 declared one candidate, Lewis of Bavaria, deposed. A long struggle between pope and emperor followed, which lasted till Lewis's death in 1347 : but it was less violent than earlier ones, and conducted rather by pamphlets and treatises than by force of arms. The chief lawyer who wrote to support Lewis, and the temporal power generally against the spiritual, was Marsilio of Padua. The poet Dante had written a Latin treatise, the De Monarchia, in which he claimed divine origin and jurisdiction for the supreme temporal power, the Holy Roman emperor : Marsilio of Padua went further in his Defensor Pacis, and came down even more strongly on the side of the emperor. A later pope suspected that Wycliffe had drawn his opinions about the relations of the temporal and spiritual powers from Marsilio of Padua.

John XXII proved himself to possess energy and ability, and besides struggling with the emperor, and his allies, the Spiritual Franciscans, he introduced great changes in the administrative system of the curia. He was unpopular for the heavy taxation he succeeded in raising from the local churches: but he led personally an austere and simple life, and astonished his contemporaries by his disapproval of papal nepotism (appointment of relations to church offices). They compared him caustically to Melchisedech, "who had neither father nor mother nor line of descent,"—and consequently, no relations. The later Avignon popes call for no special mention, except in the matter of Innocent VI's attitude to the Golden Bull, of 1356. This document was issued by the emperor Charles IV, and laid down conditions for the future election of the emperor by the seven electors. Innocent VI protested because no mention was made of any papal right to veto or confirm the election, but Charles IV threatened to confiscate church property if measures were taken against him, and Innocent was forced to acquiesce.

The Avignon papacy had very important results both for the church in general, and for the papal curia itself, especially in administrative matters. The see of Rome was already the central source of canon law, the supreme court of appeal, the supervisor of the clergy, the central organ of leadership and administration in Latin Christendom. But in the course of the Avignon papacy the links between the central government and the local churches, and the governmental machine at Avignon itself, were both strengthened and elaborated: nor was the period lacking in papal efforts for the spiritual reform of the church.

The most general result of the papal transference to Avignon was increased expense, and increased raising of funds to meet it. The popes by leaving Rome lost their palaces, villas, and large sources of revenue: they would in any case have been badly in need of funds. But their expenses also were now far greater. They needed to finance petty wars in Italy, to protect their patrimony, and to oppose the Ghibellines: to finance certain Crusades, and to build themselves a suitable residence at Avignon. This they actually established on a scale of unprecedented dignity and artistic splendour. Nor was this all, for the Avignon popes held themselves bound to act as the patrons of the universities, of letters and of the arts in general : many of the funds harshly raised were splendidly spent. To meet the needs of a hugely increased revenue, a system was elaborated which was chiefly the work of John XXII, but which went back to Clement V in origin. The financial machinery of the papacy was made immensely more effective : considered as a bureau of finance, the advance in method and organisation was very great,—the equivalent of the departmental advance in organisation of the four-teenth century monarchies. A much larger revenue was raised : the papacy was much richer after its residence at Avignon than before. But the raising of these new funds was bad for the local churches, for they were generally taken from what had been episcopal sources of revenue, or from the lesser clergy.

Five special results were entailed by the new methods to raise the papal revenue. The French clergy and benefices became specially impoverished : they were the nearest and most accessible to taxation. Many benefices were already ruined by the Hundred Years' War : vicarages were burnt, and church lands desolated by the rival " com-panies " : increased clerical taxation completed their impoverishment.

Secondly, the right to collect " procurations " passed from the bishops to the popes, especially in France. Canonists defined procurations as " a moderate cost of food and lodging due to the bishop who visited a church, or to anyone who visited in his name," and by the four-teenth century they had become fixed money payments. John XXII began to collect procurations himself from any churches which had not been visited by an archbishop or bishop before his death, sending out papal collectors to take the fees. On one ground and another popes gradually assumed the right to all procurations, the local prelates sometimes surrendering them voluntarily in return for some temporary gain. Urban V made this custom of the papal reception of all procurations general for France. The bishops became poorer, the papal court richer. The disastrous consequence was that bishops gradually ceased to visit, since the fees that paid the travelling expenses of their retinue were not forthcoming, a lapse of custom which soon entailed relaxation of standards among the local clergy. Nicholas de Clemanges, an ecclesiastic anxious for reform, spoke of the appropriation of procurations as the " greatest wound of the church."

Thirdly, the papacy became richer by an increased levy of clerical tenths. A tenth part of the movable goods of bishops and clergy was sometimes levied, by the consent of the archbishops and bishops, for the secular governments : during the thirteenth century it was several times collected by papal agents to finance the Crusades : " in subsidium Terrae Sanctae." In the fourteenth century it was levied nominally for the Crusades, but as the Holy Land was now hopelessly lost, really for general papal projects and wars. It was levied by the council of Vienne, 1311, for six years following, and several times afterwards during the residence at Avignon.[1]

Fourthly, the general payment of annates goes back to the Avignon papacy. Annates, earlier termed *annualia* or *annalia*, consisted of the papal right to take the " first year's fruit," or revenue, from all benefices collated by the holy see. It was a right in earlier centuries only enforced in times of special need, but the demand had latterly become more frequent. It was now to be extended to other benefices. Innocent VI made all benefices subject to it which had been exchanged at the court of Avignon— the greatest centre for such exchanges. Gregory XI added all benefices whose elections had ever been confirmed by the pope : and by 1400 a very large proportion of all benefices had been accepted as regularly subject to annates.

Lastly, the great increase of papal provisions helped to enrich the curia, while rendering it very difficult for the local bishops to govern their dioceses, since their right to reward good service by promotion was limited. It had never been complete, for apart from the questions of private patronage, kings and local potentates had frequently demanded that the clerks of their civil service should be rewarded with benefices. The papal claim to provide clashed both with this custom, and the bishops'

[1] The work of Mr. W. E. Lunt has shown that, in England, a surprisingly large proportion of those papal tenths went to the king; see his *Financial Relations of the Papacy with England*, 1939.

own rights. In 1344 Clement VI proclaimed that " the right of disposition (appointment) went back ultimately to the Roman pontiff, in the case of all churches, dignities, offices, and ecclesiastical benefices," which was an extraordinary straining of earlier canon law. The need of funds lay at the back of the claim. Hosts of poor clerks flocked to the court at Avignon, and offered small inducements for appointment to a benefice important in the aggregate. Moreover, Clement VI perceived that a reputation for munificence enhanced papal prestige. "No one," he said, " ought to retire discontented from the presence of a prince . . . my predecessors knew not how to be popes."

The general results of the Avignon papacy included not only financial developments, but attempts to reform and further to centralize the church. The universities, the friaries, and the increased possibility of peaceful scholarly life, had drawn away from fourteenth century monasticism many of those who would earlier have been its best recruits. The Hundred Years' War in France and civil wars in the empire had destroyed many monasteries, and left the monks to lead uncloistered, disreputable lives at large. Benedict XII in 1336 issued the so-called " Benedictine Bull " for the reform of the black monks : it urged the return of all monks whose houses had been destroyed to some other house of the order : it urged what amounted to the formation of the independent houses into an order, by the holding of triennial chapters for the heads of houses : it urged the teaching of Latin to novices, and the sending of the most promising students to the universities. The welfare of the Austin canons was similarly dealt with. Efforts were made to suppress heresy, especially by the use of the Inquisition against the Cathari, the Béguines and the Spirituals. In various ways a reform of the secular clergy was attempted. Synods were ordered to be held frequently : the holding of benefices with cure of souls in plurality was forbidden : non-residence was forbidden : and efforts were made to educate the secular clergy by founding universities in France and Italy,—their number was increased in the next century. The answer to the query, why these reforms, and particularly those of

Benedict XII, were not more successful, lies in the general fourteenth century desire to evade them, coupled with the pope's loss of spiritual prestige at Avignon and during the papal schism that followed. Benedict XII himself was compared to Nero for his severity, and his reign was too short for his reforms to take root. All later popes granted too many dispensations from them for any general results. The next pope to Benedict was particularly lenient to the religious orders, and although the Benedictine bull remained law till the council of Trent, the reform of the Benedictine houses was almost nullified.

ꞌ Centralisation in the church had been proceeding since the days of Gregory VII : in certain respects it was never greater than in the fourteenth century. Apart from increased papal appointment to benefices, and judicial appeals to the curia, the popes were in close touch with both the universities and the religious orders. They regulated the granting of university degrees in theology and canon law, and kept a watch over the degrees granted : the English calendar of papal letters has one or two cases of scholars delated to the pope " for holding fantastic opinions at the universities,"—though no action followed. The religious orders looked to the papacy as their special protector, and were in close touch with the papal court : even the Friars Preacher had a special " cardinal protector " there.

During the Avignon papacy the organisation of the curia became more elaborate and methodical ; it was divided into four main departments. (1) The Apostolic chamber dealt with finance ; it was headed by the chamberlain, who appointed the papal collectors and supervised their accounts, and the secretaries (scribes), who did the work of the department. The treasurer was in actual charge of the funds. The apostolic chamber had also its own law-court, headed by the auditor and vice-auditor. (2) The chancery dealt with the papal correspondence. It comprised a bureau of petitions (supplications), a bureau of examinations (for clerks who came to the curia to demand benefices), a sealing department (the leaden seal affixed to papal letters gave them their name of " bulls "), and a record department which registered letters received. A college of secretaries was gradually created to deal in this manner with papal correspondence, and expedite business and the examination as to the morals and learning of seekers after benefices proved useful. (3) The third department, the law-court, was in a special sense the curia. All bishops had originally presided over their own law-court : by the fourteenth century this court, known as the consistory court, was presided over by the bishop's legal delegate. The papal consistory was of course more elaborate than that of an ordinary bishop or archbishop : it could consist of a session of pope and cardinals, or the pope's legal delegate and certain cardinals, or the separate courts presided over by the different cardinals. The preliminary stage of certain cases was still sometimes heard by the pope himself in the court of audience, or rota. The marshal of the curia, originally a domestic servant of the papal household, had also his own court, which was reformed in the period. (4) The papal penitentiary dealt with the penance and absolution of those whom local bishops or archbishops were not competent to absolve. The canon law recognised two tribunals : the *forum externum* or consistory court of the bishop, and the *forum internum* or confessional. The latter of course could not reach the offender unless he repented and voluntarily came before it for sentence. In the *forum internum* the parish priest could absolve for relatively insignificant sins : but those of serious nature, or which caused public scandal, were reserved to the bishop, unless they were further reserved to the papal penitentiary. The holy see did not draw up a complete list of reserved cases, and the number varied from time to time. The second Lateran council reserved to the pope the absolution of any who " suadente diabolo " laid violent hands on a clerk : in 1287 bishop Quivil of Exeter stated in his diocesan synod a list of twenty offences which required papal absolution. These included assault on clerks, arson, destruction of church property, usury and simony. The journey to Rome was, however, often remitted, and the bishop allowed to deal with the penitent, when the transgression was slight, or when the penitent was old, sick, poor or otherwise reasonably hindered. In practice also, the papal penitentiary was often informed by letter, granted absolution, and handed the culprit over to the bishop for salutary penance. As a mark of favour to certain bishops, the popes frequently granted bulls, authorising them to absolve from a certain number of reserved cases, without reference to Rome : so that in practice papal cases were to a large extent left in the hands of the local bishops. The question whether the local bishop or the pope dealt with the matter depended as much on the status of the offender as the moral gravity of the offence, because public scandal increased as the offender rose in the social scale.

The papal residence at Avignon had been a scandal to the church, but it was to terminate in a greater, the Great Schism of 1378–1417. Of all the efforts made to induce the popes to return to Rome, those of Catherine of Siena, the Dominican tertiary and saint, were perhaps the most remarkable. Her letters to Gregory XI, imploring him to return, were marked with the greatest frankness. " Open the eyes of your intelligence," she wrote, " and look steadily at the matter. You will then see, Holy Father, that it is more needful for you to win back souls than to recover your earthly possessions." The emperor Charles IV, known for his piety and ecclesiastical zeal as the " parsons' kaiser," had long urged the same course, and in 1377 pope Gregory XI was persuaded to return to Rome, though his life there was personally unsafe from the violence of the Roman nobles. He died, however, in the year following, and Charles IV used all his influence to get a non-French pope elected. This would have suited his own German politics, and secured the papal residence at Rome. An Italian of fiercely anti-French views was elected in 1378 as Urban VI : but the French cardinals seceded, and elected a rival pope as Clement VII. Clement VII forthwith returned to Avignon. For two months the emperor tried to rouse Europe to the danger of the situation. A French pope, he argued, would be dominated by the French king, Charles V, and Charles V could dominate half Europe. His brother was duke of Burgundy, and that brother's wife heiress to the count of Flanders : another brother claimed the succession in Naples, and the kings of Hungary and Poland were also members of the same family. But in November, 1378, Charles IV died, his task uncompleted, and the papal Schism became permanent and formal.

The Schism lasted for nearly forty years. Urban and Clement died, but successors were elected to each pope in double lines. Each rival pope maintained his own curia, and papal organisation was duplicated. The emperors, the English, and most of the northern nations supported the Urbanist line of popes : the French always the Clementine line at Avignon. The allies of France, as Scotland, Spain and Naples, also supported the Clementines : the rest of Europe was divided. Charles IV and Catherine of Siena had succeeded only to fail : the existence of two popes each competing for the allegiance of Christendom, and dividing it geographically, as no earlier schism had done, was a greater scandal than ever. Vested interests rendered it impossible to persuade either line of popes to yield spontaneously, and it was the perception that some extraordinary expedient would have to be adopted, to deal with the extraordinary situation, that gave rise to what was known as the Conciliar movement. Crises in Christian history had been dealt with, in the last three or four hundred years, by general councils summoned by the pope, as the councils of Clermont, the third and fourth Lateran, Lyons and Vienne : no such means of summoning a general council was now open. The summons of a general council without papal summons was the means at length adopted for the healing of the Great Schism.

CHAPTER XV

THE FOURTEENTH CENTURY DIOCESE AND PARISH IN ENGLAND

Bishops and the civil service—The officers of the diocese—Appointment to benefices : episcopal supervision—Diocesan synod and consistory—Spiritual duties of the bishop—The parish priest : administrative and social duties—The parish priest: spiritual duties

THE ecclesiastical division of the country into provinces, dioceses and parishes was common to Europe, as was also the intermediate division of the diocese into archdeaconries and rural deaneries, and the general constitution of cathedral and collegiate churches. But general similarity of organisation in the middle ages was never strained to an exact uniformity, even within the limits of a single country. Church institutions were of ancient and natural growth, and custom crystallised in different regions in different centuries, producing a very complex whole. The small Italian diocese was not worked by as elaborate a machinery as the large English or German one. The sixth and seventh century archpriest of France persisted in many instances with powers something like those of the English rural dean : he was scarcely known in England. Local churches had their own liturgies, rites and calendars of saints' days. Of those curious Saturnalian adaptations, the feast of the boy bishop and the feast of the ass, the first was common to England and France, the second unknown in England. Festivals which became common to the whole church usually began as local observances. It seems therefore clearer in discussing the ordinary working life of the fourteenth century church, both in this chapter and the next, to consider England

only, though the description would broadly apply to the
rest of western Europe as well.   The round of the greater
festivals, the sacraments, the Latin mass and offices, the
diocese and parish, were common to Latin Christendom.

The English dioceses in the fourteenth century included
Canterbury, Rochester, Chichester, Winchester, Salisbury,
Exeter, Bath and Wells, London, Norwich, Ely, Lincoln,
Worcester, Hereford, Coventry and Lichfield, York,
Carlisle, and Durham : the Welsh bishoprics were those
of S. Asaph, Bangor, S. Davids and Llandaff.   The boun-
daries of the English dioceses were much as they remained
till the sixteenth and nineteenth centuries, when fresh
processes of subdivision began.   The medieval diocese of
Lincoln, however, stretched right across the centre of
England, and included the university of Oxford.

The fourteenth century bishop might, like Grandison
of Exeter, have risen to promotion from the ability he
had displayed as canon or dean of some church : he might,
though much more rarely than in early centuries, have
been a monk : and he might in the majority of cases have
risen through the royal civil service.   The king still
depended on the clergy in large part for his trained officials.
A lay chancellor was appointed first in 1340, but during
the greater part of the fourteenth century the chancellor
was an ecclesiastic.   These civil servants usually remained
in minor orders for many years, while they were rewarded
with canonries and benefices without cure of souls : they
were frequently only ordained priest when elected through
royal influence to some bishopric.   When bishop Sandale
was elected to Winchester in 1316, he had been in the
king's service many years, and already held two cathedral
offices, eight prebends, and ten rectories.   Bishop William
of Wykeham, who was perhaps of more service to the
English church than any other fourteenth century bishop,
was of humble birth, attended only the Winchester grammar school, and began life as the clerk of the constable
at Winchester : he entered the royal service, and practically created the post of head clerk of the office of works
through his administrative ability.   Before this, each
royal castle had a clerk-paymaster in charge of building
and repairs ; Wykeham finally supervised all the local

o

clerks-in-charge. He attended to state business as a privy councillor, and was so useful that Froissart applied to him the biblical verse : " Everything was done through him, and without him nothing was done." When he was elected bishop of Winchester in 1367 he had accumulated an extraordinary number of prebends all over England, the deanery of S. Martins-le-Grand, and the archdeaconry of Lincoln. When he had become bishop he was at once made chancellor : but while he continued to play a considerable part in politics till his death, he did not neglect his cathedral or his diocese. Bishop Stapeldon of Exeter both reorganised the royal exchequer, and carrie& out conscientiously his diocesan duties. The administrative duties of a bishop made it in many respects useful that he should have had the training of a civil servant : but nevertheless, by the end of the fourteenth century pious churchmen considered the connexion between the civil service and the episcopate too close. A fourteenth century bishop was almost certain to be no rogue and no fool : but he was equally unlikely to be a saint. When a cheerful worldling like Chaucer wanted subjects for pleasant satire, he picked out the pardoner, the monk and the friar ; but a serious and orthodox reformer like Gower inveighed rather against the general " worldliness " of prelates and the superior clergy, their desire for bishoprics and benefices, and their willingness to shear rather than shepherd their sheep.

The diocesan work of a bishop, apart from any secular duties which he might continue to perform, was administrative, judicial, and spiritual. He supervised the diocesan personnel, property and revenue, (as well as securing certain payments from his clergy for the state and the pope) : he was responsible for the church courts of his see : and he performed certain spiritual duties, or got them performed by another bishop.

The personnel of his diocese consisted of his cathedral chapter, the archdeacons, the rural deans, the parish clergy, unbeneficed clerks, the regular clergy, and the lawyers of his consistory. Cathedral chapters, whether secular or monastic, were no longer in close touch with their bishop, though individual members were often used by him in the government of the diocese. The cathedral canons had houses round the close, (which had been the semi-monastic enclosure of the Carolingian period), but resided part of the year in the country parishes often attached to their prebends ; or often, they instituted a vicar or a " curatus," took the balance of their prebendal income, and resided at the court, the papal curia, or one of the universities. Monastic chapters were resident. But in either case, the bishop maintained a separate household, and lived at his palace, and at his various manors. Jealousy between bishop and chapter was frequent : a chronicler wrote that " it was natural and customary for the monks of Rochester to annoy and slander their well-deserving bishops, who were always compelled to have a staff ready to defend themselves against the monks," and difficulties between a bishop and his secular chapter were equally possible. The election of the dean of a secular cathedral, or the prior of a monastic one, was made by the chapter, after the bishop had issued his congé d'élire : and the bishop's control over it varied greatly in different sees. The election of abbots, priors and provosts of monasteries and collegiate churches was also supervised by the bishop, unless the monastery were exempt from his control and under papal protection.

The number of archdeacons varied in size with the diocese. Up till the ninth century each bishop had had but one archdeacon, whose administrative supervision was exercised over the whole diocese. It became usual in the ninth century in France, however, for bishops to appoint more than one archdeacon, and for sees to be broken up into local or territorial archdeaconries. The same thing happened in Germany a little later. There is very little evidence for the existence of territorial archdeacons in England at the time of the Norman Conquest, but they appeared soon after in most dioceses. In that of Canterbury, however, a general archdeacon of the older type was retained, and the see was not divided into two archdeaconries till 1841. It is still the function of the archdeacon of Canterbury, in his character of general assistant to the archbishop, to induct the bishops of the southern province into possession of their bishoprics.

By the fourteenth century most English bishops had two or more archdeacons, each exercising authority over a well-defined area. The archdeacon was appointed by the bishop, but his office was a benefice, like a rectory or a vicarage, from which he was irremovable except of his own will. Originally he had been merely the assistant of the bishop, but his rights had become so fixed on the continent that he was a serious rival to him. Even in England, where their rights never reached this pitch, some archdeacons, like the archdeacon of Richmond, possessed all the jurisdictional rights of the bishop within their own area. The archdeaconries were subdivided into rural deaneries. The clergy of each rural deanery met in chapter about once a month, and were generally presided over by the archdeacon : but they received episcopal mandates through the rural dean. It was the bishop's duty to supervise and register the admission of these officials, and also admissions to parish churches, chapels, and even hermitages. He also appointed an " official " to preside over his consistory, though this was an office revocable at will : and if he were absent from the diocese (to attend parliament or for other reason), he appointed a vicar-general to perform most of his administrative acts.

To some livings the bishop " collated " or appointed himself : but most were in the hands of some private patron or corporation. In that case the patron presented a candidate to the bishop, who ordered the archdeacon to inquire in the chapter of the rural deanery whether the patron had the right to present, and whether the candidate were suitable, had other benefices, and was in orders. If the report were satisfactory, he ordered the archdeacon to institute the candidate to the living. The council of Lyons, 1274, forbade any candidate under twenty-five, or not in priest's orders, to be instituted to a parish church : but Boniface VIII allowed bishops to dispense with this decree, and permit clerks to be instituted, and given seven years to study, before they were required to take priest's orders : though they must become subdeacons (i.e. necessarily celibate) within a year. Bishops' registers show that leave of absence for a year to study grammar and singing at some cathedral school was often granted : the candidate in this case must have been really qualifying himself for his duties. But they show that leave of absence was oftener granted for study at an English or foreign university, in which case the living was being used as an university scholarship. Any absentee rector or vicar was bound to pay a stipendiary priest or " curatus " to do his parochial work in his absence, and the latter was of course removable at his will.

The bishop's income was largely derived from his manors, for which he appointed bailiffs and stewards, and which he must not allow to depreciate. The cathedral, churches, hospitals, and monasteries of the see he supervised by appointing special commissioners, or normally through his archdeacons. Parish churches, and their tithes, could only be " appropriated " to monasteries or cathedral chapters by his licence, and it was his duty to see that the " vicars " of churches thus appropriated had a house and garden and enough to live on. The chief duty of the archdeacon on visitation was to see that the churches were kept in repair, and supplied with the necessary books, vestments and altar vessels, and that their lands were not " wasted."

The bishop supervised his diocese by the process of visitation. In fourteenth century England it was held the canonical right of the bishop to visit his whole clergy every three years : but most bishops could not cover their diocese and attend to their other duties in that time, and in some sees visitation was infrequent. Bishops could visit their cathedral chapter, their consistory, their collegiate churches, their monasteries and their parishes, all with the intention of inquiry and reform. Canon law allowed them to visit with a train of thirty horses, a number they sometimes exceeded : thirty shillings, or rather over, was a normal sum to demand from a parish in lieu of lodging and entertainment. Several parishes were often visited together, which decreased expense. The bishop held his visitation in church, and summoned all rectors, vicars and chaplains, and three or four laymen from each parish visited. The clergy were asked to show their letters of orders and institution, and the dispensations for any special privilege they were enjoying.   The laymen were then asked whether the rectors and vicars fulfilled their duties and led a good life.   Did they visit the sick and take the sacrament to the dying ?   Were they often absent from the parish?   Did they wear the clerical dress ? frequent taverns ?   play dice ?   engage in secular occupations, etc. ?   The conduct of the laity was then inquired into.   Did they work on the Lord's day or festivals ? Did they commit any of the seven deadly sins ?   Did they publicly brawl or frequent taverns, etc. ?   The property and ornaments of the church were then examined, and repairs of the fabric or lack of books ordered to be made if necessary.

If the bishop wished to legislate for his see, or further explain the canons of some recent provincial synod, he drew up statutes and had them " read and published " in his diocesan synod.   He could, however, issue them simply as an edict, from his palace or manor.   The synod was an assembly of the clergy of the diocese, including priors and abbots, held in the fourteenth century once or twice a year and lasting three days.   The ostiarius exercised the last relics of his proper function by keeping the door of the sacred synod, and the archdeacon opened the proceedings with proper prayers.   The consent of the clergy to the bishop's statutes was not asked : canons were " promulged," not voted upon.   They covered the whole range of subjects under the bishop's supervision. Business matters, however, were also decided upon, and these were discussed by the clergy, who could also make any complaint to the bishop.   A diocesan synod in 1300 discussed such matters as the payment of a pension to a certain abbot, the enclosure of nuns, whether a certain rector ought to be deprived, the questions of some undedicated chantries, and whether it were better to satisfy the bishop of Llandaff for his expenses in coming to Gloucester.

The bishop's consistory court held sessions about once a month, and they lasted three or four days.   They were held usually in some part of the cathedral : but sometimes a consistory was regularly held in two or three of the chief towns of the diocese as well.   More often there was only

Iona(Hii)
Sodor

Melrose

Lindisfarne

Carlisle   Durham

Whithern

⚜ YORK

Lincoln

Bangor   S.Asaphs

Lichfield

Ely   Norwich

Coventry
Cambridge

Hereford   Worcester

Menevia
St.Davids

Oxford
Llandaff   Dorchester

Bristol   London

Bath
Rochester
Wells   Salisbury   CANTERBURY
⚜Winchester

Exeter   Chichester

ENGLISH AND WELSH BISHOPRICS c 1300

one court, with one set of rolls and registers, but it was to some extent itinerant. The judge of the court was the " official," who was often a canon of the cathedral as well, and he had an assistant known as a delegate or commissary. Each consistory had a certain number of advocates, trained canonists, and possibly civilian lawyers as well, and these acted like modern barristers. It had also a certain number of proctors, licensed by the bishop, who can be compared to the modern solicitors. Both proctors and advocates were hired by litigants to take charge of or argue their case. The consistory had also an examiner, who took the testimony of witnesses, to be presented in written form to the judge, a registrar, one or two notaries public, and an apparitor or summoner, with his henchmen, (most unpopular personages). But a good deal of legal business was done outside the consistory. The official or his delegate could hear cases " pro tribunali sedente," in the presence of witnesses and a notary public, as could the bishop himself: and the bishop could appoint special commissaries to hear a particular case. Citations to appear before the bishop personally, wherever he should be in his diocese, were a favourite medieval grievance.

Each archdeacon had a court, modelled upon the consistory, to which he appointed an official and delegate, advocates, proctors, registrars and summoners. In 1341 archbishop Stratford ordered that, on account of the " pestiferous crowd of summoners," archdeacons should keep only one for each deanery : and another bishop denounced the " damnable presumption of summoners " who cited people for crimes without instructions, to extort money from them. Each diocese had also many " peculiars," or local jurisdictions and courts, particularly that of the cathedral chapter. The appeal from the archdeacon's court lay to the consistory, and from the consistory to the archbishop's court.

The bishop's spiritual work consisted in the conferring of orders, of confirmation, in blessing abbots and abbesses, and in hallowing churches, and reconciling them after bloodshed. The numbers admitted to orders, even holy orders, were very much larger in proportion to the population than nowadays. Bishop Stapeldon of Exeter ordained

1005 persons at his first ordination, and 1427 during the first year of his episcopate. By papal privilege a priest could give the tonsure and lower orders, but only the bishops could confer the higher. Ordination to the higher orders was given four times a year, in the Ember weeks, generally in the cathedral, but also at other important churches. Candidates were summoned to present themselves the Wednesday before, to be examined for three days orally by the archdeacon, as to their character, learning, and whether " they firmly grasped the catholic faith, and could express it in simple language." They must be eighteen before they could be admitted to the sub-diaconate, nineteen for the diaconate, and twenty-four for the priesthood. Servile birth, illegitimacy and bodily defects were bars to ordination, though the bishop could dispense illegitimates for admission to the minor orders, and the pope to the higher. Bishops could only ordain to the higher orders those with a title to a living, or who had sufficient patrimony on which to maintain themselves. This usage had survived since the time when all the clergy of the see were the bishop's familia, for whose maintenance he had to provide. The actual ceremony of ordination was long : it might last from nine in the morning till three or four in the afternoon, while bishop and ordinands were all fasting. The candidates for each of the seven orders were presented by the archdeacon, instructed in the peculiar functions of the order, received its symbol, and were blessed by the bishop with appropriate prayers. All the different orders were conferred at the beginning or in the course of the mass, at which all communicated. Candidates might receive the three minor orders in one day, but not the minor orders and a major, or two major orders. All candidates had to seek ordination from the bishop of their diocese or to obtain letters dimissory from him to be ordained by some other bishop.   .

The bishop also dedicated churches and consecrated altars in person, with the appropriate rite ; if a church or cemetery thereafter were polluted by bloodshed, it could not be used till it had been " reconciled " by being sprinkled with holy water. Reconciliation involved a good deal

of expense and fees for the parishioners, and a financial motive was added to the religious one for the prevention of brawling.

The rites for all these spiritual acts of the bishop together with those for blessing abbots, abbesses, veiling nuns, enclosing hermits and anchoresses, blessing the chrism, etc., were recorded in the *pontificale* of the see. This book, like the missal, breviary, and other service books, had the same structure and important ceremonies and prayers in all the dioceses, but had local variations. Each diocese had its own "use," but in the north of England the York use, and in the south of England the Sarum or Salisbury use, obtained wider than diocesan acceptance. The bishop had final liturgical authority, but normally exercised it only by ordering " processions," (litanies sung during procession), at critical times, as when the king summoned parliament, went abroad, was ill, or engaged in war; or when the kingdom was swept by famine or pestilence.

The work of the parish priest had its administrative side, but it was much more largely spiritual and social. A rector had to see to the collection of all the tithes : a vicar had often the right to the lesser tithes, excluding the " great tithe " of corn. The medieval church was not run on a system of voluntary finance : the parish priest could excommunicate for non-payment of tithe, and the secular courts would enforce the obligation. The parish priest also tilled or let out the glebe land of his church. He was bound to keep the chancel of his church in repair, and see that the church-wardens repaired the nave : he was also bound to see that no fairs or morris dancings were held in the churchyard and that it was not otherwise profaned.

It was his duty to relieve the poor, and strangers, as far as he could himself : though his stipend was usually too small to permit of much almsgiving. But as there was no state system of poor relief, it was his especial duty to exhort his parishioners to care for the poor, and to exhort the dying to leave alms for this purpose. All manuals for priests and laymen stressed the " six[1] works of mercy bodily, and the six works of mercy spiritually," and they

---

[1] Sometimes seven.

formed a stock syllabus for medieval sermons. The six works of mercy bodily included : feeding the hungry, giving drink to the thirsty, harbouring the houseless, clothing the naked, visiting the sick, visiting prisoners and burying the dead. All collections of homilies and " exempla " contain exhortations to charity. One story in the collection of the Knight of La Tour-Landry dwelt on the wickedness of luxury while the poor were starving. There was a lady, it said, that had two " litell doggis," and loved them so that she took great pleasaunce in the sight and feeding of them : and " she made every day dress and make for them dishes with sops of milk, and often gave them flesh. But there was once a friar that said to her, that it was not well done that the dogs were fed and made so fat, and the poor people so lean and famished for hunger. And so the lady for his saying was wroth with him, but she would not amend it." So the lady came to a bad end, as she deserved. " And therefore here is a good ensample that ladies nor gentle-women should not have their pleasaunce in such beasts, not give them that the poor people might be sustained with, that die for hunger, the which be God's creatures and made to His likeness." The personal care of the sick and poor, their succour in famines and pestilences, was always urged as a Christian duty on medieval women. Extra food, beyond what was needed for the meal, was often cooked in monasteries, and even in castles, for the beggars at the gate, especially at festival times, and the lives of medieval saints like S. Elizabeth of Hungary show in what esteem those corporal works of mercy were held. The Elizabethan system of compulsory poor-relief grew from the medieval system of almsgiving for the poor in church. Other important parts of the priest's social work were the reconciliation of parishioners who had quarrelled, and sometimes the duty of acting as chaplain to a parish gild, which was half burial-club and friendly society, half devotional in character. He might also help with the Corpus Christi and other gild plays : miracle and mystery plays were fairly frequent, and indeed the only drama in fourteenth century England. It was his duty to bless the crops, with processions through the fields, at Rogation tide, (to have trodden down growing corn was a sin to be mentioned in confession), and to offer the first fruits of the harvest at Loaf-mass, or Lammas. His manual would contain special blessing for sick children, or animals, or houses and natural objects for which the divine protection was desired, and he would exorcise evil spirits and ghosts. But it was his duty to warn his people not to use spells and incantations, or gather herbs by moonlight, saying the Paternoster backwards, or use sortilege or necromancy.

The spiritual work of the parish priest consisted of the instruction of his people and the administration of the sacraments. He was supposed to preach on the Sunday gospel at the parish mass, or to instruct his people in the creed, commandments, sacraments, seven works of mercy, seven virtues, and seven deadly sins ; Grosseteste in the thirteenth century found many curates unable to preach, and required that in this case the curate should ask some neighbouring cleric charitably to expound the meaning of the Sunday gospel to him, so that he might rehearse it in English to his parishioners : " or else resign he up his benefice." But clerical education was better and Sunday sermons common in parish churches by the end of the fourteenth century.

The priest would normally say mass every day : the setting of hands on a " mass-dial," which still remains outside some churches, indicated the time of the " morrow-mass." Lords and ladies heard mass every day in their chapels, but the peasantry could only attend on Sundays and festivals. A book of instructions for pages, after telling them how to help their master to dress, ran :—

> Prince or prelate if it be, or other potentate,
> Ere he enter in the church, be it early or late,
> Perceive all things for his pew, that it be preparate.
> Both cushion, carpet, curtain, beads and book, forget
>   not that.

There were several unofficial manuals for the use of lay-folk at mass, generally in verse, like the *Lay-Folks' Mass-Book*. This had been first written in old French,

when all gentle-people spoke that tongue, but it had soon
been transferred into English. It did not translate the
Latin prayers of the missal, but explained the course of
the service, and supplied English prayers at certain parts.
Men ought, the manuals said, to come into church quietly
and kneel down, and " holden no parliament " with their
neighbours. They should stand up at the gospel out of
reverence, even if they understood it not, and cross themselves in the creed, and not walk about in the churchyard
during the sermon. This was followed by the English
" bidding of the beads," when the priest asked for the
prayers of the congregation for all holy church, and their
mother church, and this church in which they prayed :
for archbishops and bishops, and especially the bishop of
this see : for himself and the clerks that served the church :
for the Holy Land, that God would deliver it. At the
elevation of the host men might pray,

> Lovèd be Thou, king,
> And thankèd be Thou, king,
>   Jesu, all my joying !
> Give me grace to sing
> The song of Thy loving.

Only monks, nuns and priests made their communion at
all frequently : all, however, received it after confession
at Easter.

Though the priest himself said the canonical hours or
offices daily, these were strictly speaking no concern of the
laity. It is only in fifteenth century manuals that exhortations to attend the Sunday mattins and vespers begin.
Earlier, lay people completed their Sunday duty by attendance at the parish mass at nine o'clock. In cathedrals
and collegiate churches mass would be said at the parish
altar, at the head of the nave : mattins and vespers would
be said by the canons beyond the screen, in the chancel,
the canon's part of the church. The long service of
mattins would be said or sung, on Sundays as on week-
days, at a very early hour, vespers in the afternoon.
These liturgical offices were not designed for lay-people,
nor very suitable for them. They were in Latin : a single

office was part of a daily and larger scheme, and incomplete in itself : and monotony was avoided by the application of the fourfold interpretation of scripture, in which the lay listener would scarcely be instructed. The psalms of which the offices were mainly composed were preceded by a solitary verse or antiphon, which varied with the season, and changed their whole colour and meaning. To the person who recited them, the psalmist's words might be the words of Christ in His passion, of the martyr in his torment, or the groans and tears of his own soul, according to the day and the antiphon. Words like " The good shepherd giveth his life for the sheep " might be green and cool like the shepherd's psalm one day, and take on a new tinge of blood for the feast of S. Thomas of Canterbury the next. But all this could scarcely be felt by the lay person listening in the nave to Sunday vespers.

One of the earliest English manuals was intended to help the priest, the " shrift-father " of his parish, in hearing confessions : it was a translation of a treatise on the vices and virtues, and was called the *Again-bite of In-wit,* (a literal translation of the Latin for *Remorse of Conscience*). The priest on Shrove Tuesday or in Lent heard all his people's confessions. It was then his duty to ask them whether they could say the creed, Paternoster, ten commandments, etc., in Latin or English. If they were ignorant, he questioned them about their sins, under the heading of the seven deadly sins, (pride, wrath, envy, sloth, covetousness, gluttony and lechery), and he then gave them advice, penance and absolution. There were no " confessionals " in the middle ages : the priest sat, and the penitent knelt before him, generally somewhere in the chancel. The fourteenth century font at East Dereham, Norfolk, has carvings of the seven sacraments. In the picture of penance, the priest sits on a stool inside the altar rail, a penitent kneels before him, a prosperous looking merchant tells his beads very close by, at the head of a queue of kneeling figures, and two plump, attentive angels hover close to the priest's head, listening with interest to the confession. It gives the impression of a rather crowded sacrament.

The priest was bound to baptize the children of his parishioners, to hasten to administer the sacrament to any sickly, new-born infant, and to instruct the midwife to baptize it herself if he could not get there in time. He must see that she baptized it in the name of the Father, and of the Son, and of the Holy Ghost, and did not merely bestow upon it some vague blessing. Most baptisms took place in church: the naked infant was plunged in the font, which was large enough for this purpose, and its forehead was anointed with the sacred chrism and bound round with a white cloth. The child's sponsors made the Christian renunciations and promises on its behalf, and were thereafter related by "spiritual affinity" both to it and to each other. To have "lifted up the same child from the font" was a canonical impediment to marriage, though a dispensation could be obtained.

Confirmation was administered to quite young children by the bishop, as he travelled round his diocese from manor to manor. The child was blessed and anointed with the chrism: the "seven gifts of the Holy Ghost" was another frequent subject of exposition by medieval priests and manuals. The administration of confirmation in the early medieval centuries must have been casual in the extreme, a careless bishop blessing the children without troubling to dismount, and the children themselves running about among his retinue, between the horses' legs. By the fourteenth century the bishop usually blessed the children in church, or in the chapel of his manor. Parents were exhorted by the priest to bring their children to the bishop, but no regular appointments were made and no record was kept. A chronicler, wishing to commend a virtuous bishop, wrote that " he confirmed, as it were, an innumerable multitude of children."

The medieval marriage service was short, consisting merely of the troth-plight with the ring, before the church door. It is found in the old missals, because it usually preceded the nuptial mass. The feast that followed was the " bride-ale."

The sacrament of orders only concerned the parish priest's work through the boys of his parish. The tonsure and minor orders were often given by the bishop in the chapel of his manor, apart from the four yearly ordinations, and the priest may have brought boys to receive them. His own " parish clerk " would be an adult in minor orders, and probably married. It was his business to keep a look-out for ordinands, though he no longer kept a school to teach them grammar himself.

When a parishioner was sick, it was his priest's duty to visit him, exhort him to make a will, hear his confession, give him the viaticum, and anoint him with the holy chrism. He should gently exhort him, saying : " While thy soul is in thy body, put all thy trust in Christ His passion and in His death, and think only thereon. . . . With His death mingle thyself, and wrap thee therein, nought thinking on thy wife, ne on thy children, ne on thy riches, but all on the passion of Christ ; and have the cross before thee, and say thus : ' I wot well thou art not my God, but thou art imagined after Him, and makest me have more mind of Him after Whom thou art imagined. Lord, Father of heaven, the death of our Lord Jesus Christ, Thy Son, which is here imagined, I set between thee and my evil deeds : and the deserts of Jesus Christ I offer thee for that I should have deserved.' " As death drew near, the priest prayed with long litanies beside the sick man's bed, calling upon God and the saints to help him, while his friends and relations answered to each invocation : " Intercede for his soul." The last words that many a dying person would hear in this life would be the beautiful Latin commendation for the departing soul : " Set forth, O Christian soul, from this world, in the name of God the Father Almighty, Who hath created thee : in the name of Jesus Christ His son, Who suffered for thee : in the name of the Holy Spirit, Who was poured out upon thee : in the name of angels and archangels : thrones and dominations : princes and powers and all celestial virtues : in the name of cherubim and seraphim : in the name of patriarchs, prophets, apostles, martyrs, confessors : in the name of bishops, priests, deacons and all the grades of the catholic church : in the name of monks and anchorites and virgins : let thy place be to-day in peace, and thy habitation in holy Zion."

CHAPTER XVI

SCHOOLS : HOSPITALS : ANCHORAGES

Illiteracy and its results in the middle ages—Song, grammar and cathedral schools—Hospitals—Lepers—Hermits—Anchors and anchoresses

THROUGHOUT the middle ages the connexion between the church and literary education remained very close. Such education was not regarded as a general preparation for life, but as equipment for a career : and that career in its broadest sense the service of the church. This was a legacy of the dark ages, when for hundreds of years the only class taught to read and write, and to take possession of the human heritage of learning by a knowledge of Latin, was the clerical militia. A clerk, by definition, was one whose lot it was to serve the Lord. Gradually, certain other classes had been taught reading, writing and Latin, for practical ends. Kings, dukes and such like must be able to sign their names. By the fourteenth century an Italian writer recommended that even women, down to the daughters of marquises, should be educated, so that they might sign charters : for those beneath them in the social scale there was no need. Bailiffs and reeves, even of a humble description, had usually, in the fourteenth century, picked up enough reading, writing and figures to be able to keep accounts. Notaries public, at the end of the fourteenth century, were beginning to be described in records as " literate laymen," as were some other witnesses to documents. Nobles and knights were laymen, but at the end of the fourteenth century they could read and write : so could " solemn merchants " in the towns. But it

was still true at the end of the fourteenth century that
ability to read and write was confined mainly to those
in orders, those with the clerical tonsure, and those who
by attendance at a grammar school or university were
" scholares," and entitled to benefit of clergy. The records
of the Châtelet at Paris, about 1400, with its jurisdiction
and prisons, show that many arrested persons claimed
benefit of clergy "falsely," and that in proof of their
clerkship they were asked to produce the letters given
them when they were shorn, or bring witnesses to that
event. One clerk escaped by recitation of the psalm,
" The Lord is the lot of my inheritance," which he would
have recited with the bishop who was shearing him ; and
in England this proof was accepted in the late fifteenth
century, and the verse became known as the " neck-verse."

It is sometimes forgotten in considering medieval
religion, that it had adapted its methods for the service
of a society where the majority could not read or write.
Most people were peasants, countrymen, small craftsmen,
and illiterate : there was a very much larger cultural
gap between them and the medieval university student,
than there would be between corresponding classes to-day.
Popular illiteracy was not the fault of the church, which
did educate the masses as far as she could, but it was the
necessary accompaniment of the stage of civilisation to
which Europe had so far advanced. National education
depends on marginal national energy : on the balance of
leisure and effort left over when primary needs have been
satisfied : and this in the middle ages was too small to
allow of it. England did not get national education
till 1870 : three quarters of the native population of India
are to-day illiterate, after two hundred years of our rule.
Ninety-five per cent, of the population of Russia was
illiterate in 1914. It was not the printing-press which
made national education possible, for that was discovered
in the fifteenth century : it was coal. The industrial
revolution brought many evils, but it made national
education possible, by increasing the balance of energy
after primary needs were satisfied. In the middle ages
the winds on the sea, the ox for ploughing, the horse
for travelling, the stream for grinding corn, were the

only sources of power additional to the energy of the human body. Life was physically tiring, not only for the peasant reaping his corn with a sickle, but even for the king, travelling endlessly about on horseback. There was no margin for general education.

This illiteracy of the lower classes accounts for some charges made against medieval religion. Parish priests were often drawn from the peasant class, and comparatively ignorant men. Their stipend was not more than the income of a fairly prosperous villein : the council of Oxford, 1222, settled the stipend of vicars at five marks a year. The windows and pictures and images in churches, which shocked the later Puritans, were a means of teaching the illiterate, as were miracle plays and the like. Superstitious practices which prevailed in popular religion were made possible by general ignorance, though some were increased also by the cupidity of the baser elements in the church : Chaucer represented his pardoner as trying to palm off his " piggis' bones " for relics on the country-folk, not on clerks and canons.

There was, however, by the fourteenth century, and much earlier, an educational ladder for the children of humble parents. There were a certain number of little parish or ABC schools, sometimes taught freely by the parish clerk, occasionally by the parish priest : and the latter sometimes taught children for fees, by a private bargain made with their parents. But the great organ of education was the grammar school, now to be found in most market towns. These schools had generally been founded by some benefactor, who bestowed or bequeathed a house for the school, and sometimes a small endowment to provide a salary for a grammar master : sometimes the master charged small fees. The school was not the private venture of the master, (although sometimes a grammar master taught school for a year or two in a town, and then passed on), but the school of the town, or some gild, or set of trustees. It usually had a class for the ABC children, who learned their letters and " song " together, like the " little clergeon " in the *Prioress's Tale*, and one for the boys learning grammar. These last were taught the Latin classics, and the old disputations and exercises which had belonged to the first subject of the seven liberal arts, rhetoric. In 1357 the bishop of Exeter complained to his archdeacons that boys were badly taught : it would be better if they were made to construe and understand mattins and the hours of the Blessed Virgin, which they now said daily in after life without proper understanding.

The cathedrals had, by the end of the fourteenth century, both a grammar and a theology school. The curriculum in the grammar school was the same as elsewhere. In the theology school the chancellor lectured on the *Sentences* of Peter Lombard, which involved a certain amount of pastoral theology, and on the biblical text. While Wycliffe's English Bible was being translated by his followers at Oxford, a quite independent glossed English version of the gospels was being made, perhaps by someone who had come under his influence while at Oxford. Its nature and glosses render it likely to have been the work of some lecturer in a theology school, and the north midland dialect suggests a connexion with the cathedral schools at Lincoln. The inferior clergy of a diocese, vicars and stipendiary curates, had seldom a university degree, as the episcopal registers show : most were probably the product of the cathedral school.

While Wycliffe's followers were agitating, at the end of the fourteenth century, for a doctrinal reform to cure the evils of the church, there was also a school of orthodox churchmen who recognised the need for reform, and saw the best hope of it in a better education for the clergy. William of Wykeham is typical of this class. He provided a complete school and university education for his scholars, all of whom were maintained free of cost, and intended, with few exceptions, for the priesthood. He endowed and built " Saint Mary College of Winchester " for seventy poor scholars to be taught grammar, and allowed ten " sons of noble and powerful persons, special friends of the said college," to share their education with them. These lay boys were the germ of the public school, and by including them Winchester was the first of its class. But the seventy scholars were the raison d'être of the college : and they could proceed when ready to " Saint Mary College of Winchester in Oxford," which Wykeham also founded and endowed.   In 1343 the bishop of Durham appropriated the large endowments of the parish of Houghton for the maintenance of a parish vicar, a small college consisting of a resident rector and four chaplains, and four university scholarships.   Private patrons maintained young clerks at school and at the university. Chantry priests began to teach small schools.   Chantries were endowments to maintain a priest to say mass for the souls of the testator, his ancestors and family, and the souls of all the faithful ;   endowment deeds now began to insert clauses that the chantry priest should teach freely such scholars as came to him.   The teaching depended on the learning of the priest, but probably was of the same nature as that of the grammar school.   Chantries became very numerous in the fifteenth century, and though all chantry priests were not bound by the terms of the endowment to teach, the chantry schools were fairly frequent, and made education more accessible.

The medieval counterpart of modern "social services" and welfare institutions consisted of the hospitals, not solely for the sick, but for all kinds of unfortunates. Besides private almsgiving to the poor, the church encouraged the foundation of permanent houses for their relief.   The ancestor of the frequent medieval hospital, almshouse, bede house, God's House, or whatever its name, was the hospitium or xenodochium of the fifth century episcopal familia.   The bishop was directed by the canons to spend a certain proportion of the revenue of the see on the poor, and this alms was largely given in stipends to the poor of the hospitium.   When bishops began, from the ninth century onwards, to bestow a separate revenue on their chapter, they also began to give a separate endowment to a hospitium in their cathedral city, or to arrange that the cost of the hospitium should be a charge on the endowment of the cathedral.   Royal benefactors also gave the bishops land and endowments especially for their hospitium.   By the fourteenth century every cathedral city had a hospitium, and generally three or four for special objects, built by private donors or different bishops of the see :   other towns had them as well, though in less numbers.   In the fourteenth century

Canterbury had eight hospitals, York eighteen, London seventeen, Norwich fifteen and Exeter four, and more were founded in the fifteenth century. They varied very much in size, but generally provided maintenance for a warden or mistress, one or two chaplains or sisters, and food and lodging for the poor whom they sheltered for the night, a week or two, or permanently.

The earliest hospitals provided temporary shelter indifferently for wayfarers and the sick : Flixton, in Holderness, was founded c. 925 " to preserve travellers from being devoured by the wolves and voracious forest beasts." Athelstan helped the minster clergy to entertain the needy by founding the hospital of S. Peter at York : bishop Oswald founded the hospital at Worcester. Every bishop was asked at his consecration : " Wilt thou show mercy and kindness, to the poor, to the stranger, and to all in want ? " and many founded hospitals, not only in their cathedral city, but elsewhere in their diocese. Archbishop Theobald of Canterbury in 1141 aided two brethren to build a hospital at Dover, for crusaders and the many pilgrims to the Holy Land. Monasteries also sometimes maintained a hospitium outside the abbey walls : Battle abbey near Hastings maintained thus " the house of the pilgrims which is called the hospital." Pilgrims and the sick were received together : a chain of hospitals was founded after 1170 along the way to Canterbury, to the shrine of S. Thomas : from Southwark in one direction, and from Dover in another. After the Black Death vagrancy increased, and the hospitals were filled, not merely with pilgrims and the sick, but with casual workers and runaway serfs ; it was at this point that town statutes and hospital regulations began to require that in receiving the poor, more attention should be paid to the sick than to the whole.

Besides these early hospitals of a general type, some were founded for special objects. That at Kingston-upon-Hull was called a God's House, and provided a habitation " for thirteen poor men and women broken down by age, misfortune or toil, who cannot gain their own livelihood." The hospital of S. John's, Canterbury, maintained " a hundred brothers and sisters, blind, lame, deaf and sick." Boroughs often founded hospitals of this description, the right of entrance being generally limited to the freemen of the town : bishop Bubwith founded one at Wells, and stipulated that burgesses fallen into poverty should have the "more honourable places and beds." The merchant gilds also founded such hospitals, the merchant adventurers at York, the taylors at Winchester, the fraternity of the Holy Trinity at Newcastle-upon-Tyne.

Special hospitals for the relief of Jews, who after their conversion could no longer earn their living by usury, and were cut off from their friends, were founded in London, (the Domus Conversorum), Oxford and Bristol. There were many houses for poor priests and poor clergy, and they were much needed in the fourteenth and fifteenth centuries, when the number of unbeneficed clergy and chantry priests was large. Some hospitals took only women and children : Gilbertine nuns often maintained such a house for children only. Grammar scholars were sometimes lodged in the ordinary hospitals : that of S. Cross, Winchester, took in seven. Special hospitals for the insane were not founded till the fourteenth century, before which such patients were received with other sick folk. The most famous of all hospitals for the insane was that of S. Mary of Bethlehem without Bishopsgate, which received about ten mad patients in 1403. In 1451 a London citizen described it as " A church of our Lady that is named Bedlam. And in that place be found many men that be fallen out of their wits. And full honestly they be kept in that place, and some be restored unto their wits and health again. And some be abiding therein for ever, for they be fallen so far out of themselves that it is uncurable unto man." The hospital to become most famous for the treatment of the sick was that founded c. 1123 by Rahere, the beautiful Norman church and cloister of S. Bartholomew, Smithfield.

Medieval England had at least two hundred special hospitals for lepers, or lazar-houses. Leprosy was known in England before the Crusades, but it became much worse in consequence of them, and was very frequent between 1000 and 1250. After 1400 it was rare, and after 1500 practically extinct. After c. 1250 every big town and many villages had a leper-house ; many were insufficiently endowed, their discipline harsh, and the life within them wretched enough. They had, however, their own chapels and chaplains : it is a popular fallacy that lepers made their communion through " leper-windows " in the parish church. Leprosy cut off the sufferer from all share in ordinary life : when the disease was discovered, the patient was made to withdraw to a leper-house, or if he had property, to a little house of his own, wear a special dress and avoid all human intercourse. Even for such unfortunates the medieval church had a message of vocation, delivered by the parish priest in a special office which preceded the sufferer's seclusion. The parish priest went in surplice and stole to the sick man's house, brought him with comfort and exhortation to the church, sprinkled him with holy water, and bade him make his confession in church, " and never again." Then he made him kneel before the altar beneath trestles covered with a black cloth (like a dead man in his coffin at a requiem mass). Here he heard mass for the last time in church, with special prayers, epistle and gospel, and then was led by the priest and cross-bearer into the church yard. A pause was made, and the priest counselled him out of holy scripture, teaching him the words of Isaiah about Christ : " Yet we did esteem him as a leper, smitten of God and afflicted," and saying to him : " If in weakness of body thou art made like unto Christ by means of suffering, thou mayst surely hope that thou wilt rejoice in spirit with God." Then, casting earth on his feet with a spade, as at a burial, he bade him : " Be thou dead to the world, but alive again unto God." Then, commending him to the prayers and alms of the people, he led him across the fields to his house. Here he solemnly charged him never to enter church, market, mill, bakehouse or assembly again, to keep nine other rules to avoid spreading the disease, and to say his prayers and have patience, for Christ would be with him.

Hermits, anchorites, and anchoresses were another frequent feature of medieval life. The hermit dwelt as a solitary, but was not "enclosed : " anchorites and anchoresses were, the word itself signifying one who dwelt in a cell " beside the choir." Before either hermit, anchor or anchoresses established themselves, they had to seek permission from the bishop, show that they had sufficient endowment, or some prospect of maintenance, and were suitable in character. Anchorites and anchoresses must have sufficient to support one or two servants, as they could not fetch food for themselves. Many had cells in towns, where alms would be bestowed on them : and many hermits did work like caring for bridges or travellers, or directing travellers on wastes. They might be priests or lay-people, and their primary work was prayer, though they might give spiritual counsel to those that sought it. An anchorage generally consisted of two or three rooms beside the chancel of a church, so that the enclosed person might, through a little slanting window in the wall, hear mass, and pray before the blessed sacrament, which hung in its pyx above the altar. The anchorite's own cell had also two other windows, one into the servant's cell, for the passage of food, one covered by a curtain with a big cross on it, for conversation with visitors.

There were many hermits in Anglo-Saxon England, and some of the most saintly bishops and monks withdrew to the desert at the end of their life. One of the most remarkable of the later hermits was Richard Rolle, a Yorkshireman who went to the university of Oxford, and left it to take up the life of a wandering hermit near his own birthplace. He was not a priest, he made no regular profession as hermit, and he lived on the alms of different patrons, moving his habitation from time to time. He spent the last years of his life in a cell near the little Cistercian nunnery of Hampole, and he died in the Black Death. He was one of the first to use Middle-English, as well as Latin, for his writings : he translated the psalter, with Peter Lombard's gloss upon it, he wrote beautiful English lyrics, and English treatises on *Our daily Work*, on *The Form of Perfect Living*, and other subjects. *Our daily Work* was intended for lay people, advised them on their conduct throughout the day, their prayer, work, and almsgiving, and counselled them : " Before thou goest to bed, hold a chapter with thine heart at night, and ask it in what things it is better than it was? : : :

What temptation hast thou withstood this day ? In what art thou meeker than thou wast ? In what more chaste, more sober, more patient, more temperate, more loving thy God in thy brother, or what more liking in God hast thou than thou hadst ? " *The Form of Perfect Living* was written for an anchoress, and answered some of her questions. " Thou speakest so much of love," said the anchoress, " tell me, what is love ? . . . Love is a burning yearning after God, with a wonderful delight and certainty. God is light and burning. Light clarifies our reason, burning kindles our will, that we desire naught but Him. Love is a life, joining together the loving and the loved. . . . Love is the thing through which God loves us, and we love Him, and each of us loves other. Love is the desire of the heart, aye thinking on that it loves : and when it has that it loves, then it joys and nothing can make it sorry. Love is yearning between two, with lastingness of thoughts. . . . If thou wilt ask, how good is he or she, ask how much he or she loves."

An even earlier Middle-English treatise was the *Ancren Riwle*, or rule for anchoresses, written originally in the twelfth century in old French. Between 1127 and 1135 the abbot of Westminster provided for the enclosure as anchoresses of three young friends of his, ladies from the court, waiting maids on good Queen Maud, wife of Henry I. Their names were Emma, Gunhilda and Christina, and one was only fifteen. He had a hermitage built for them near a church at Kilburn, and he placed them under the direction of Godwin, who had been grammar master of Salisbury cathedral, and had already retired to lead a hermit life at Kilburn. The abbot received certain endowments from the young anchoresses' friends, and agreed that the convent of Westminster should in return make a regular allowance of food and corn and cloth to maintain the anchoresses, sending it at stated intervals on a donkey. The *Ancren Riwle* was drawn up for the guidance of these ladies, probably by Godwin, their master : in course of time more ladies joined them, and the anchorage was turned into a priory of Austin canonesses, Kilburn priory. The *Ancren Riwle* contained interesting and explicit directions: the anchoresses might consider that they were keeping the "rule of S. James," since they kept themselves unspotted from the world, though belonging to no regular order. They must never be idle, but sew and read and do manual work when not saying the office or praying: they must not gossip at the window: they must not practise austerities unknown to their master, and have enough skins to keep themselves warm in winter: they must keep their maidservants from idleness and gossiping: they must not teach little girls,—if any little girl were in danger of being taught along with boys, their servant might teach her: they must not have more than one cat, for more might lead to quarrelling.

Fifteenth century Norfolk, with its rich wool merchants and trade with the Netherlands, was a land of many churches, chapels, hospitals, and anchorages. Two Norfolk anchoresses have left English writings. Margery Kemp of Lynn wrote how she marvelled that any man could be finally lost: " Lord, of Thy great goodness, have mercy on my great wickedness, as certainly as I never was so wicked as Thou art good . . . for Thou art so good, that Thou mayest no better be: and therefore it is great wonder that ever any man should be departed from Thee without end." "She might not endure to behold a leper . . . specially if he has any wounds appearing on him: so she wept as if she had seen our Lord Jesu, with His wounds bleeding: and so she did, in the sight of her soul . . . she had great mourning and sorrowing that she might not kiss the lepers when she met them in the way, for the love of our Lord: which was all contrary to her disposition in the years of her youth and prosperity, for then she abhorred them most." Juliana, an anchoress of Carrow, near Norwich, left a record of the sixteen "shewings," or revelations of divine love, which she had received. "I saw," she said, "that each kind compassion that man hath on his even-Christians with charity, it is Christ in him: " and in another shewing about prayer: "All-thing that our Lord hath ordained to do, it is His will that we pray therefore, either in special or in general. . . . He said: *I am the ground of thy beseeching*." " For this is the natural yearning of the soul

by the touching of the Holy Ghost : God, of Thy goodness, give me Thyself, for Thou art enough to me . . . and
if I ask anything that is less, ever me wanteth : but only
in Thee I have all." " *It is sooth*," said Christ to her in
another shewing, "*that sin is cause of all this pain : but
all shall be well, and all shall be well, and all manner of thing
shall be well.*"

CHAPTER XVII

MEDIEVAL HERESY AND THE INQUISITION

Medieval attitude to heresy—Academic heresies : the Averrhoïsts —Manichaean and pantheist heresies : Cathari, etc.—Witchcraft and sorcery—Bible-reading heretics : Waldensians, Béguines, Lollards—Early punishments for heresy—The episcopal Inquisition and early papal commissions—Gregory IX and the mendicant Inquisition—Procedure of the Inquisition

THE popular attitude to heresy in the middle ages was quite alien from the modern. It was universally accepted that religious certitude, that truth, was in the possession of the church by revelation, and that she was its guardian by divine commission. Two opposing religious beliefs could not both be true, and that which was untrue should be rooted out and purged away. Heresy was, by definition, an individual choice in religious matters, whereby some aspects of truth were stressed at the expense of others, or alien beliefs grafted upon the whole body of Christian truth. The Christian faith was a balanced and complex whole, guaranteed by the acceptance of Christendom. There was an antecedent improbability, apart from divine revelation, that in matters of faith the whole body of Christians would be wrong, and the leader of a small sect of heretics right. Neither heretic nor orthodox believed religious toleration desirable : the heretic, like the orthodox, believed himself in possession of the whole Christian truth, and wished to convert all men to it. The orthodox masses resented his existence not only as an insult to truth, but as an anti-social menace. Christendom was one state, the city of God, and heresy involved not merely religious division, but social upset and political strife. Only baptized Christians could be heretics, and heresy was a rejection of an accepted relationship, a rebellion against spiritual authority, a revolt which in feudal times seemed to undermine the foundations of society. Except in Provence, and later in Bohemia, the heretic was always an object of hatred to the masses, and the crowd delighted to seize and burn him before the procedure was authorised by the church.

The body of medieval heresy was a very complex whole, and the simple Bible-reading type of heretic, popularly supposed to have been the chief victim of persecution, was in a small minority ; though from the eleventh century he undoubtedly existed. A comprehensive catalogue of the various forms of heresy would need to be long, subtle, and complicated : but if a general search of the records of the Inquisition and earlier ecclesiastical documents were made, the really general and widespread heresies would soon stand out, comparatively few in number. They were those founded upon latent Manichaeism, and pantheism : academic heresies which affected only the universities : a whole group which were nothing but the expression of morbid psychological cravings : that of the Spiritual Franciscans : witchcraft and sorcery cases : and the group of heresies nearest akin to sixteenth century protestantism, inspired by popular reading of the gospels.

The condemnation of academic heretics, generally either extreme realist or extreme nominalist, has been mentioned earlier, in the case of Roscelin, Abelard and Berengarius of Tours. Arnold of Brescia, a pupil of Abelard, not only shared his master's heterodoxies, but added to them belief in the ancient republican ideals of the city of Rome. He held that the papal authority within the city was a usurpation, and further, that the whole temporal power of the papacy and the wealth of the bishops was unchristian. He wished the clergy to return to a state of apostolic poverty, and led a revolution in Rome to establish a commune or republic. He was captured in 1155 and burnt as a heretic, but a small sect of Arnoldists survived.

Another academic heresy was that of the Averrhoïsts. Of the Arabian philosophers who had studied Aristotle before western scholars, Avicenna had combined Aristotelian thought with a nominalist view of the question of universals. Averrhoës, († 1198), had far more influence on Christian philosophers, and accepted all Aristotle's teaching in its completeness : he taught that matter was uncreated and eternal, while God, the First Cause, was the latent force or impulse in the universe. Emanating from the First Cause was the *active* intellect, while the human intellect was moved or *passive*. It had no personal immortality, but was absorbed at death into the universal mind. Religion and philosophy must be kept severely apart, and while religion had utilitarian value, philosophy was a higher human study or activity. Averrhoïsm spread into Castile, Aragon and Sicily, and had a powerful following among Christian scholars by the mid-thirteenth century. In 1210 a council of Paris prohibited the reading of Aristotle, or (Averrhoïst) commentaries upon him. The papal legate renewed the prohibition in 1215 : but in 1231 Gregory IX made the prohibition provisional, till the books of Aristotle could be examined and purged of Arabian corruptions. Thomas Aquinas himself, and the Dominican order, were accused of Averrhoïsm from their study of Aristotle, and particularly by Franciscan scholars and the English archbishop Peckham. Aquinas cleared himself of the charge and reconciled Christian philosophy with Aristotle : but a school of Latin Averrhoïsts existed for some time afterwards, in spite of condemnations for heresy. In 1270 Siger of Brabant contended for Averrhoïsm against Aquinas, and his doctrines were formally condemned. Siger made no attempt to reconcile Aristotelian theory with Christian revelation, but denied personal immortality, the biblical story of creation, and the free will and moral responsibility of the individual. In the fourteenth century the university of Padua became the centre of Averrhoïst influence, though even Paris was affected by the teaching of the Averrhoïsts. Raymond Lull and Petrarch were its chief adversaries, Petrarch regarding Averrhoës as a mad dog, ever raging against the Christian faith. To the fourteenth and fifteenth centuries, Averrhoës came to be regarded as the personification of insolent unbelief : and the saying was fathered upon him that Moses, Christ and Mahomet were three impostors, who had deceived the world in turn.

The Manichaean Cathari and Albigeois have been mentioned earlier, and were widespread and particularly dangerous. They flourished especially in Provence, or the country of the *langue d'oc*, because this borderland of the Mediterranean, between the Rhone and the Pyrenees, had a civilisation unique in Europe. It had been the centre of the old Visigothic kingdom, stretching both sides of the Pyrenees, and throughout the middle ages it was in close touch with Moorish Spain. It had a vernacular literature earlier than elsewhere in Europe, vivid, luxuriant, and not untinged with eastern sensualism. It was the land of the troubadours, and of the poetry of the romance and adventures of love : the ascetic side of medieval Christianity, and the priests who taught it, were unpopular. The Albigensian creed taught that there was no immediate need of discipline or asceticism, for there was no heaven or hell. Those who received the *Consolamentum*, and died soon thereafter, or the perfect who led a life of complete asceticism, went straight to glory : but the rest of mankind on death, through the transmigration of souls, merely entered upon another life on earth. The moral influence of the creed was bad, for while it taught that righteousness involved complete separation from the material and sensual, and that marriage was as evil as promiscuity, it allowed all its followers to indulge in any form of material and sensual evil provided they promised to receive the *Consolamentum* before death. England remained largely unaffected by these early medieval heresies : but in 1166 two Cathari were tried at Oxford, whipped and branded, and driven out from the city, probably to perish in the snow.

Pantheist heresy developed in academic circles from the position of extreme realism, and the works of Scotus Eriugena were condemned on this score some centuries after his death. The fourteenth century German Dominican and mystic, Meister Eckhart, was accused of pressing his doctrine of the immanence of God to the point of pantheism : but modern comparison of his sermons with the works of Hugh and Richard of St. Victor scarcely supports the theory that he pushed the immanence doctrine farther than the orthodox mystics. His sermons used to be taken down in German by the nuns to whom he preached, and possibly the fact that they were the first writings to treat of such high matters in the vernacular gave rise to suspicion. But pantheism produced sometimes small and erratic heresies. Some taught that no one filled with the Holy Ghost could commit sin : while the Brethren of the Free Spirit held that Satan participated in the divine essence. They were sometimes known as Luciferans, and practised horrible and debased rites at the initiation of novices. They persisted from the late thirteenth century till the Reformation.

While Manichaean and pantheist heresy sometimes led to disgusting practices, there were quite a number of small heresies which a modern psychologist would regard as simply and solely the expression of pathological instincts. The Adamists conducted their religious rites in a state of nature. The Flagellants made their appearance in the thirteenth century, but were more important just after the Black Death. Strings of penitents marched through Hungary, Germany, Flanders and Holland, chanting litanies, and each man scourging the shoulders of the man in front : they proclaimed complete certainty of salvation to all who should persevere in flagellation for thirty-three days. Scourging was the one necessary sacrament. They were condemned in 1349. Bands of dancing fanatics appeared at the same time, marching from place to place, and dancing with rhythmical convulsions on the village greens : when their followers sank down exhausted, the leaders spurred them on with cries of " Afresh, afresh ! "

Witchcraft and sorcery were heresies cognisable by the Inquisition : Roger Bacon unique among his contemporaries and much later philosophers believed, however, that reputed sorcery was either fraudulent or a delusion. Sorcery was commonly held to be invoking demons, trafficking with Satan : witches were held to transport themselves through the air and hold Sabbats where they worshipped the prince of darkness. Canonists like Gratian dismissed these stories as fiction, but in the fifteenth

Q

century the inquisitor Sprenger wrote asserting the undoubted existence and powers of witches. Women, he explained, were naturally discontented, impatient creatures, easily captured by the devil and used as his instruments. They undoubtedly transported themselves, or at least their spirits, to Sabbats, held somewhere in the Brocken, and there practised horrible rites. Witches were universally held to be able to produce sterility and abortion, transform men and women into beasts, and create tempests : they could transform themselves into the likeness of animals, particularly cats. The Inquisition was urged in the fifteenth century to get rid of these pests, and an outburst of witch-burnings followed. The practice of witch-burning of course survived the Inquisition, and persisted well down into modern times.

The Spiritual Franciscans have been mentioned earlier. Their heresy was primarily disobedience to the bull *Quorundam* of John XXII, which had forbidden them to wear the smaller hoods and gowns by which they distinguished themselves from the Conventuals. But the Spirituals were soon involved in doctrinal heresies as well. In 1323 John XXII declared it heresy to assert that Christ and His apostles had held no property, which the Spirituals maintained. Through John of Parma and Peter John Olivi, moreover, the Spirituals were involved in suspicion of sharing the heresy of Joachitism, the " Everlasting Gospel." Abbot Joachim of Flora worked in the half-Greek district of Calabria, and was under Greek influence : he had a great reputation as a prophet, was respected by Grosseteste, and his works were declared orthodox after inquisition in 1200, and by Honorius III in 1220. But about 1254 a work known as the *Eternal Gospel* appeared in Paris, consisting of his authentic works, and a strange *Introduction*, which was by some Franciscan, perhaps John of Parma. Joachim had foretold that the world would go through three cycles, the first that of the Father, the second that of the Son, the third, still future, that of the Holy Ghost. The *Introduction* stressed the complete failure of the Christian dispensation, and the imminent establishment of a completely new religion, that of the Holy Ghost. The final era was to be founded in 1260, the Franciscans were to be its chief inaugurators, and the religion of S. Francis and the Holy Ghost was to supersede the Christian church.

The Waldensians, and to some extent the Beghards of the Netherlands and the empire, were heretics originally of a distinct type, though their proscription tended to throw them into contact and under the influence of other heretics. The Waldensians tended to approximate to the Albigensians, the Beghards to the Spirituals, or to the Brethren of the Free Spirit. The Waldensians were the original stock of heretics of this type. An inquisitor recounted their origin : " A certain rich man of the city of Lyons, called Waldo, was curious when he heard the gospel read, since he was not much lettered, to know what was said. Wherefore he made a pact with certain priests, the one, that he should translate to him the Bible : the other, that he should write as the other dictated. Which they did. . . . Which when the said citizens had often read and learned by heart, he proposed to observe apostolical perfection as the apostles observed it : and he sold all his goods . . . and gave his money to the poor, and usurped the apostolic office by preaching the gospel, and those things which he had learnt by heart, in the villages and open places, and by calling to him men and women to do likewise, and teaching them the gospel by heart, . . . who, being simple and illiterate men and women, wandered through villages and entered houses and preached in open places, and even in churches, and provoked others to the same course." The teaching which Peter Waldo and his disciples sought to spread was the result of excluding from Christian usage all sacraments, institutions and customs not found in the Bible—penance, prayers to saints, image worship, oath-taking, and the taking of life— the two last a literal following of the texts " Swear not at all," and " Thou shalt not kill." The Waldensians arrived at the same conclusions as the later Lollards, though there is no evidence that Wycliffe directly borrowed from their teaching. One result, however, followed their lay origin : they came to hold that lay people might validly administer the sacraments as well as preach: the later Lollards, being well supplied with Wycliffite priests, used lay people only for preaching. The Waldensians were at length forbidden to preach by the archbishop of Lyons, and declared heretics by papal edict in 1184. They soon spread, however, up the Rhone, into the Rhine valley and the Netherlands, and thence into the empire. They encountered in 1203, in the city of Liège, the followers of the mission preacher, Lambert le Bègue, (the Stammerer), also devout but unlettered lay people, who set great store on the use of vernacular scriptures. Lambert's followers were called from his surname, in Dutch, Beghards, (whence the English word " beggar "), in Latin, Beguini or Beguinae. They were loosely organised, and lived sometimes a wandering life, sometimes (especially in the case of women) in small communities, supporting themselves and living separately, but with common chapel and services. Throughout the thirteenth and fourteenth centuries authorities differed as to whether the Béguine life was orthodox or not : many communities lived under episcopal approbation, but others were condemned as heretical, as early as 1209. Their mode of life made them liable to infection from wandering heretical teachings, like the Waldensians, the Spirituals and the Brethren of the Free Spirit. They were termed Lollards by the beginning of the fourteenth century, from a Dutch word meaning to mutter or mumble : while Beghard originally implied no suspicion of heresy, Lollard always did so. Certain Lollards, " wandering hypocritical fellows," are mentioned in Brabant as early as 1309, and one was burned in 1322. The English Wycliffites, or Lollards, were to be scholars as well as wandering preachers.

" In those days," wrote an English chronicler of the year 1382, " flourished master John Wycliffe, rector of the church of Lutterworth, in the county of Leicester, the most eminent doctor of theology of those times. In philosophy he was reckoned second to none, and in scholastic learning without rival. This man strove to surpass the skill of other men by subtlety of knowledge and to traverse their opinions." Wycliffe was, in fact, the most eminent scholar of the university of Oxford, from 1372 when he took his doctorate till his condemnation in 1382 by archbishop Courtenay. The rectory of Lutterworth had been given him by his patron, John of Gaunt, to whom his ecclesiastical theories seemed to promise a weapon against the French popes, and for the confiscation of church property : Lutterworth lay on the direct road between Oxford and John of Gaunt's castle of Leicester, where his protection sheltered a group of Wycliffe's followers. Wycliffe spent most of his time at Oxford, and was preeminently a university don, not a fourteenth century John Wesley ; he paid a stipendiary " curatus " called John Horn to take charge of the parish work at Lutterworth. He was important politically, as siding with the party of John of Gaunt against the Black Prince and William of Wykeham : he had the university of Oxford at his feet, and the chancellor John Rygge as his admirer, and he inspired a popular preaching movement which converted large numbers of the lower classes and a considerable proportion of the English knights. His " poor preachers " were not formed into an order, for Wycliffe held that all orders save the " religion of Christ " were wrong or unnecessary : his followers had no rule and no habit. They consisted at first of his admirers at Oxford, scholars who preached when they were free on greens and market places, and in churches when they were invited by patron, mayor or parish priest. They were at first all priests, and though they were joined by lay preachers after Wycliffe's death, there is no evidence that unordained Wycliffites attempted to administer the sacraments. Indeed, from their point of view, there was already too much emphasis on the sacraments in church teaching, and plenty of priests to administer them : what was wanted was more preaching.

The three points most notable in Wycliffe's teaching were his theory of " dominion by grace," his acceptance of the Bible as the sole rule of faith, and his teaching about the sacraments. He wrote an immense array of Latin treatises on these matters, supporting his contentions from the scriptures and the early Fathers, and guarding himself carefully from overstatement, or from being thought to urge that all his theories could at once be put in practice, in an imperfect world. His early Oxford followers were equally careful and academic. His

secretary John Purvey, who was the most notable leader
of his followers after his death, was a scholar of the same
caution. But Wycliffe's other followers were far more
extreme : they made rough English paraphrases of some
of his propagandist works, and interwove their own more
violent recommendations : they were not appealing to
scholars, but the lay knights of parliament, and the man
in the street. Hence there was a marked difference in
tone in the Wycliffite movement under Wycliffe and
Purvey, down till Purvey's recantation in 1401, and in
its later phase under Oldcastle. Indeed, Purvey's own
followers, between Wycliffe's death in 1384 and 1401,
were more violent than himself, and reproached him as
" neither hot nor cold."

Wycliffe opposed the current theory that " dominion,"
lordship either spiritual or temporal, was derived from
God through intermediaries. The feudal conception of
the ownership of land, through the tenants-in-chief and
the intermediate or " mesne " tenants to the actual holder,
had become applied to spiritual office : grace was conceived
of as derived from God through the pope and the hierarchy.
Wycliffe taught that every man was God's tenant-in-chief,
owing no vassalage to any mesne tenant. Those who
kept God's law were possessed of dominion : those who
disregarded it were ipso facto dispossessed,—either of
temporal ownership or spiritual power. Every man was
responsible for the keeping God's law, and by " God's law "
Wycliffe meant the Bible. This teaching was liable to
lead to anarchy both in the temporal and spiritual sphere,
for it allowed the right of a man's neighbours to seize his
property if they considered that he did not keep God's
law, and it logically rendered any form of organised church
unnecessary. Wycliffe's followers were feared for the
social as well as the spiritual effect of this teaching, and
some of the later Bohemian Wycliffites carried his social
theories to extremes. But Wycliffe himself never
demanded that the implications of " dominion by grace "
should be followed to their logical conclusion : he held
that it justified disendowment of all church property, and
that a large measure of such disendowment would be
useful : that it nullified much of the teaching of the canon

law : and that it would not lead to ecclesiastical anarchy, because there could be but one inference about church organisation drawn from the scriptures.

Wycliffe had thus thrown overboard the appeal to the visible and historic church as final authority, and he found an alternative one in the written scriptures. The church had always taught that the Bible was the foundation and criterion of discipline and dogma : but Wycliffe held that the appeal to scripture involved return to a simplified Christian organisation like that of the gospels and Acts. There seemed to him an impossible contrast between the Christianity of his own day, with its church courts, summoners and legal apparatus, with its splendid court at Avignon, and after 1378 at Rome as well, with its rich and businesslike bishops and cardinals, and the lives of the fishermen Christians of the gospels. The whole thing was wrong : men ought to follow the " meek and poor and charitable living of Christ," and those who followed it most nearly were the most Christian : those who " contraried it " were anti-Christian, and the worldly popes, the head of the system, who contraried it most of all, were most anti-Christian : they were in fact, Anti-Christ. Wycliffe and most fourteenth century minds had little historic sense, or perception that Christian organisation had begun to develop even in the period between the gospels and the Acts, and was bound to develop later in the process of becoming a world-religion. The criterion of an institution was for him its mention in the gospels, or elsewhere in the Bible : if it were not mentioned it was not in accordance with " God's law." The Wycliffites, in accordance with their position, upheld the uniform authority of the whole of God's law : they laid much more stress on the teaching of the Old Testament to the people than the orthodox did at the time, and Wycliffe wrote one of his most important treatises, *De Veritate Sacrae Scripturae*, to defend the truth of the Bible against those who pointed out certain inconsistencies in its text, and whom he called " these modern heretics."

Wycliffe's appeal to scripture led him to set on foot a new translation of the Bible into English. His work in this direction was not unique in Europe : in Germany,

France, Spain and Italy, as well as England, there was a contemporary movement in favour of vernacular literature. The end of the fourteenth century saw the rise of more prosperous towns, and a more numerous merchant class ; whereas only the nobles could afford to buy books earlier, rich townsmen could now buy them also. It was largely for them that the new vernacular translations of all the important medieval manuals kept appearing, and among them translations of the gospels and the psalms, always with a translated gloss : for to put " the bare text " of the scriptures into lay people's hands was considered unwise. Henry von Mügeln prepared a German glossed psalter a few years after Richard Rolle produced his English one. The Dominicans translated the greater part of the Old Testament for the French king John the Good : Raoul de Presles revised an earlier French Bible in 1384. A new German Bible was prepared for the emperor Wenzel a few years after Wycliffe's death. The Wycliffite translation was then partly inspired by a contemporary movement, but it stands out among the other translations for three reasons. It was a complete new translation of the whole Vulgate, whereas all the others were partial, and most of them of the gospels only : it was prepared by at least five Wycliffe scholars at Oxford. Again, it was an unglossed translation, which was unwarranted by contemporary custom. Thirdly, it was meant for use by a lower social class : not only knights who could buy copies, but peasants and craftsmen who could not, but who learnt the text by heart in " schools " or conventicles. The first translation made by the Wycliffites proved of little use for this, because it translated the Latin word for word : accordingly Purvey retranslated the whole Bible " according to the sentence " or meaning, into normal, flowing English. Archbishop Arundel in 1408 condemned the Wycliffites' translations, and forbade any fresh translation to be made or read by any man without diocesan licence.

Wycliffe's teaching about the sacraments and certain other institutions was all conditioned by his appeal to the scriptures, primarily in their literal sense, though he did not throw overboard the old fourfold interpretation. He had no particular attack to make on baptism, confirmation, marriage, or unction ; but the case was otherwise with orders, penance and the mass. He held that there should be no difference in grade or function between bishop and priest : and he held that their supreme duty was preaching. As the canon law had no validity, laymen might preach as well. Sacramental confession to a priest was not necessary : Christians might confess their sins one to another without all this " ear-whispering." The doctrine of transubstantiation, the words substance and accidents, were not found in the Bible : therefore he challenged them, and it was at this point that the authorities began their serious efforts to suppress his teaching as heretical. There was something to be said, both for Wycliffe and the orthodox. Wycliffe did not challenge Christ's words : " This is My body," but only asserted that the philosophical theory which explained the change in the sacred elements was not to be found in the gospels, and that it led to popular misunderstanding and superstition, to a belief in the material change of the elements. No medieval theologian would have equated substance and matter : he would have explained the change as one of the substance, while the accidents of bread and wine remained. But to the popular mind, substance meant simply matter. The church herself used " substance " in this sense at times. The *Quicunque Vult* spoke of Christ as " man, of the substance of his mother, born in the world : " the collect for the Purification spoke of him as " presented in the temple in substance of our flesh." Popular manuals found it necessary to explain that when the priest broke the host or wafer at the consecration, Christ's body was not thereby broken. But for the orthodox it might be said that Wycliffe really believed Christ was not present in the mass at all. He contended mainly that the orthodox explanation was unscriptural : but he was pressed into giving explanations of his own belief as to the mode of Christ's presence. At one time his answers were not inconsistent with the later Lutheran doctrine of consubstantiation, (the presence of both substances, of bread and wine and of Christ's body and blood, after the consecration) ; at another much more significant and disturbing. Christ was present in the sacrament of the altar, he said, as the king was regarded by the law as present in the whole of his kingdom, so that all crimes were committed in his presence. To the medieval mind this was equivalent to saying Christ was present only by a legal fiction, or only allegorically, or in fact not present at all. And in face of Christ's words, this was a very great heresy.

Wycliffe's enemies tried to bring him to trial in 1378, but failed. They renewed their attack in the summer of 1382, at Oxford, and in a sermon at S. Mary's denounced his followers for the first time as " Lollards," that is, as resembling the Dutch heretical preachers. There was a dreadful uproar, but in spite of the chancellor's efforts to protect him, Wycliffe's teaching was condemned as heretical, his followers were attacked, and he was forced to withdraw to Lutterworth, where he died eighteen months later. Lollardy could no longer remain an Oxford movement. It failed to obtain the approbation of parliament in 1395, and it attempted a military rising under Oldcastle, which failed in 1414 : Oldcastle was executed as heretic and traitor in 1417. But Lollardy maintained a twofold existence later. It existed in obscure local movements in England continuously till the Reformation : and it flourished in Bohemia.

The machinery by which the church dealt with heretics was developed gradually : the three chief stages were those of the old episcopal inquisition, the sending out of papal legates to inquire into heresy, and the setting up of the Inquisition as an independent institution in the reign of Gregory IX. The word " inquisitio," inquiry, was a common legal term : lay rulers frequently ordered local *inquisitiones* into questions of property ownership, and spiritual rulers used the same term, and roughly the same process, for inquiries into " heretical pravity." In the early days of Christianity the church herself had been persecuted, and there had been no specific punishment for heresy, certainly no death penalty : S. John Chrysostom held that " to put a heretic to death would be a crime inexpiable." In 385 Priscillian, a Spanish heretic, and his followers, were denounced to the emperor by the

Spanish bishops for heresy and sortilege, a civil offence, and burned by his command : but S. Martin of Tours and Ambrose condemned vigorously the bishops' share in the matter. In the centuries following there was neither popular heresy nor burnings : the right to safeguard the faith was inherent in the bishop's office, and he could condemn an individual teacher who fell into error by his own jurisdiction, or condemn particular doctrines as heretical with his fellow-bishops in the provincial synod.

It was not till the Cathari became dangerous, in the twelfth century, that heretics began to be punished by death, especially by burning. In 1022 king Robert of France had thirteen of the Cathari burned in his presence at Orleans. The stake had been sanctioned by Roman law as the punishment for parricide, arson, sorcery and a few other crimes : the burning of witches and sorcerers was still practised. The emperor Henry III had certain Cathari hanged in Saxony. Heresy was not a civil offence, but in both these instances the executions had full popular approval. The mob passion of cruelty was further exercised : in 1075 a Catharan condemned by the bishop of Cambrai as a heretic, without sentence, was seized by the bishop's officers and the mob, placed in a shed, and burned with it. In 1114 the mob in the bishop of Strassburg's absence dragged some heretics from his prison and burned them, and the same thing happened at Cologne : in 1145 the clergy at Liège only just succeeded in rescuing the victims of the crowd. The mob burned Peter de Bruys, a heretic of Languedoc, because it saw him make a bonfire of crucifixes. Lawless violence against heretics continued : the spectacle of a hanging was common enough, but death at the stake roused all the baser instincts of cruelty. Many of the clergy protested at this stage : Gregory VII excommunicated the inhabitants of Cambrai in 1076 ; a bishop of Liège, questioned about the handing over of heretics to the secular arm for punishment, recommended lenience, and letting the tares grow together with the wheat until the harvest. Nevertheless, the violence of the mob must have seemed to most clergy to have its fortunate side, in keeping the danger of the heretical penetration of society in check :

the clergy belonged to the ages of violence as well as the mob. The punishment of heretics so far was irregular, and even the *Decretum* of Gratian laid down no regular procedure, because his authorities disagreed. Gratian himself stated that heretics might be fined and exiled, but not killed : but later commentators upon the *Decretum* argued that they might. A council of Tours, 1163, presided over by the pope, ordered the confiscation of a heretic's goods : and the second Lateran council, 1179, which dealt with the Cathari and the Waldensians, commended the punishment of heretics " per exteras," by the secular arm. In 1184 pope Lucius III met the emperor Frederick Barbarossa at Verona, and issued a bull regularising the prosecution of suspected heretics, and the assistance of the civil authorities, while Frederick placed all heretics under the imperial ban. So far the prosecution was left to the bishop.

The pontificates of Innocent III and Honorius III, (1198–1227), were marked by the sending out of papal missionaries as inquisitors, in the effort to prevent the spread of Albigensian and Waldensian heresy in Provence, and up the Rhine into Germany. Two Cistercian monks were sent to Metz by Innocent in 1199 and a legate and another monk worked in Provence : the bishop of Osma offered S. Dominic and his friends to the legate to help the work by preaching. The efforts of all were fruitless, unbacked by the secular power, and the legate was murdered. Inquiry into heretical pravity was replaced by the Albigensian Crusade, though, as mentioned earlier, the episcopal inquisition was strengthened by the fourth Lateran council.

The machinery of the papal Inquisition was organised by Gregory IX, largely with the help of Raymond of Peñaforte. Two changes were made. The old canonical methods of dealing with heretics, by denunciation (by the archdeacon), or accusation (by a private witness), were completely dropped for the new method of inquisition. By this method, the inquisitor visited a town or a village " defamed " of heresy, and solemnly charged the inhabitants to accuse all whom they suspected : the village clergy and in some cases a special " synodal witness,"

or spy maintained in the district, would also give evidence.
This was the *inquisitio generalis*, and many accusations
were thus obtained ; those who surrendered themselves
voluntarily were adjudged to penance. An *inquisitio
specialis* followed, where those accused were questioned
as to their belief, and most stringently as to the other
heretics with whom they consorted : to be " defamed '
was treated as a priori evidence of guilt, and, while those
who confessed at first received a light penance, it was
practically impossible to prove complete innocence. The
inquisitor never allowed those defamed to depart without
penance at all. The second change made by Gregory IX
was his practice of granting inquisitorial commissions,
after 1227, only to friars, particularly to the Dominicans.
In 1223 he addressed two important bulls, one to the
French bishops, telling them that he had decided to divide
their burdens by sending the preaching friars against the
heretics of France : and the other to the friars themselves,
giving them new and extraordinary powers in their work.
Inquisitorial practice was regularised by being kept in the
hands of the two mendicant orders, and this bull may be
reckoned as the establishment of the papal and mendicant,
or as it is sometimes called, the Dominican Inquisition :
the Holy Office. It worked in succeeding centuries in most
European countries, though it was only used in England
for the trial of the Templars. The Lollards were tried
by the English bishops themselves, though the Dominicans
were active in procuring their condemnation.

The use of the Inquisition has justly been held one
of the greatest blots on the history of Christianity, its
employment of the spy system, of punishment by burning,
and of torture for procuring confession being peculiarly
irreconcilable with the spirit of Christ. Nothing could
be more horrible reading than the record kept by the
Spanish inquisitors of every word spoken by their victims
under torture. Nothing can excuse such enormities. But
a fair historical judgment should take into consideration
certain facts. The inquisitor believed an unrepentant
heretic would go to hell, into that fire which Christ said
" shall never be quenched : " he tried by all means,
short of torture itself if possible, to bring the heretic to

confession. He hoped the heretic might repent even in the flames, and be saved " yet so as by fire." For the sake of the vine of Christ, obstinately withered branches should be " cut out, and cast into the fire, and burned." In Spain, too, the Moors were national as well as spiritual enemies. Again, the Inquisition has been shown to have been far more effective against heretics by the confiscation of goods and fines than by any other weapon, even torture or the stake. Again, the law in England made use of torture, and continental civil law used it as late as the seventeenth century, and admitted curious and well-born strangers to watch. Finally, the Inquisition and the proscription of heretics from all schools together preserved the unity of the Latin church for three hundred years. The Waldensians from 1200, and the English Lollards from 1400, did succeed in maintaining their existence, in spite of proscription, till the Reformation : and but for the Inquisition there would have been other permanent organised bodies of Christians outside the Latin church. The Inquisition was justified to its contemporaries by its success.

CHAPTER XVIII

THE CONCILIAR MOVEMENT

Fourteenth century reform movements : Gerard Groot and Hus—
The conciliar idea—The council of Pisa—The council of Constance—
The council of Basle—Causes of failure

THE conciliar movement was the most important feature of church history in the first half of the fifteenth century, and its failure led to the Reformation of the sixteenth. General councils were held at Pisa in 1409, Constance from 1414 till 1418, and Basle from 1431 till 1449 : but during the whole period the questions of the summons, authority and achievements of these councils were of dominant interest. One main cause of the summons of the first council, the existence of the Schism, has been mentioned earlier : another cause was the reform movement in Bohemia, led from 1400 onwards by John Hus, rector of the university of Prag and a great preacher in the Czech language. There were in fact three movements in northern Europe whose leaders desired the reform of the church, and set about achieving it, and in each case they found opponents to accuse their methods as ill-judged, and their peculiar tenets as heresy. The movements were inspired by Wycliffe in England, by Gerard Groot in the Netherlands, and by Hus in Bohemia. The English and Bohemian movements were in very close connexion and at first similar in character: the Dutch movement had no connexion with the English but certain affinities with it, particularly in the desire to promote the lay use of vernacular prayers, offices and scriptures. The council of Constance dealt with all three movements.

The movement of the " New Devotion " was the result of the preaching of Gerard Groot (or " the Great ") in the Netherlands. He attained a great reputation at the university, and was converted by a Carthusian friend, who " let down the net of pious exhortation to draw this great fish into the ship of holy religion." He made a long noviciate with the Carthusians, and then spent the rest of his life as a mission preacher, always retaining his Carthusian austerity of life. He died the same year as Wycliffe. He gathered round himself a number of disciples, who supported themselves by copying manuscripts, teaching and alms. He founded from among their number houses of " Brethren of the Common Life," and houses of Austin canons inspired by the same principles : there were also houses of " Sisters of the Common Life." The men's houses did mission and pastoral work, and had schools for boys which became famous. They were not friaries, because Gerard shared the contemporary reaction against mendicancy : his followers were to live very simply, but earn their living by teaching and other work. The houses of the Brethren spread all over the Netherlands, Windesheim and Deventer being the best known : the canons of Mount S. Agnes at Kempen, also founded through Gerard's influence, produced Thomas of Kempen (à Kempis) and the *Imitation of Christ* in the fifteenth century. The Brothers contended especially for the right to encourage the laity to use Dutch scriptures, booklets and prayers. In 1398 they invited certain well known lawyers from the university of Cologne, together with a Benedictine abbot, to their house at Deventer, and obtained from them pronouncements in writing that it was lawful for lay people to use sacred books written in the vulgar tongue. The Inquisition noted this affair, and declared that the Masters of Cologne had acted " sufficiently impertinently " in trying to protect the Brethren. The whole subject of the lawfulness of the way of life of the Brethren and the Sisters came up at the council of Constance.

The Wycliffe movement in Oxford had from the beginning been in close touch with the Bohemian university of Prag, whose chief patron was the emperor Wenzel, father-in-law of the English Richard II. The Wycliffite

English gospels, with a translated gloss, were presented to queen Anne of Bohemia, who already had Slav and German books of the gospels. Students from Prag came to England, heard Wycliffe and his followers lecture, and took copies of his treatises back to Prag. Peter Payne, a great Lollard clerk and debater at Oxford, thought it safer to flee to Prag in 1415, and there he was made M.A. and had a long and prominent career. The chief friend and disciple of Hus, Jerome of Prag, completed part of his academic course at Oxford, and returned with Wycliffe's treatises. Bohemia itself had produced reformers of a similar type to the early Wycliffites, men like Conrad Waldhaüser, John Militz Kremsier and Matthias of Janow, who had protested against the existence of monks and friars, and the worldliness of the higher clergy. Matthias had a devotion to the Bible similar to Wycliffe's : " It has not departed from me," he wrote, " neither in the way, nor when I was occupied, nor when I was at leisure. . . . And when I saw that many men carried with them everywhere the relics and bones of divers saints . . . I chose for myself the Bible as my elect, the companion of my pilgrimage, to bear ever with me." Hus therefore inherited a tradition of reform from Bohemian sources as well as English : but his character was strong on the moral rather than the intellectual side, and he borrowed from Wycliffe very closely in his writings. His *De Ecclesia* was little more than a translation of Wycliffe. Like Wycliffe he denounced the claim of the papacy to the overlordship of the church, the worldliness of the clergy, the sin of simony. Wycliffe demanded that lay knights should step in and reform the church : Hus declared that the church could not try heresy cases. He went further than Wycliffe in his conception of predestination : both he and Wycliffe had an immense reverence for Augustine. Wycliffe's doctrine that dominion belonged only to those who kept God's law merged at times into the position that dominion belonged only to God's elect, and Hus emphasised this aspect. The Husites challenged, like the Lollards, all extra-biblical rites, institutions and customs, and they laid special emphasis on the withdrawal of the cup from the laity as non-biblical.

R

Hus was not merely a distinguished doctor, but he soon became the nationalist leader of the Slav party in the empire. The university of Prag had been founded by the emperor Charles IV, who had always favoured Bohemia as against his German subjects, and helped Prag by his patronage to become larger and more distinguished than any purely German university. Both German and Slav scholars came to Prag, and the German masters represented the bulk of the orthodox opposition to Hus and Jerome of Prag. One of the Germans brought up the question of the condemned Wycliffite doctrines, and the majority being orthodox the university again condemned them. But in 1409 the emperor Wenzel desired the support of the university for the cardinals anxious to end the Schism by a council : the German majority were unwilling to concur, since they supported the Roman pope, and Wenzel overruled them. He changed the constitution of the university, making the Slavs completely dominant, and the Germans thereupon withdrew in a body. His edict meant a triumph for Husite teaching as well as Slav nationalism, and henceforth the two became more and more closely connected. Husitism was so strong in Bohemia, that its suppression seemed to the orthodox as important as the ending of the Schism.

The holding of the councils was brought about by moderate reformers like Gerson, chancellor of Paris, Pierre D'Ailly, Dietrich Niem and Zabarella. But the main source of inspiration was the orthodox and influential university of Paris. In 1394 its members were invited to send suggestions as to the best means of ending the Schism, and among the numerous answers received, many suggested the holding of a general council. The answers were those of the most outsta ling members, and gave the best promise of success. Gerson and D'Ailly explained that the *plenitudo potestatis* of the church resided in its whole body, as represented in a general council. The civil power might lawfully summon such a council, for Constantine and other emperors had done so. The university of Paris urged on the French king that Christ had submitted to the authority of his mother and S. Joseph, and the pope, no greater than

Christ, might well submit to his mother, the church. Let cardinals, archbishops, bishops, the heads of the monastic, mendicant and military orders be called : let doctors of theology and law from the university, and the representatives of the civil power be summoned : and let such a council end the Schism, condemn heresy, and reform the church.

The question, how far this expedient was lawful, is of interest. Was this " appeal from the vicar of Christ on earth to Christ Himself, residing in the whole body of the church " in the line of Christian tradition, or was it an innovation ? Its necessity to end the Schism was in fact generally conceded, for when the council of Constance finally succeeded in ending it, the pope elected was then and later accepted as lawful. The Latin church was in an impasse with no other practical way out. But the council's claim to the *plenitudo potestatis* was felt to be an innovation, masked by antiquarian research. The undivided church had been ruled at crises by general councils : but for six or seven hundred years before 1400 Christendom had tended to split into east and west, and the split had been absolute since Michael Cerularius. Councils held had been either Greek and eastern, or Latin and western. The Latin councils, held at intervals since the days of Charlemagne, had been summoned and presided over by the pope, or his legate. The councils held were now to be Latin councils, at any rate till reunion with the Greek church could be arranged, and there was small precedent for such a council to declare itself superior to the pope, or to become the governing body of Christendom by arranging for future sessions at regular intervals. The conciliar method justified itself to scholars on antiquarian precedent, and to all more or less from the motive of immediate necessity, but it really expressed the democratic tendency of the age, similar to the desire to give a house of representatives some share in the civil government. It was the religious side of a democratic movement in Europe. Bishops desired to settle issues with the pope, to reform the curia, to win a victory over their old rivals, the papally protected friars. The lower clergy desired to reform the prelates. The laity desired to reform the clergy, to limit benefit of clergy, to confiscate clerical endowments. The claim of the superiority of the council to the pope was itself partly a lay claim, because at the back of the council was the lay emperor. Moreover, though the councils were international, and in accordance with orthodox, international, political thought, their sessions showed the rising strength of nationalism.

In 1407 the university of Paris induced the French king to withdraw his allegiance from the Avignon pope : earlier efforts to get the rival popes to meet and agree upon a solution had been no more successful than attempts to make land and sea beasts confer together, as a contemporary remarked. The rival cardinals had, however, conferred, and they now deserted the popes and summoned a general council to meet at Pisa. France and England supported the council, Wenzel agreed to support it and coerced Prag, but Germany as a whole was divided, and the Spanish kingdoms supported the Avignon pope,—now fled into Spanish territory. The council opened in March, 1409, and the existence of two parties within it became apparent. The cardinals and the majority wished to end the Schism, but not to undertake reform : Gerson, D'Ailly and the Paris doctors wanted reform as well. It was agreed that the *causa unionis* should precede the *causa reformationis*. Charges were formally brought against both popes, and both were deposed. A Franciscan was then elected as Alexander V, but this proved a mistake. Neither the Roman nor the Avignon pope acknowledged the deposition, and the university of Paris expelled the mendicants in answer to certain bulls of Alexander V, conferring privileges on his own order. When Alexander died, the Cardinals elected a clerical brigand as John XXIII, and the three rival popes continued. The council of Pisa had failed : yet it was significant.

The next council met at Constance on 1 November, 1414. While the assembly at Pisa had been one mainly of prelates, that of Constance included princes as well as ecclesiastics. It was almost as much a great diet of the medieval empire, as a council of the medieval church. It was presided over by the emperor Sigismund, and became the meeting place for the national interests of

Europe. The summons to it had been issued not merely by the cardinals, but at Sigismund's request by John XXIII himself. The council was divided ecclesiastically between reformers and conservatives. The latter wished merely to end the Schism, the former taught that the council had authority superior to the pope, and should carry out reforms ; but they feared the doctrines of Wycliffe and Hus as much as the conservatives. The council achieved the ending of the Schism, the vindication of the Brethren of the Common Life, and the condemnation of Hus : it failed to reform the church at large.

John XXIII regarded the council with misgiving, but hoped to stir up trouble between it and the emperor, and avoid his own deposition. He nearly succeeded in his aim over the question of Hus, but things went against him, and he decided to flee. The council deposed him in May 1415, and declared the church without a head. After considering the whole question of Hus and heresy, they elected cardinal Odo Colonna as pope Martin V, and Europe received the news of the ending of the Schism with enthusiasm. The council had hoped to proceed with reform after the election ; they had already discussed such matters as the reorganisation of the curia, and the college of cardinals : papal dispensations and indulgences : the suppression of provisions and annates. To secure reform they had passed a decree in 1417 that a council should be held again in five years, another within seven years, and that afterwards a council should meet regularly every ten years. The superiority of a general council to the pope would be vindicated if the decision to summon it did not rest with him. But when Martin V was elected, (November, 1417), he denied that a general council was superior to the pope and declared that the whole question of reform must be left with him. " No one may appeal from the supreme judge, that is, the apostolic see or the Roman pontiff, vicar on earth of Jesus Christ, or may decline his authority in matters of faith." Gerson and his party in indignation asserted that such a declaration would nullify all the acts of the council, including Martin's own election : but the members of the council wanted chiefly to get home again. Though the council aimed at being universal, its procedure had been borrowed from the university of Paris, and the members had been voting by nations. On many questions it had been found that national interests clashed. Pope Martin now drew up separate concordats, making small concessions in the direction of reform, and offered them to each nation. They accepted them, and Martin dissolved the council in May, 1418.

The reformers at Constance approved the way of life of the Brethren of the Common Life, in spite of the arguments of certain Dominicans that certain practices were heretical. But curiously enough, Gerson and D'Ailly were less willing to let lay people use vernacular Bibles than the Brethren of Deventer had been. Gerson feared mistranslations and the effect of popularisation of the bare text. Men would almost certainly be "deceived by a false understanding of scripture : even as there are many men who understand scripture according to their own private opinion, and not according to the exposition of holy doctors, which they know not, or are unwilling to consider. . . . It is most dangerous to give to simple men and women, who are quite unlearned, books of the holy scripture translated into French, because they may forthwith fall into many errors by a misunderstanding." The Brethren themselves accepted the reformers' views, and while contending in the fifteenth century for the use of German and Dutch books of vices and virtues, lives of Christ and the saints, etc., did not argue that the use of vernacular gospels or missals was lawful, except with special licence.

The Husites had been attacked before the council. Alexander V had charged the archbishop of Prag to put down heresy, and Wycliffe's writings had been publicly burned at Prag: (they were also burned in Rome in 1413). Hus had been summoned to answer for his heretical opinions at Bologna, but he refused to go, appealing from the pope ill-informed to the pope better-informed. Moreover, when John XXIII had tried to raise money for an Italian war by the sale of indulgences, he had protested vigorously, and the papal bull had been burned in the public square at Prag. He was summoned to Constance by the council, and relying on the emperor Sigismund's safe conduct, he went. He expected to maintain his opinions in theological debate : he was tried as a heretic, the council virtually resolving itself into an inquisitorial court, and following inquisitorial methods. Hus's decision to go was a bold one, and though he trusted Sigismund, he left letters beforehand to be opened in the event of his death. The explanation of Sigismund's betrayal lies in the fact that he found himself in a dilemma. The cardinals were determined to try Hus, and to have protected him would have wrecked the council, and the chance of ending the Schism : so he sacrificed Hus. Legally, the cardinals' case was good : Hus came to the council as " suspect " or " defamed " of heresy, and such a man in law had neither rights nor privileges till he had purged himself. No secular safe-conduct could stand, according to the contemporary rules for dealing with heretics.

The council demanded of Hus a complete abjuration of all the heresies with which he was charged : Hus stoutly declared that the charges misrepresented his teaching, and refused. The English Lollards had declared as bitterly that the list of heresies presented to them for acknowledgment and confession had been garbled versions of their teaching : but the *De heretico comburendo* act of 1401 had made them willing for the most part to recant them, as their own teaching. Hus's teaching was most vulnerable with regard to the sole " dominion " of the righteous, or the predestined. No man living in a state of mortal sin had any right to exercise authority. The doctrine had perilous implications, and Sigismund reminded Hus that no man lives without sin. Hus was not condemned formally for any heresy or error, but for his refusal to abjure. " Serene prince," he said to Sigismund, " I may not offend God and my conscience by saying that I hold heresies that I have never held ; " and he wrote in a letter shortly before his death : " Assuredly it is fitting for me rather to die than to flee a momentary penalty and fall into the hand of the Lord, and afterwards, perchance, into everlasting fire and shame. And because I have appealed to Christ Jesus, the most potent and just of all judges, committing my cause to Him, therefore I stand by His judgment and sentence, knowing that He will judge every man not on false and erroneous evidence but on the true facts and merits of his case." Hus was degraded from the priesthood, and burned outside the walls of Constance on 6 July, 1415. The council had condemned the teaching of Wycliffe just before his trial in June, and declared communion in both kinds heretical between his trial and his death. Jerome of Prag was burned the year following.

The council of Basle met to promote reform, heal the Greek schism, and above all to deal with Husite heresy in Bohemia,—the only reason why the papacy desired its aid. Bohemia had been furious over Hus's betrayal, and his doctrines, popular before, at once became the programme of the national Slav party in Bohemia. The nationalists were quite unwilling that Bohemia should sink back into being merely a part of Sigismund's mainly German empire, and they took up arms to demand the whole Husite programme. Under John Ziska, a capable soldier, they soon became the dominant military party in Bohemia, which was plunged in civil war. They demanded especially freedom of laymen to preach, and the reception of holy communion by the laity in both kinds, whence they were termed Utraquists. At the same time they demanded social and democratic reforms, and seized the land of hostile lay nobles and the church by force : the movement partook of the nature of a peasants' revolt. There were different shades of opinion within the party : the moderate Husites or " Calixtines " wished for gradual reform, the extreme radical and democratic party, the Taborites, were frankly revolutionary, hostile to every kind of authority. To the Calixtines religious grievances, and to the Taborites social grievances counted for most. In 1420 Martin V proclaimed a Crusade against the Husites, but Bohemia under Ziska defeated all the German armies sent against her. In 1427 a fourth Husite Crusade was proclaimed, and though Ziska was by now dead of the plague, Prokop his successor defeated even larger imperial armies as completely. The English cardinal Beaufort, who accompanied the Crusade, tore the imperial colours to pieces in his rage at the crusaders'

flight. The complete failure to suppress the Husites by
military means gave birth to the idea that " heresy should
be met with argument, not with arms," and that a council
should deal with the Husites. In accordance with the
decrees of Constance, Martin V had allowed unimportant
councils of Italian prelates to meet at Pavia and Siena,
and a council was due to be held at Basle in 1431. Martin
dreaded a fresh council beyond the Alps, but he summoned
the council and appointed cardinal Cesarini to preside
over it as his legate : he died himself on the eve of the
council.

The important sessions of the council of Basle were
held between 1431 and 1438, when it quarrelled with the
pope. The members avoided the error of voting by
nations, and divided themselves into four deputations,
each of which discussed a separate subject. One dealt
with the restoration of peace (the Husite problem) : the
second, doctrine and faith, (which affected both Greeks
and Husites) : the third, reform, and the fourth, general
business. The council succeeded in arranging the Bohemian question, thanks to the conciliatory temper of
Cesarini. Prokop himself was summoned to a three
months' discussion, and thereafter delegates of the council
negotiated with the diet at Prag. An agreement called
the *Compactata* was arrived at, by which Bohemians and
Moravians were allowed to receive the communion in both
kinds, and a nominal liberty of preaching was conceded,
so long as the sacraments were only administered by
ordained priests, and the authority of bishops was obeyed.
The question of the benefit of clergy was left vague, but
it was clearly stated that the church might possess endowments, with which it was sacrilege for laymen to interfere.
These concessions satisfied the moderate Husites, but
not the extremists. It was necessary to win a military
victory over the Taborites before Sigismund could enter
Prag in triumph, and feel his power restored in Bohemia.
The pope somewhat reluctantly confirmed the concessions
in 1435.

Meanwhile the council had won no credit for its other
work. Its negotiations with the Greeks for reunion had
failed, and certain measures of reform which it carried

were discredited by others which seemed a clear encroachment upon papal rights. It declared annates abolished in
1435, and legislated for the reform of the curia in 1436 :
but it also appointed legates, conferred the pallium
and even issued a decree of indulgence. The Greeks
showed themselves more willing to negotiate with the
pope than the council : ill-feeling became more acute,
Cesarini declared himself on the pope's side in November
1436, and in the middle of the next year the schism
between the pope and the council became complete. Of
the only two possible mediators, Cesarini left Basle in
December 1437, and Sigismund died in January 1438.
While the more responsible members of the council went
off in 1438 to the council of Ferrara, whither the pope
had summoned the Greek delegates to discuss reunion,
(see chapter XIX), other members held later sessions at
Basle, and elected an antipope. Though council and
antipope had from the first little chance of securing the
allegiance of Europe, they found a certain support in
Germany, and their existence enabled the emperor
Frederick III to bargain for papal concessions before
disowning them. He sent an order to the civic magistrates
to dissolve the remnant of the council in 1449.

Although the council had not carried its programme
of reform, England, France and the Empire protected
themselves individually as regards the points about which
they felt most. The English statutes of Provisors and
Praemunire remained on the statute-book. In 1438 a
synod of French clergy accepted the Pragmatic Sanction
of Bourges, which applied to France many of the reforms
which the council had desired for the whole church, and
which in particular checked the flow of French gold to
Rome. In 1439 a German diet followed the French lead,
and drew up the Pragmatic Sanction of Mainz. Annates
were abolished, papal reservations and provisions forbidden, and local self-government quickened by arrangements for the regular holding of provincial and diocesan
synods. These concordats of Martin V saved the situation
for the papacy, which when the great jubilee was held
in 1450 seemed stronger than ever. Pius II, who as the
humanist Aeneas Sylvius had done most to secure the

rapprochement of Frederick III with the papacy, published a bull formally condemning the practice of appealing from the pope to a general council. Sixtus IV confirmed it in 1483, and five years earlier formally annulled the decrees of the council of Constance. The principle of the constitutional reform and future government of the church through her own members had failed.

The reasons for the failure of the conciliar movement are various. The council of Constance might possibly have carried some reform before electing a pope. Martin V showed extraordinary skill in playing off sectional jealousies to his own advantage : national jealousies, and especially those between England and France, and between the northern nations and Italy : and the clerical jealousy of the bishops and prelates. The extravagance of some of the claims of the council of Basle made it finally " a laughing stock to Christendom." Moreover, a " parliamentary " experiment in church government was untimely : it had been discredited by the corresponding lay movements in the fourteenth century, and the future lay with the " new monarchy," with strong national kings like Henry VII and Louis XI. To the new monarchy the Renaissance papacy was in some sense an analogue.

CHAPTER XIX

THE RENAISSANCE

The Renaissance spirit—The early Renaissance—The fall of Constantinople—Orthodoxy at the end of the fifteenth century—Factors working for change

WHEN the Christian church became the religion of the Roman Empire she was not eager that her ministers should devote themselves to the Greek and Latin literature which was no small part of the imperial heritage. She apprehended two dangers from such contact, the one plain and evident, the other obscure. She hated the classical pantheon and mythology, and could not dissociate the beauties of Greek and Latin literature from the worship of idols and daemons. S. Augustine lamented that he found the fables of Dido and Aeneas more attractive in form than the Christian gospels. Gregory the Great wrote to Didier of Vienne, the most learned bishop in Gaul, that he was grieved to hear that Didier lectured on the pagan classics : such studies did not befit even a religious layman, much less a bishop. The church's fear of classical paganism was to die, as paganism died : but her more obscure fear was to prove not ill-founded in the fifteenth and sixteenth centuries— the fear of the Greek spirit. Christianity grew from a Hebrew stock, with a strong conception of morality : the Christian teaching about sin, redemption, a future life and an imminent judgment demanded restraint on the part of the individual, and some measure of asceticism. The "perfect" Christian life was in every century conceived of as demanding great renunciations. These conceptions clashed with the Greek watchword of moderation, of "nothing too much:" the Greek reverence for beauty : the Greek acceptance of the joys of the senses as good in themselves, coupled often with sensual indulgence of a baser nature. Pagan and Christian philosophy made terms : pagan and Christian morals could not be made to square. Hence, when Europe began to pass out of the dark ages there was no general desire on the part of scholars to lift the veil that hung between them and the art and literature of ancient Greece.

Nevertheless, it would be a mistake to think that all medieval people were pious and ascetic, or that an anti-ascetic spirit did not find expression in literature. The romance of *Aucassin and Nicolette* comes from twelfth-century Provence, and in a famous passage Aucassin, threatened with hell if he persists in his love for Nicolette, replies that to hell he will go. " For none go to Paradise but I'll tell you who. Your old priests and your old cripples, and the halt and the maimed, who are down on their knees day and night, before altars and in old crypts : these also that wear mangy old cloaks, or go in rags and tatters, shivering and shoeless and showing their sores, and who die of hunger and want and misery. These are they who go to Paradise : and what have I to do with them ? Hell is the place for me. For to hell go the fine churchmen, and the fine knights, killed in the tourney or in some grand war, the brave soldiers and the gallant gentlemen. With them I will go. There go also the fair gracious ladies who have lovers two or three beside their lord. There go the gold and silver, the sables and the ermines. There go the harpers and the minstrels and the kings of the earth. With them will I go, so I have Nicolette my most sweet friend with me." In less sceptical individuals, the same anti-ascetic spirit allowed them to enjoy the good things of life, while compounding for a possibly uncomfortable hereafter by money offerings. Chaucer's irony played upon the complaisant friar who measured repentance not by tears, but by such gifts : " They may not weep, although them sorë smart."

Italian scholars and writers were first to realise the importance of Greek, and most notable among them Petrarch and Boccaccio. Dante had given the finest expression to the medieval attitude to life and the universe in the *Divina Commedia :* Petrarch prided himself on never having read it, because it was not in Latin. He and Boccaccio both learned the rudiments of Greek, and found in the classics the key to the interpretation of life. To Petrarch the works of the ancients contained " all wisdom and rules of right conduct : " the true aim for man should be the quest of imperishable renown. Italy he found " the fairest country under heaven," and he desired that she should become the instructress of the human mind. By a revival of ancient practice he was crowned poet-laureate on the Capitol by the Roman Senate, and when he died in 1374 an Italian empire of letters had been fairly founded. In Florence, Rome, Milan, Naples, the Renaissance was abroad. In Florence Italian scholars had brought the Greek teacher Manuel Chrysoloras to the university, and persuaded him to stay and teach Greek : when Cosimo dei Medici began his rule of Florence in 1434, his chancellor Leonardo Bruni had been one of his scholars, and was the first Italian really to master the Greek language. Under Cosimo and Lorenzo architects, sculptors and painters as well as scholars were attracted to Florence : in a competition for the gates of the baptistery Ghiberti produced the bronze gates of which Michael Angelo said : " They are so beautiful that they would do well for the gates of Paradise." Cosimo was the patron of the Platonist, Niccolò Niccoli, and on his death placed the manuscripts Niccolò had left him in the convent of S. Mark, for the use of students. While the early Renaissance scholars had despised Italian, Lorenzo dei Medici and his circle admired it, wrote poems in it, and treatises in its defence : the support of vernacular literature became a frequent characteristic of Renaissance effort. At Florence the high spring time of the Renaissance came with more of spiritual beauty, and less of coarseness and sensuality than elsewhere : in Lorenzo's circle were Platonists like Marsilio Ficino his tutor, Poliziano and Pico della Mirandola, poets who wrote in Italian and made commentaries on Dante, and painters like Ghirlandaio and Sandro Botticelli. In Milan the children of Francesco Sforza, the ruler, had Greek tutors and became prodigies of learning.

In Rome humanism invaded the papacy with Nicholas V, (1447-1455). Like Cosimo dei Medici, he was without much classical learning himself, but a great patron of men of genius, among them Fra Angelico and Lorenzo Valla. The latter had been a scholar of Leonardo Bruni, from whom he had learned Greek, had wandered as a teacher to various universities, and had become the secretary of Alfonzo V of Aragon and Naples. In his *De Voluptate* he contrasted the principles of the Stoics with those of Epicurus, and openly sympathised with those who claimed the right to the free indulgence of all natural appetites. He openly declaimed against the monastic life. In 1439 he had written a treatise on the so-called Donation of Constantine, and exposed the real nature of the document, and his zeal had shown similarly that other works supposed to be early Christian were but forgeries, like the letter of Christ to Abgarus. He ridiculed the Latin of the Vulgate, and accused S. Augustine of heresy : he had been even summoned before the Inquisition, and only escaped by the special intervention of Alfonzo. But his curious views and activities weighed nothing with Nicholas compared to his scholarship and his humanism : he made him apostolic secretary, and none could say thereafter that the curia was obscurantist or lacking in the humanities. Nicholas's supreme object, in fact, was to bring the papacy to the forefront of the Renaissance movement, and use the triumphs of pagan art in the service of the church. His reign saw the fall of Constantinople, and the failure to unite Europe in a Crusade to restore it was the tragedy of his successor Pius II, (1458-1464), also a humanist. The latter, by birth Aeneas Silvius Piccolomini, was not merely a patron of learning, but a scholar himself, and one of the most interesting characters of the century. His early life was devoted to diplomacy, letters, and travel, in the course of which he visited England and Scotland ; he supported the earlier Conciliar movement at Basle, was active at the council of Florence in 1438, and thereafter as papal secretary. From 1442 he was poet laureate and secretary to Frederick III, and for his success in securing his neutrality and bringing the council of Basle to an end he was made bishop of Siena. He wrote poems, a novel, a witty and immoral play, *Chrisis*, and a diary or *Commentaries* in which he mingled shrewd political observations with frank descriptions of his private vices. When by skilful intrigue he obtained the papacy in 1458, the humanists rejoiced that so ripe a scholar should ascend the papal chair, his very title Pius bearing a reference to the Virgilian hero after whom he had been named. Though the new pope abandoned with his elevation the licence of his past, calling on friends to forget it, (" Aeneam rejicite, Pium accipite "), his love of natural beauty and delight in archæology led him to wander round Italy, endearing himself in the process to numbers of his fellow countrymen.

The Renaissance thus had gone far indeed before the fall of Constantinople in 1453. The latter was itself an ecclesiastical event of the first magnitude, apart from its effect on the Renaissance. The city had been long threatened. Islam had been strengthened in the east by the rise of the Ottoman Turks, and throughout the fifteenth century the Byzantine emperors had appealed more and more desperately for help, at least in money, to protect their capital. The Greek emperor Manuel II had toured round Europe asking for help in 1400, and in the December of that year he had crossed the channel in hope of raising funds. Though the hard-up Henry IV had no money to spare, he had welcomed his imperial visitor cordially enough. Manuel stayed at Canterbury with the archbishop, and spent Christmas with the king, remaining in England nearly two months, and his visit was a source of ecclesiastical interest, both to Lollards and orthodox. The Lollards were not slow to point out that Manuel's chaplains said the daily mass before him according to the Greek rite and in the Greeks' mother tongue : even lay knights as well as clerks took part in the Greek offices, for the same reason. The Lollards addressed petitions to Henry in the January parliament " asking that it should be generally permitted to have the law of God [the Bible] in their mother tongue," as the Greeks had in theirs. Whereupon the Greeks were questioned : " Whether the common people, and the ignorant, in their country did indeed understand the scriptures, and the divine words [which they] recited together with the learned ? " To which they answered, " No : holy scripture is edited in a language totally unknown to the common people, and the common people have a Greek which is totally different from that Greek in which the divine word is retained." Which satisfactory reply the Dominicans duly noted, and the king had it preached in a sermon at Paul's Cross the Sunday before Septuagesima, 1401, for the refuting of the Lollards.

It was the increasing danger from the Turks, coupled with the perception that nothing but the ending of the Schism between east and west would rouse Europe to send help, that led the Greek patriarch to send delegates to the council which met at Ferrara in 1438, and was transferred to Florence on the outbreak of the plague. The pope himself presided, and the old subjects of dispute, the addition of the *Filioque* clause to the original form of the Nicaean creed, the use of leavened or unleavened bread in the eucharist, the doctrine of purgatory, were all discussed. The vital difference was that between the Latin doctrine of the papal supremacy and the Greek conception of autocephalous churches. The Greek delegates yielded on all points, a decree of union was drawn up, and the papal triumph seemed complete. But the Greeks at home regarded the action of their delegates as a betrayal, the schism remained unhealed, and Europe sent no help against the Turk.

The Greek patriarchate survived the conquest of Constantinople, though S. Sophia and all the churches save one were given over to Mahometan worship. The Sultan Mahomet II allowed the patriarchate to continue, and even protected it from interference. But as the Turks added Serbia, Wallachia and Bosnia to their conquest the Greek church was made a captive church, and Christianity the religion only of the conquered peasants. In the west Pius II tried to reawaken the crusading spirit, and retake the city. He summoned a congress to Mantua in 1459, but the rivalries of the secular rulers of Europe rendered a united Crusade impossible, nor could the oratory of Pius stir them to united effort. In his last days Pius himself undertook a Crusade, but death overtook him at Ancona, averting what could only have been failure.

S

The fifteenth century was the eve of the Reformation : yet in its latter half both personal religion and the old institutions seemed in most parts of Europe flourishing. The conservatives seemed to have persuaded Europe to be content with the national concessions of reform at Basle. In England a devout conservative ruled, in the person of Henry VII. His mother, the lady Margaret Beaufort, guided by John Fisher, her confessor, founded divinity lectureships at both universities, and Christ's college and S. John's college at Cambridge. Bishop Alcock anticipated Wolsey by dissolving the nunnery of S. Rhadegund at Cambridge, in a very struggling condition since the Black Death, and using its buildings and endowments to found Jesus College. Judging from the wills of the period, and the episcopal registers, parish life flourished : bequests were plentiful for churches and their ornaments, for friaries, for hermits and anchoresses, for hospitals and almshouses. The records of visitations show a certain number of complaints from parishioners on the score of the absenteeism, ignorance or secular preoccupations of their rectors, but not a large proportion. The records of monastic visitations show that both men's and women's houses were impoverished, and the greater the poverty the worse the discipline : but while actual vice was found in some cases, the records show that it was exceptional. The secular work undertaken by nunneries for a living, the slackness of the monks in coming to mattins, and above all the debts of both, engaged the visitor's attention far more. Nevertheless, there were clearly more men's houses than were needed for true monastic vocations : the nunneries were always overflowing, because there was no other alternative for gently born women to marriage. Bishops had difficulty in keeping the number in the men's houses up, and in the women's houses down.

In Germany and the Netherlands, Italy and Spain, religion also was in different respects flourishing. In Germany and the Netherlands monastic conditions were definitely worse than in England, as appears from the episcopal commissions to John Busch, a Brother of the Common Life, to visit and reform various houses. But parish and diocesan life flourished : synods were held, mission preachers rebuked superstition and sin, and above all, emphasis was laid upon the popularisation of the gospels. Synods ordered priests to preach frequently and " to be cautious in their sermons, and not to utter useless and vain tales, offensive to pious minds, but rather to preach on Sundays and holy days the holy scripture of the Old and New Testament, plainly and intelligibly. First, let them explain the text in the vulgar tongue, as it lies, adding a commentary ; or verse by verse, even as they know to be suitable for their people's capacity." The laity were told that their Sunday obligation to hear mass extended to hearing the sermon. Since the mid-century printing-presses had been set up in all the Rhine towns, and printed German booklets and manuals for the laity were beginning to pour forth in some numbers. The first German Bible was printed in 1466, and between then and the publication of Luther's New Testament in 1522 fourteen editions of the German Bible were printed, and four in Dutch. They were mostly in use in nunneries : orthodox opinion still considered their free use by lay people dangerous, and no German manual was found to recommend such use till 1508. The Husites, Béguines and Waldensians continued to use them, as the Lollards used English Bibles in manuscript, (there was no fifteenth century printed English Bible). Both in England and on the continent it was possible for well-born lay people to use vernacular scriptures with episcopal licence.

In Italy everyday religion had suffered from Renaissance scepticism and Renaissance morals : but the success of the Dominican Girolamo Savonarola at Florence showed that the old medieval Puritanism was not yet dead. Florence repented in sackcloth and ashes of the Renaissance which she had so cherished, and in obedience to the preacher and terror of judgment to come adopted a life of Puritan strictness. In 1497, to mark the abolition of the Lenten carnival, the citizens made a " bonfire of the vanities," burning masks, manuscripts of songs and poems, and valuable jewels. A merchant who offered an immense sum for the doomed vanities was refused, and his portrait added to the pile. Such fervour was too strained to last. In Spain the reign of Ferdinand and Isabella, covering

the last half of the century, was of great importance to
local religion, and the future of European Christianity in
the sixteenth century. Up till their reign, the Spanish
peninsula had been divided into four small kingdoms,
including Portugal, and three of these were now united.
Ferdinand and Isabella saw in religion a bond of political
union, and used all their efforts both to strengthen and
reform it. The work was carried out by cardinals Ximenes
and Torquemada. The former both as Franciscan provincial, and as archbishop of Toledo from 1495 till 1517, had
the greater influence upon Spanish Christianity at large :
it was mainly because the Spanish church underwent
internal reform at his hands that abuses were relatively
absent in the sixteenth century, and that protestant
reformers could effect little in the peninsula. He both
reformed his own order, and by his patronage of learning,
especially at the university of Alcalà, improved the condition of the secular clergy. Thomas de Torquemada was
Grand Inquisitor of Spain from 1483 till 1498. Till this
reign the Inquisition had not been strong in Spain, though
in the thirteenth century the redoubtable Raymond of
Peñaforte had secured its establishment in Aragon, and
a council of Tarragona, 1242, had laid down rules for the
guidance of inquisitors. But in Aragon it had not been
active, and in Leon, Castile and Portugal it had been
unknown. Civilisation was partly Saracen, and the
existence of a large class of semi-converts, the Marranos
from Judaism and Moriscos from Islam, made for intercourse and toleration. Torquemada himself was for
twenty years prior of the Dominican priory of Segovia, and
during that time confessor to the Infanta Isabella : when
she became queen of Castile in 1476 he remained her
personal counsellor. Through his influence she and
Ferdinand saw in the Inquisition a means to cleanse
Spanish Christianity, and no less to unite their subjects
in an effort to expel the Moors. In 1478 Sixtus IV
empowered Ferdinand and Isabella to organise the
Inquisition in all their domains : but little was accomplished till Torquemada took charge of the work. In
1483 the pope appointed him Grand Inquisitor for both
Castile and Aragon. In 1484 he assembled all the Spanish

inquisitors, issued statutes for them, and henceforth personally directed the whole business of the Inquisition. Largely through his persistent request, the Jews were expelled from Spain in 1492, for though the Inquisition had no jurisdiction over any but Christians, the Jews had proved effective helpers of the Marranos and heretics. About two thousand persons were burned by Torquemada's efforts, and his name became a synonym for inquisition at its worst : the term " auto de fé " (act of faith) obtained European cognizance as a heretic-burning. It should be remembered, however, that the fifteenth century Spanish Inquisition was unique in Europe, under monarchical far more than papal control, and used for secular ends.

If orthodoxy were thus about 1500 in so apparently strong a position, what were the real religious grievances, and what the symptoms of impending change ? They may be classified under four headings. There were the grievances ventilated but left unredressed by the Conciliar movement : those inspired or fortified by Renaissance scholarship : the reaction against Renaissance morals : and the demand of a growing nationalism to settle its own affairs.

The old legacy from the Councils, the questions of provisions, procurations, annates, the reform of the papal curia, etc., persisted throughout the fifteenth century, as only partially settled by the national concordats, written or implied. Anti-clericalism was growing.

Far more important was Renaissance distrust of Christian original sources, Renaissance contempt for superstition and ignorance, and Renaissance repudiation of asceticism, especially as criticism could be now popularised by the printing press. Renaissance recoveries of Greek and Latin classical texts, and its contempt for medieval Latin and knowledge of the classics, had inspired suspicion of the Vulgate, and the Latin translations of patristic works and early canons. There was a desire to get back to Christian original documents, the Greek New Testament, the Greek Fathers, the Greek collections of canons. This led almost at once to the discovery that certain Latin authorities hitherto universally accepted were not authentic. Lorenzo Valla's work has been mentioned :

but the papacy and the church in general were less willing to believe that the Isidorian collection of canons, with its early papal decretals, were forgeries. Nicholas of Cusa in 1464 and cardinal John de Torquemada, (uncle of the inquisitor), in 1468 declared that these early decretals were false, and Renaissance scholars agreed with them, as did Erasmus and several orthodox canonists in the sixteenth century : but portions of the Pseudo-Isidore were embedded in the *Decretum*, the very foundation of canon law, and the papacy refused to be enlightened. The official editions of the *Corpus Juris* in 1580 still upheld their genuineness. These discoveries created a general suspicion and distrust of Christian documents in the minds of the educated, which corresponded to the effect of the popularisation of vernacular Bibles on the lay mind. Fifteenth and sixteenth century popular reformers made the same discoveries about the non-mention of the pope in the New Testament, and other *prima facie* discrepancies, as did Waldensians, Béguines and Lollards earlier. The scriptures and their teaching became the subject of enormous discussion, not only among the learned, but as sir Thomas More lamented later, in pothouses and alehouses as well.

The Renaissance attitude to asceticism and monasticism needs no emphasis. Medieval fast days included not only all Fridays, but Lent, Ember days, Rogation days, and the vigils of saints, a very considerable proportion of the year altogether, and their observance, even by lay people, demanded not merely abstinence from meat but a very meagre diet. As to monasticism, Wycliffe had parted with the medieval conception of the value to the community of lives of prayer and contemplation : but the anti-monastic, anti-ascetic impulse was necessarily strengthened by the followers of Epicurus and his philosophy.

Stronger force still was the Renaissance contempt for ignorance and superstition, and the practices which seemed to flourish at the expense of an ignorant and gullible multitude. The humanists' contempt for ecclesiastical Latin because it was not Ciceronian was no doubt unreasonable : medieval Latin was a living, spoken language, bound to develope on its own lines. When they declaimed, however, against priestly and monastic ignorance of the Latin offices, they were doing a real service ; though that ignorance was probably not as general or as extreme as their satire implied. Many quite orthodox reformers in Germany and England agreed with them as to the need of a better education for the inferior clergy. But where the orthodox reformer joined issue with the humanist was with regard to certain doctrines, rites and usages which the latter criticised as superstitious. This applied particularly to the invocation of saints, the reverence paid to relics, the sale of indulgences, and the doctrine of purgatory as connected with prayers and masses for the dead. (Philosophical dispute as to the mode of Christ's presence in the mass had of course been going on for centuries). With regard to all these doctrines, the real accusation against them was the financial ends which they were made to serve. The invocation of saints was age-old, and consistent with the conception of the unity of all the members in the body of Christ, and the Christian teaching about immortality. The medieval Christian asked not only the dead saint, but the living saint for his prayers : as Henry II in the storm prayed to God by the merits and intercessions of S. Hugh. But when the medieval sinner made money offerings to secure the inter-cession of some saint, and of the Blessed Virgin above all, and looked on the matter as a kind of celestial insurance, reformers were sure to point out sooner or later that his action was commercial rather than devout, and the humanist laughed at the futility of such procedure. He laughed too at the superstition, commercialism and deceptions connected with the veneration of relics : as he laughed at the value attached to priestly blessings and exorcisms, at the credulity which sought for miraculous cures. He had many orthodox reformers with him when he protested against the sale of indulgences, which had by now lost all connexion in the popular mind with canonical penance, and could be obtained by the penitent for money on many occasions, particularly the papal jubilees of 1450 and 1500. There appeared a rank unfair-ness about the attainment of salvation, if the rich man could buy the prayers of the saint, and remission of the temporal punishment of his sins in purgatory by an indulgence, while the poor man could not. The complaint was similar about prayers for the dead and masses of requiem. The church had always prayed for her children at the moment of death and beyond : centuries before Monica had asked for the prayers of Augustine at the altar, and the offering of Christ for sinners had been pleaded there for the departed soul. But in the fifteenth century the rich left bequests in their wills to pay for thousands of requiem masses, and the salvation of those who could so pay was popularly considered more secure than that of those who could not. Men left large sums in their wills to be paid at the time of their burial to priests, monks and nuns to say mattins and vespers of the dead for them, to poor bedesmen to say Paternosters and Aves, to priests to say mass on the day, to anchorites and anchoresses for prayers, to monasteries and friaries to say mass for thirty days after death, and to keep a yearly obit. John of Gaunt, Wycliffe's patron, left immense sums and explicit directions for such purposes. The commercialism that accompanied all these practices found strong condemnation from the humanists, as did the superstition which made abuses possible.

A third source of grievance was actually a reaction against an effect of the Renaissance itself—the impetus to immorality. The binding of large numbers of men to a celibate life, without much preparation, and when most country priests led lives of great monotony and isolation, had always produced a certain number of immoral priests and illegitimate children. But clerical morality in Italy under Renaissance influence became a byword, and the papal curia a scandal to Christendom. The popes were using all their efforts to build up the papal states into a strong principality ; the papal court had little more spiritual character than those of the other Renaissance princes of Italy. Nepotism was rampant, the cardinals spent and gambled away fortunes, and the lowest depth was reached when Rodrigo Borgia, notorious for immorality and cupidity, procured the papal chair by the rankest simony in 1492. " We believe in a just God," wrote some German knights to this pope, " Who will punish with eternal fire all sins such as robbery, sacrilege, pride, violence, vanity, abuse of Christ's patrimony, concubinage, simony, and other horrible crimes, through which the Christian religion totters and Christians are scandalized." While creatures like Alexander VI and his son, Cesare Borgia, ruled at Rome, the claim of the popes to be regarded as the vicars of Christ, their judgments identical with His, appeared monstrous.

And finally, stronger perhaps than all these, the new monarchy was strengthening itself all over Europe, a most formidable though unrecognised enemy of any international system, either political or religious. The Italy which produced Savonarola produced also Machiavelli, the prophet of the new order. In the *Prince* Machiavelli preached the complete divorce of ethics and politics, and urged on rulers a far-sighted selfishness, both with regard to their own subjects and to neighbouring states. All men were governed, he taught, by motives of selfishness, cupidity and fear : "men will forgive the murder of their children rather than the loss of their money." Though the book was condemned by the church, the new rulers of Europe were ready to be guided by its principles, if not with the licence of a Cesare Borgia, at least to the extent of subordinating all questions to their own dynastic interest. Whereas most Christians in the fifteenth century had desired an internal reform of the church and been unable to achieve it, sixteenth century reformers were to succeed through the political support of rulers who desired to be supreme in all spheres within their states. The old Byzantinism of the east was to find fresh expression in the principle of "cuius regio, eius religio." But at the end of the fifteenth century, while change proceeded gradually, the forces of revolution still slept.

SELECT BOOK LIST

[The order is roughly chronological]

FOR GENERAL REFERENCE

The chapters dealing with Church History in the *Cambridge Medieval History*, vols. ii, iii, iv, v, vi; the volumes dealing with the English Church in the *Antiquaries' Series: Histoire de l'Église depuis les origines jusqu'à nos jours*, Fliche, A. et Martin, V., Paris, begun in 1934, still incomplete; *Docs. of the Christian Church*, ed. Bettenson, H.

EUROPEAN CHURCH HISTORY

FOURNIER, P., et LE BRAS, G. *Histoire des Collections Canoniques en Occident.* 2 vols. 1931, 1933.

CHADWICK, O. *John Cassian.* 1950.

BECK, H. G. J. *The Pastoral Care of Souls in South-East France during the Sixth Century.* Anal. Gregoriana, 1950.

DUDDEN, F. H. *Gregory the Great.* 2 vols. 1905.

ROBINSON, C. H. *How the Gospel Spread through Europe.* S.P.C.K. 1919.

BERLIERE, U. *L'Ordre Monastique.* 1921.

GRIEVE, A. *Willibrord.* 1923.

BROWNE, G. F. *Boniface of Crediton.* 1910.

BUTLER, E. C. *Benedictine Monachism.* 1919.

COULTON, G. G. *Five Centuries of Religion.* Vol. I to vol. IV. 1919, 1950.

GRUNEBAUM, G. E. VON. *Medieval Islam.* Cumberlege. 1947.

DUCHESNE, L. *Les premiers temps de l'État Pontifical* A.D 754–1073. 1904. Translated by Mathew, A. H.

Hussey, J. M. *Church and Learning in the Byzantine Empire,* 867–1185. 1937.

Smith, Lucy M. *The Early History of the Monastery of Cluny,* 1920. *Cluny in the Eleventh and Twelfth Centuries.* 1930.

Evans, Joan. *Monastic Life at Cluny,* 910–1157. 1931.

Waddell, Helen. *The Wandering Scholars.* 1927.

Whitney, J. P. *Hildebrandine Essays.* 1932.

Fliche, A. *Grégoire VII.* 1920. 2nd ed.

Macdonald, A. J. *Lanfranc.* 1926. *Berengars of Tours.* 1930.

Dickinson, J. C. *Origins of the Austin Canons.* 1950.

Morison, J. C. *The Life and Times of St. Bernard.* 1884.

Cuthbert, Father. *Life of St. Francis of Assisi.* 1912.

Sabatier, P. *Vie de S. François d'Assise.* Translated by Houghton, L. S. 1894.

Jarrett, Father Bede. *Life of St. Dominic.* 1924.

Mandonnet, Father Pierre. *Saint Dominique.* 1937.

Poole, R. L. *Illustrations of Medieval Thought and Learning.* 1920.

Rashdall, H., ed. by Powicke and Emden. *Universities of Europe in the Middle Ages.* 1936.

Wulf, M. de. *History of Medieval Philosophy.* Translated by Coffey, P. 1909.

Gilson, E. *Études de philosophie Médiévale.* 1922.

Turberville, A. S. *Medieval Heresy and the Inquisition.* 1920.

Luchaire, A. *Innocent III.* 6 vols. 1908–1911.

D'Arcy, M. C. *Thomas Aquinas.* 1930.

Douie, D. L. *The Nature and Effect of the Heresy of the Fraticelli.* 1932.

Rivière, J. *Le problème de l'Église et de l'État au temps de Philippe le Bel.* 1926.

Boase, T. S. R. *Boniface VIII.* 1933.

Ullmann, W. *Medieval Papalism.* 1950.

Lunt, W. E. *Papal Revenues in the Middle Ages.* 1934.

Mollat, G. *Les Papes d'Avignon.* 1912.

CREIGHTON, M. *A History of the Papacy from the Great Schism to the Sack of Rome.* 6 vols. 1897.

VALOIS, N. *Le Pape et Le Concile, 1418–1450.* 2 vols. 1909.

WORKMAN, H. B. *The Dawn of the Reformation.* 2 vols. 1901–1902.

ENGLISH CHURCH HISTORY

PATTERSON, M. W. *A History of the English Church.* 1909.

MAKOWER, F. *Constitutional History of the Church of England.* 1895.

THOMPSON, A. HAMILTON. *The Historical Growth of the English Parish Church.* 1911. *English Monasteries.* 1913. *The English Clergy and their organization in the later Middle Ages.* 1947.

DUKE, J. A. *The Columban Church.* 1932.

GRAHAM, ROSE. *English Ecclesiastical Studies.* 1929.

KNOWLES, DOM DAVID. *Monastic Order in England.* 1940. *Religious Orders in England.* 1948. *Map of Monastic Britain*, Ordn. Survey. 1950.

SELLAR, A. M. Translation of the Venerable Bede's *Ecclesiastical History of the English Nation.* 1912.

ROBINSON, J. A. *The Times of St. Dunstan.* 1923.

CHURCH, R. W. *Saint Anselm.* 1888 and later editions.

EDWARDS, K. *The English Secular Cathedrals in the Middle Ages.* 1949.

JENKINS, CLAUDE. *The Monastic Chronicler and the Early School of St. Albans.* 1922.

BROOKE, Z. N. *The English Church and the Papacy from the Conquest to the Reign of John.* 1931.

HUTTON, W. H. *Thomas Becket.* 1926 ed.

CLARKE, E. *The Chronicle of Jocelin of Brakelond.* 1903.

POWICKE, F. M. *Stephen Langton.* 1928.

WEBB, C. C. J. *John of Salisbury.* 1932.

GIBBS, M., and LANG, J. *Bishops and Reform, 1215–1272.* 1934.

MOORMAN, J. R. H. *Church Life in England in the Thirteenth Century.* 1945.

Power, E. E. *English Nunneries.* 1922.

Cheney, C. R. *Episcopal Visitations of Monasteries in the Thirteenth Century.* 1931. *English Bishops' Chanceries,* 1100–1250. 1950.

Cranage, D. H. S. *The Home of the Monk.* 1926.

Maitland, F. W. *Roman Canon Law in the Church of England.* 1898.

Smith, A. L. *Church and State in the Middle Ages.* 1913.

Cuthbert, Father. Translation of Thomas of Eccleston's *De Adventu Fratrum Minorum in Angliam.* 1909.

Little, A. G. *Studies in English Franciscan History.* 1917.

Offer, C. J. *The Bishop's Register.* 1929.

Capes, W. W. *The English Church in the Fourteenth and Fifteenth Centuries.* 1900.

Poole, R. L. *Wyclif and Movements for Reform.* 1899.

Deanesly, M. *The Lollard Bible and other Medieval Biblical Versions.* 1920.

Workman, H. B. *John Wyclif.* 2 vols. 1926.

Gwynn, A. *The English Austin Friars in the time of Wyclif.* 1940.

Smith, H. Maynard. *Pre-Reformation England.* 1938.

LEADING EVENTS, 451-1500

451	Council of Chalcedon. (Fourth oecumenical.)
496	Baptism of Clovis.
537	Inauguration of S. Sophia.
543	Death of S. Benedict.
553	Council of Constantinople. (Fifth oecumenical.)
590	Accession of Gregory the Great.
597	Mission of Augustine.
614	Persians capture Jerusalem.
632	Death of Mahomet.
664	Synod of Whitby.
680	Council of Constantinople. (Sixth oecumenical.)
722	Boniface's mission to Germany.
726	Edict against images.
754	Donation of Pepin to the papacy.
776	Conquest and conversion of Saxony.
787	Council of Nicaea. (Seventh oecumenical.)
800	Coronation of the emperor Charles the Great.
817	Council of Aix-la-Chapelle makes Chrodegang's rule obligatory.
c. 863	Mission of Cyril and Methodius to Moravians.
867	Schism of Photius.
870	Council of Constantinople. (Eighth oecumenical.)
910	Foundation of Cluny.
997	Accession of S. Stephen and conversion of Hungary.
1017	Observation of " truce of God " begins.
1022	First burning of heretics by civil power.
1046	Henry III " cleanses the papacy."
1054	Schism of Michael Cerularius.
1059	Lateran council regulates papal elections.
1071	Battle of Manzikert : Seljuks take Jerusalem.
1073	Hildebrand accedes as Gregory VII.
1077	Henry IV submits at Canossa.
1084	S. Bruno founds Grande Chartreuse.

1095	Council of Clermont : First Crusade preached.
1098	Foundation of Cîteaux.
1100	Foundation of Latin kingdom of Jerusalem.
1107	Concordat of Bec.
1122	Concordat of Worms.
1147	Second Crusade.
c. 1148	*Decretum* of Gratian.
1155	Arnold of Brescia burnt.
1170	Murder of S. Thomas of Canterbury.
1179	Third Lateran council.
1184	Waldensians condemned.
1187	Saladin takes Jerusalem.
1189	Third Crusade.
1198	Accession of Innocent III.
1199	Cistercians sent as inquisitors to Metz.
1201	Fourth Crusade.
1204	Foundation of Latin empire of Constantinople.
1208	Albigensian Crusade begins.
1213	John surrenders to Papal legate.
1215	Fourth Lateran council.
1220	Dominican rule confirmed.
1223	Franciscan rule confirmed. Mendicant Inquisition organised.
1230	*Decretals* of Gregory IX.
1254	The *Introduction* to abbot Joachim's Eternal Gospel issued.
1264	Feast of Corpus Christi instituted.
1274	Council of Lyons : death of S. Thomas Aquinas.
1296	Issue of *Clericis Laicos*.
1298	*Liber Sextus* of Boniface VIII.
1302	Issue of *Unam Sanctam*.
1303	Outrage at Anagni.
1305	Accession of Clement V.
1336	Issue of the " Benedictine Bull."
c. 1340	Richard Rolle's English psalter.
1349	Black Death : Flagellants in Germany.
1351	Statute of Provisors.
1353	Statute of Praemunire.
1378	Great Schism begins.
1384	Death of Wycliffe.
1401	*De Heretico Comburendo* statute : Purvey recants

1409   Council of Pisa.
1414   Council of Constance meets.
1415   Burning of Hus.
1417   End of Great Schism.   Execution of Oldcastle.
1420-7   Husite Crusades in Bohemia.
1431   Council of Basle meets.
1433   Bohemian *Compactata*.
1438   Pragmatic Sanction of Bourges.   Council of Ferrara-Florence.
1439   Pragmatic Sanction of Mainz.   Lorenzo Valla exposes Donation of Constantine.
1447   First humanist pope, Nicholas V.
1453   Fall of Constantinople.
1464   Suspicion thrown on Pseudo-Isidorian decretals.
1483   Torquemada becomes Grand Inquisitor of Spain.
1493   Rodrigo Borgia becomes pope Alexander VI.
1497   " Bonfire of the Vanities " at Florence.

POPES, 440–1503

(Most of the antipopes are omitted)

Leo I, 440
Hilary, 461
Simplicius, 468
Felix III, 483
Gelasius I, 492
Anastasius II, 496
Symmachus, 498
Hormisdas, 514
John I, 523
Felix IV, 526
Boniface II, 530
John II, 532
Agapetus I, 535
Silverius, 536
Vigilius, 537
Pelagius I, 555
John III, 560
Benedict I, 574
Pelagius II, 578
Gregory I, 590
Sabinian, 604
Boniface III, 607
Boniface IV, 608
Deusdedit I, 615
Boniface V, 619
Honorius I, 625
Severinus, 640
John IV, 640
Theodore I, 642
Martin I, 649
Eugenius I, 655
Vitalian, 657

Deusdedit II, 672
Donus, 676
Agatho, 678
Leo II, 682
Benedict II, 684
John V, 685
Conon, 686
Sergius I, 687
John VI, 701
John VII, 705
Sisinnius, 708
Constantine I, 708
Gregory II, 715
Gregory III, 731
Zacharias, 741
Stephen II, 752
Paul I, 757
Constantine II, 767
Stephen III, 768
Hadrian I, 772
Leo III, 795
Stephen IV, 816
Paschal I, 817
Eugenius II, 824
Valentine, 827
Gregory IV, 827
Sergius II, 844
Leo IV, 847
Benedict III, 855
Nicholas I, 858
Hadrian II, 867
John VIII, 872

T

Marinus I, 882
Hadrian III, 884
Stephen V, 885
Formosus, 891
Boniface VI, 896
Stephen VI, 896
Romanus, 897
Theodore II, 897
John IX, 898
Benedict IV, 900
Leo V, 903
Christopher, 903
Sergius III, 904
Anastasius III, 911
Lando, 913
John X, 914
Leo VI, 928
Stephen VII, 929
John XI, 931
Leo VII, 936
Stephen VIII, 939
Martin III, 942
Agapetus II, 946
John XII, 955
Leo VIII, 963
Benedict V, 964
John XIII, 965
Benedict VI, 972
Benedict VII, 974
John XIV, 983
Boniface VII, 984
John XV, 985
Gregory V, 996
John XVI, 997
Sylvester II, 999
John XVII, 1003
John XVIII, 1003
Sergius IV, 1009
Benedict VIII, 1012
John XIX, 1024
Benedict IX, 1033

Gregory VI, 1044
Clement II, 1046
Damasus II, 1048
Leo IX, 1048
Victor II, 1055
Stephen IX, 1057
Nicholas II, 1058
Alexander II, 1061
Gregory VII, 1073
  [Clement III, antipope,
    1080–1100]
Victor III, 1086
Urban II, 1088
Paschal II, 1099
Gelasius II, 1118
Calixtus II, 1119
Honorius II, 1124
Innocent II, 1130
[Anacletus, antipope, 1130–
    1138]
Celestine II, 1143
Lucius II, 1144
Eugenius III, 1145
Anastasius IV, 1153
Hadrian IV, 1154
Alexander III, 1159
Lucius III, 1181
Urban III, 1185
Gregory VIII, 1187
Clement III, 1187
Celestine III, 1191
Innocent III, 1198
Honorius III, 1216
Gregory IX, 1227
Celestine IV, 1241
Innocent IV, 1243
Alexander IV, 1254
Urban IV, 1261
Clement IV, 1265
Gregory X, 1271
Innocent V, 1276

Hadrian V, 1276
John XXI, 1277
Nicholas III, 1277
Martin IV, 1281
Honorius IV, 1285
Nicholas IV, 1289
Celestine V, 1294
Boniface VIII, 1294
Benedict XI, 1303
Clement V, 1305
John XXII, 1316
Benedict XII, 1334
Clement VI, 1342
Innocent VI, 1352
Urban V, 1362
Gregory XI, 1370
Urban VI, 1378
Boniface IX, 1389
Innocent VII, 1404
Gregory XII, 1406

Alexander V, 1409
John XXIII, 1410

Avignon popes of the Schism—

Clement VII, 1378
Benedict XIII, 1394
Gregory XII, 1406–1409
Popes of Schism end here.

Martin V, 1417
Eugenius IV, 1431
Nicholas V, 1447
Calixtus III, 1455
Pius II, 1458
Paul II, 1464
Sixtus IV, 1471
Innocent VIII, 1484
Alexander VI, 1492
Pius III, 1503

EMPERORS AND KINGS OF THE ROMANS

Charles the Great, 800
Louis I, or the Pious, 814
Lothar I, 840
Louis II, 855
Charles the Bald, 875
Charles the Fat, 876–888
Otto I, 936
Otto II, 973
Otto III, 983
Henry II, 1002
Conrad II, 1024
Henry III, 1039
Henry IV, 1056
Henry V, 1106
Lothar II, 1125
Conrad III, 1138
Frederick I, 1152

Henry VI, 1190
Otto IV, 1197
Frederick II, 1212
Conrad IV, 1250
Great Interregnum, 1254
Rudolf I, 1273
Albert I, 1290
Adolf, 1292
Henry VII, 1308
Lewis V, 1314
Charles VII, 1347
Wenceslas, 1378
Sigismund, 1410
Albert II, 1438
Frederick III, 1440
Maximilian I, 1493

ARCHBISHOPS OF CANTERBURY

Augustine, 597
Laurentius, 604
Mellitus, 619
Justus, 624
Honorius, 627
Deusdedit, 655
Theodore, 668
Brihtwald, 693
Tatwin, 731
Nothelm, 735
Cuthbert, 741
Bregwin, 759
Jaenbert, 766
Aethelhard, 793
Wulfred, 805
Feologild, 832
Ceolnoth, 833
Aethelred, 870
Plegmund, 890
Athelm, 914
Wulfhelm, 923
Odo, 941
Dunstan, 960
Aethelgar, 988
Siric, 990
Aelfric, 995
Aelfheah, 1005
Lifing, 1013
Aethelnoth, 1020
Eadsige, 1038
Robert of Jumièges, 1051
Stigand, 1052

Lanfranc, 1070
Anselm, 1093
Ralf d'Escures, 1114
William of Corbeil, 1123
Theobald, 1139
Thomas, 1162
Richard of Dover, 1174
Baldwin, 1185
Hubert Walter, 1193
Stephen Langton, 1207
Richard, 1229
Edmund Rich, 1234
Boniface of Savoy, 1245
Robert Kilwardby, 1273
John Peckham, 1279
Robert Winchelsey, 1294
Walter Reynolds, 1313
Simon Meopham, 1328
John Stratford, 1333
Thomas Bradwardine, 1349
Simon Islip, 1349
Simon Langham, 1366
William Whittlesey, 1368
Simon Sudbury, 1375
William Courtenay, 1381
Thomas Arundel, 1397
Henry Chichele, 1414
John Stafford, 1443
John Kemp, 1452
Thomas Bourchier, 1454
John Morton, 1486
Henry Deane, 1501

INDEX

(For proper names, see under Christian name: e.g. Berengarius of Tours, Lorenzo dei Medici.)

Printed in Great Britain by
UNWIN BROTHERS, LIMITED, LONDON AND WOKING